Mountain Biking the Puget Sound Area

Help Us Keep This Guide Up to Date

Every effort has been made by the author and editors to make this guide as accurate and useful as possible. However, many things can change after a guide is published—trails are rerouted, regulations change, techniques evolve, facilities come under new management, etc.

We would love to hear from you concerning your experiences with this guide and how you feel it could be improved and kept up to date. While we may not be able to respond to all comments and suggestions, we'll take them to heart and we'll also make certain to share them with the author. Please send your comments and suggestions to the following address:

The Globe Pequot Press
Reader Response/Editorial Department
P.O. Box 480
Guilford, CT 06437

Or you may e-mail us at:

editorial@GlobePequot.com

Thanks for your input, and happy trails!

Mountain Biking
the Puget Sound Area

A Guide to the Best Off-Road Rides in
Greater Seattle, Tacoma, and Everett

by local mountain biker
Santo Criscuolo

Foreword by Gary Klein,
Founder, Klein Bicycles

FALCON®

GUILFORD, CONNECTICUT
HELENA, MONTANA
AN IMPRINT OF THE GLOBE PEQUOT PRESS

Text design by Nancy Freeborn

Maps created by XNR Productions Inc. © The Globe
Pequot Press

The author thanks the following individuals for providing
some of the photos: Mike Walker, Eric Layland, Romeo
Solomon, Ivan Agerton, Kristen McLaughlin, Troy Hopwood,
and Doug "Elvis" Bruce.

Library of Congress Cataloging-in-Publication Data is
available.

ISBN 0-7627-2554-0

Manufactured in the United States of America
First Edition/First Printing

Contents

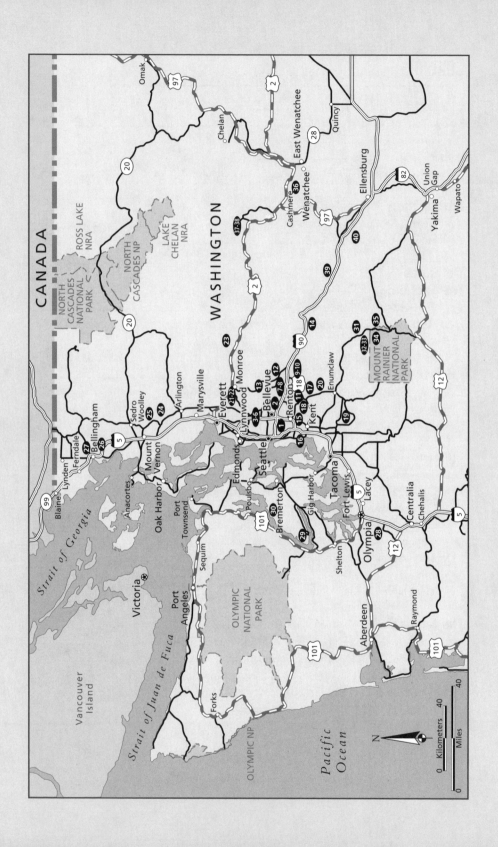

Map Legend

90	Limited access highway
2	U.S. highway
18	State highway
———	Paved road
═══	Gravel road
═ ═ ═ ═	Unimproved road
- - - - -	Singletrack trail
··············	Doubletrack trail
▓▓▓▓▓	Featured trail
++++++++	Railroad
•——•——•	Powerline
—·—·—	Pipeline
[_ _]	Parks
✕	Airport
≍	Bridge
🚌	Bus stop/shuttle
⛺	Campground
•—•	Gate
⛳	Golf course
◙	Overlook/viewpoint
🅿	Parking
)(	Pass
▲	Peak
🎪	Picnic area
🚻	Rest room
🏫	School
🚴	Trailhead
∥	Waterfall

START

● Easy   ■ Moderate   ◆ Difficult   ◆◆ Very Difficult

The North End

Olympia and the Kitsap Peninsula

Highway 410

The Outer Limits—Or just because they are so good we couldn't leave them out

The Art of Mountain Biking

Repair and Maintenance

Foreword

Washington natives may not realize how beautiful their state is. I have lived in Massachusetts and California and grew up in Texas and Louisiana. Nowhere else is the landscape as green, vibrant and breathtaking as in the Northwest. Nowhere else I have lived is the weather and culture as conducive to year-round cycling.

I moved to Chehalis in 1980 because the cycling was excellent, with many small back roads—like back east but without the traffic and smog. Permanent snow and glacier-covered peaks soar upward from the beautiful Puget Sound and its many water-based activities. The variety of terrain is amazing. Lush rain forests near the ocean change to desert as you travel east—and all of it offers fantastic riding.

Some of my favorite trails are located in Capitol Forest. Hundreds of miles of motorcycle and horse trails wind throughout this working forest and up and down the Black Hills of the south Puget Sound area. After twenty years of riding in the region I still get a thrill out of the whoop-de-do sections, banked turns, and gnarly downhills. I am sure you will as well.

Santo has done an excellent job pulling together detailed ride descriptions, maps, tips, and information about Capitol Forest as well as many other rides in the state. His guide is a good read and it will definitely help you enjoy mountain biking more than ever. See you out on the trail.

Gary Klein, Founder
Klein Bicycles

Preface

I love mountain biking. In fact, I love it so much that you could say I am a bit of a fanatic. Everything about mountain biking is, well . . . cool: cooler than rock legend Bono of the super group U2, Laurence Fishbourne as Morpheus in *The Matrix,* and John Travolta as Vincent Vega in *Pulp Fiction* combined.

Dirt and grease under my fingernails; colored ferules, carbon-fiber gizmos, titanium gadgets, sealed cartridge bearings; ripping down thin twisting ribbons of dirt, struggling up torturous climbs, negotiating nasty switchbacks and brutal rock gardens, copping air, riding until my lungs feel as though they are filled with napalm; hydration systems, tasteless energy bars, baggy shorts, Smith Sliders. The quiet and calm after a race official shouts "One minute!"—and the total chaos that ensues sixty seconds later; www.dirtworld.com, mud-splattering face shots, the thin layer of sweat that forms as you ride in a Puget Sound rain forest in the middle of summer; purple and yellow bruises, angry gashes and gouges; www.petefagerlin.com. Packing up your bike and gear to fly somewhere (anywhere) to ride; fat-tire brethren lending total strangers a map, tools, or spare tubes out on the trail; the police officer who pulled me over for doing 80 mph in a 55 mph zone, then asked about my full suspension ride and the race I was headed to instead of giving me a ticket; Devils Gulch, cars loaded down with bikes, red tires, anything XTR. The Sea Otter Classic, crossing the finish line, 24-Hour racing; Marla Streb, Tinker Juarez; the rhythm and grace that I feel every so often when the bike becomes an extension of my body . . . I think you get the point by now.

I have laid tracks in British Columbia, Alberta, Oregon, Idaho, California, Arizona, Utah, New Jersey, New York, Alaska, Mexico, and Costa Rica. I've pedaled alongside Tinker Juarez, Alyson Sydor, Brian Lopes, Marla Streb, and Cadel Evans. I have raced in more than a hundred different events and have tested, reviewed, and written about nearly as many bikes and bike accessories (I was one of the original founders of Dirt Northwest and Dirtworld.com.) While I haven't been everywhere or seen everything, I have been lucky enough to ride more than most, and the conclusion I have reached after twenty years in the saddle is that there is no other place on earth like the Puget Sound when it comes to mountain biking.

Whether it is the porcelain-smooth singletrack of Devils Gulch; the inspiring views of Mount Rainier, Saint Helens, Adams, and Baker, the Cascades, and the Olympics; the confusing maze of trails on Galbraith Mountain; the wicked trenches of Walker Valley; the intestine-like turns of the Tapeworm; the banked curves, whoop-de-dos, and sticky pudding-like mud of Capitol Forest; the alpine lakes of Crystal Mountain and the mountain meadows of Mad Lake; the root-infested Skookum Flats; the treacherous DH descents of The Summit or the lung-bursting climbs of the Cascade Triple Crown (11,000 feet in a single day), the Puget Sound area offers one of the largest varieties of mountain bike adventures in North America. If you can ride here, you can ride almost anywhere.

Granted, none of the current big-name riders are from the Seattle area, and precious few of us are lucky enough to be able to ride from our backdoor to the trailhead—which is exactly why the Puget Sound does not make it onto the North American mountain bike community radar. But this is exactly how the locals want it—fewer visitors from outside the area results in fewer riders on the trails. How can anyone argue with logic like this?

So why write a book that will potentially put more riders on the trails? Over the years, mountain biking has been a significant part of my life. I want to give back to the sport that has given so much to me. Biking has taken me all over the world, introduced me to new cultures, established lifelong friendships, created good times, and helped me through the worst of times. I owe the sport and I hope that *Mountain Biking the Puget Sound Area* will help you get even just a little of what I have gotten, and still get, out of mountain biking. Good luck—and good thrill hunting.

Santo Criscuolo

Acknowledgments

I love sports analogies, and this is one of my favorites: Lance Armstrong is the greatest American cyclist in history. After beating cancer, he won the Tour de France—four years in a row at the time of this printing. Not only did he win but he also crushed the Europeans in a sport they claimed to own. As a result, Armstrong has secured wealth, glory, and fame. Most Americans think that cycling is an individual sport, but no one knows better than Armstrong that there would be no yellow jersey in the Tour de France without his selfless teammates Frankie Andreu, Vjatceslav Ekimov, Tyler Hamilton, Roberto Heras, George Hincapie, Victor Pena, Jose Rubiera, Benoit Joachim, Steffen Kjaergaard, Kevin Livingston, Christian Vande Velde, and Cédric Vasseur. They are called *domestiques,* or *helpers,* and they performed the grueling behind-the-scenes labor that made it possible for Armstrong to lead the peleton into Paris. While publishing a book is not winning the Tour de France, it is grueling in its own fashion. Only one rider gets to wear the yellow jersey. And only one name goes on the cover of the book. But none of this would be possible without the following *domestiques:*

My mother, who purchased my first mountain bike. My sister Samantha for always being there for me, no matter what. Bill Harnett, Phil Hawley, Kristen McLaughlin, and Earl Lindl for their constant friendship and support. Andy Walker for introducing me to the sport, teaching me to lay off the front brakes, pushing me to go faster, and being my first mechanic and one of my closest friends. Chris "McGyver" Genau for his awesome skills as a publicist and for being the best mechanic I have *ever* had. Troy Hopwood for hauling my bike all over the Puget Sound area, being my default photographer, and always being willing to ride a new trail. Eric Layland, Cyril Jay-Rayon, and the rest of the Dirtworld.com crew. Karl Weatherly for making me look like a star in his photos and Chase Jarvis for taking an awesome cover shot. Keith Rollins for introducing me to the Crystal Mountain trails. Doug "Elvis" Bruce for always being willing to ride. Mike Walker for numerous adventures and gear from Smith Sport Optics. Dimitri Keating from Old Town Cycles, Bill Rudell from Cannondale, Chris Destefano from Shimano, and Carmela Livorsi from Specialized. Eric Carlson from Smith Sport Optics. Jerome "Bis" McCarthy, Krista Schimpf, Ivan Agerton, Romeo Solomon, Christian McGlaughlin, Joy Walker, Patrick and Lorie Walker, Tripp Meister, Bret Burlew, and Chris Thompson for being great riding partners. Heather Dennis from Saint Edwards State Park, Tom Eksten from the King County Parks Department, Sean Tobin from Wallace Falls State Park, and the Backcountry Bicycles Trails Club for working to improve our trails and keep them open.

Scott Adams and the rest of the Falcon Publishing team.

And finally, special thanks to Gary Klein from Klein Bicycles.

Thank you all.

Introduction

Welcome to *Mountain Biking the Puget Sound Area!* There's no better way to get to the heart of the woods faster or to experience the exhilaration of a winding downhill trail than in the saddle of a mountain bike.

This guidebook is designed to expose you to some of the best mountain biking available in the Puget Sound region. Each of the fifty-three (53) rides (including Options) comes with a detailed map and instructions on how to reach the trail, where to ride once you arrive, and general information about the area, such as where to grab a burger and a cold drink afterward. The rides range from easy jaunts accessible to first-time mountain bikers and families (many of the rides in this guide are also dog friendly) to hardcore rides that'll lead you up and over some of the most extreme biking terrain in the region. Check the information at the beginning of each chapter to be sure that the ride you choose fits your ability level. Be honest with yourself about your skills and conditioning. It is easy to get in over your head on a mountain bike, and the results can be serious. And since many of these rides venture into the backcountry, make sure you are prepared to be self-sufficient once you leave the trailhead.

Although a huge part of mountain-biking fun lies in the speed of the descent, take the time to notice and enjoy the scenery along the way. The Puget Sound region is gorgeous and has more to offer outdoor enthusiasts than many other regions in Washington. Please be aware that other people use these trails, too. Access to these trails is a privilege, and with that privilege comes responsibility: Be courteous to others, and do what you can to ensure the good standing of mountain bikers on every route.

Puget Sound Weather

The Cascade Mountain Range divides Washington, giving the state two distinct weather faces. Temperate marine air dominates the western half of the state; drier, more volatile air dominates the east. The marine air west of the Cascades brings mild temperatures, overcast skies, and frequent rain from October through May. Hence, Seattle's infamous rain reputation. What's lesser known, however, is that June through September is absolutely gorgeous (locals say that July 4 marks the beginning of a four-month dry season). And it's rarely too hot to ride in western Washington—summer highs seldom reach 90°Fahrenheit.

Winter conditions are also mild. It's unusual for snow to hamper riding at low elevations; however, riding on higher mountain trails during winter months can be dicey. Even in summer, snow will occasionally fall in the Cascades. Regardless of the season, it's a good idea to pay attention to weather forecasts before heading out.

Flora and Fauna

The lush western side of the Cascades provides for a wide range of ecosystems and wildlife in a relatively small area. Throughout western Puget Sound, stands of Douglas fir are neighbors to western hemlock, cedar, oak, and maple trees. Below tree cover (in the areas that haven't been clear-cut) live native mosses, ferns, salmonberries, salal, rhododendron, vine maple, prickly devil's club, and nettles. Wetland areas offer even more variety, including the odiferous skunk cabbage, fragile trillium, and bleeding heart.

Western Washington's wildlife includes a host of songbirds and reptiles. Although rarely encountered along the trail, there is always a chance to see deer, black bear, or cougar; mountain bikers are more likely to see smaller mammals like rabbit and squirrel.

Wilderness Restrictions and Regulations

In 2000 Washington and Oregon national forests and scenic areas teamed up in an effort to make it easier to obtain trailhead passes. Trailhead fees are now $5.00 per day, or you can buy an annual Northwest Forest Pass for $30—good at all participating national forests and scenic areas in Washington and Oregon. Trail park passes can be purchased at local ranger stations, participating outdoor retail outlets, and some trailheads. For more information about participating national forests and locations for purchasing a Northwest Forest Pass, visit www.fs.fed.us/r6/feedemo or call (800) 270–7504.

Before you head into the backcountry, find out what type of permit you'll need and what restrictions are in place for the area you're going to visit. If you're planning an overnight trip into a wilderness area, call ahead to the local ranger station to see if a permit is required.

Getting Around Puget Sound

Area Codes

Washington currently has five area codes: 206 for the Seattle area; 253 for Tacoma and south Seattle suburbs, including Auburn; 425 for north Seattle suburbs, including Everett; 360 for western Washington, except Seattle and surrounding areas; and 509 for Spokane and eastern Washington.

Roads

To contact the Washington Department of Transportation, call (800) 695–7623 or visit www.wsdot.wa.gov. For mountain pass reports, visit www.traffic.wsdot.wa.gov/sno-info.

By Air

One major airport services the Puget Sound area: **Sea-Tac International Airport.** A travel agent can best advise you on the least expensive and/or most direct way to connect from wherever you're departing. They can also arrange transportation from the airport to your destination.

To book reservations online visit your favorite airline's Web site, or search one of the following travel sites for the best price: www.cheaptickets.com, www.expedia.com, www.previewtravel.com, www.priceline.com, www.travelocity.com, www.trip.com—just to name a few. Many of these sites can connect you with a shuttle or rental service to get you from the airport to your destination.

By Bus

Washington is well covered by bus service; however, intercity bus services often require that you box your bicycle. The major carriers are **Greyhound** and **Northwestern Trailways.** Schedules and fares are available online at www.greyhound.com or by calling (800) 231–2222. Greyhound charges $15 to carry a boxed bicycle. **Olympic Bus Lines** runs between the Olympic Peninsula and Seattle. Contact them through their Web site at www.tourtheolympics.com or by phone at (360) 452–3858. Nearly all local buses in Washington are equipped with bicycle racks.

By Ferry

Washington State Ferries has many routes that cross Puget Sound. Most connect Seattle with the Islands and the Olympic Peninsula. Visit their Web site at www.wsdot.wa.gov/Ferries, or call (888) 808–7977 (in Washington).

Visitor Information

For visitor information or a travel brochure, call the **Washington State Tourism Division** at (800) 544–1800, ext. 800, or visit www.tourism.wa.gov. The state's official site is www.access.wa.gov.

How to Use This Guide

Mountain Biking the Puget Sound Area features fifty-three mapped and cued rides, some with one or more options, covering the Seattle, Tacoma, Everett area and a bit beyond. The book has been split up into six regions: The East Side, The South End, The North End, Olympia and the Kitsap Peninsula, Highway 410, and The Outer Limits. Each area is described at the beginning of each section of the book. For the individual trails, the most pertinent information rises quickly to the top, so you don't have to waste time poring through bulky ride descriptions to get mileage cues or elevation stats. They're highlighted for you. And yet a FalconGuide doesn't read like a laundry list. Take the time to dive into a ride description and you'll realize that this guide is not just a good source of information; it's also a good read. In the end, you get the best of both worlds: a quick-reference guide and an engaging look at mountain biking in western Washington. Following is an outline of the guide's major components.

What you'll find in this FalconGuide. Each region begins with a **Section Intro,** where you're given a sweeping look at the lay of the land and a taste of the adventures that will be featured in the section.

Now to the individual chapters. The **ride specs** are fairly self-explanatory. Here you'll find the quick, nitty-gritty details of the ride: where the trailhead is located, the nearest town, ride length, approximate riding time, technical difficulty, type of trail terrain, and what other trail users you may encounter. You'll also find information on trail contacts, park schedules, fees, and maps available for the area. **Finding the Trailhead** gives you dependable directions from a nearby city right down to where you'll want to park. **The Ride** is the meat of the chapter. Detailed and honest, it's the author's carefully researched impression of the trail. While it's impossible to cover everything, you can rest assured that we won't miss what's important. The **Miles and Directions** section provides mileage cues to identify all turns and trail name changes, as well as points of interest. **Ride Information** contains a hodgepodge of information, including where to stay, what to eat, and what else to see while you're riding in the area.

The Maps

We don't want anyone to feel restricted to just the routes and trails that are mapped here. In fact, many of the areas are so jam packed with trails that we couldn't describe each and every one. Instead, we provided directions to the entrance and highlighted some of our favorite trails. Then it's up to you; we hope you have an adventurous spirit and use this guide as a platform to explore the Puget Sound region's backcountry and discover new routes for yourself. For an entirely new perspective you can always ride the routes in reverse or even after the sun goes down.

You may wish to copy the directions for the course onto a small sheet to help you while riding, or photocopy the map and cue sheet to take with you. Or just slip the whole book in your pack and take it all with you. Enjoy your time in the outdoors—and remember to pack out what you pack in.

Route map: This is your primary guide to each ride. It shows all the accessible roads and trails, points of interest, water, towns, landmarks, and geographical features. It also distinguishes trails from roads and paved roads from unpaved roads. The selected route is highlighted, and directional arrows point the way.

The East Side

The entire wired world, at least anyone who has ever sat in front of a Microsoft-enabled PC, is familiar with the East Side even though they may not realize it. The region is a collection of several communities—Bothell, Redmond, Kirkland, Bellevue, and Issaquah—that are all located "east" of Lake Washington. Smack dab in the middle (Redmond) lies the center of Bill Gates's Microsoft Empire. It is no surprise then that when the East Side is mentioned, locals are likely to think of young millionaires, software, outrageously expensive real estate, BMWs, and Land Cruisers before they think of mountain biking. Cyclists are surprised to learn, however, that the East Side is home to more than double the amount of trails than any other area in the Puget Sound region. And despite the low elevations and lack of seriously long descents, the rides are some of the most technically challenging in the state.

Lakes, rivers, and streams rolling down and out of the Cascade Mountains, not to mention Puget Sound itself, combine to turn the area into a virtual rainmaking machine. In June and July, many of the trails are still moist and even muddy. Early in the season, they are downright nasty. Download a few inches of precipitation on the ferociously root-infested descents of Tiger Mountain or the sprawling tight turns of the Tolt McDonald Park, and these trails may cause your hard drive to crash. The mud and grit, sand and silt, eat bikes up and tear riders down on a daily basis. Then there's the Mountain Bike Center at The Summit. In 1997 World Cup downhill maniacs like Missy Giove, Leigh Donavon, and Shaun Palmer broke bones and bikes. Treacherous is an understatement, and if there is a downhill-only area in Washington, The Summit is it. Many of the pros said it was one of the most brutal courses they had ever ridden anywhere in the world.

The East Side also has plenty of rides for the novice cyclist. With a golden tax base, the local communities have plenty of money to build safe, sane, and tame satin-smooth trails. The Redmond Watershed, Pioneer Park, and the Redmond Puget Power Trail are all excellent trails for virgin fat-tire riders. The terrain is flat; the trails are buffed and as wide as I–5. The East Side offers something for riders of all abilities.

1 Pioneer Park

Start: Park and Ride across SE 68
Length: 5 miles of trails
Approximate riding time: 1 to 1½ hour
Technical difficulty: Novice
Trail surface: Hard-pack dirt, mud, gravel
Trail contacts: Mercer Island Parks Department, (206) 236-3545
Fees and permits: None
Schedule: Park is open year-round. However, from November until June mud makes the trails practically unridable.

Maps: *Washington Atlas and Gazetteer,* page 79, D6-7; USGS Bellevue South
Land status: Mercer Island Parks Department
Nearest town: Mercer Island
User density: Heavy
Other trail users: Joggers, hikers, equestrians
Canine compatibility: Leashed dogs permitted
Wheels: Single-speed, BMX, hard-tail, and light suspension
Hazards: Mud, other trail users

Finding the Trailhead

From I-5 head east on I-90 to Mercer Island. From I-405 take I-90 west to Mercer Island. From either direction take the Island Crest Way exit to Southeast Sixty-eighth Street. Turn right onto Sixty-eighth and park in the Park and Ride at the shopping center. Be respectful; do not litter, and keep music levels to a minimum.

The Ride

Finely manicured trails and a lack of climbing make Pioneer Park the perfect place for fretting first-time fat-tire enthusiasts. The park is home to 3 to 5 miles of criss-crossing trails that Mercer Island residents usually have to themselves. Located on the south end of the island, Pioneer Park covers 113 acres and is full of old-growth cedar, Douglas fir, big-leaf maple, and alder.

As one of the first luxurious neighborhoods in Seattle, Mercer Island might be best known for its "old" money and the power that comes with it. When I-90 was expanded in the late 80s/early 90s, Mercer Island residents threw so many attorneys and so much money against the project that it quickly became one of the most expensive 3-mile stretches of interstate in the country. Millions of dollars' worth of extra sound barriers and landscaping were required to end the legal battles so that the upgrades and expansion could be completed.

Today Mercer Island tax dollars are being used much more efficiently. More than thirty parks covering nearly 500 acres are located on the island. Pioneer Park is by far the largest and perhaps the most popular. Like all the Mercer Island parks, Pioneer is maintained nearly as well as the greens at nearby golf courses. Mountain bikers will find three distinct sections separated by Island Crest Way and Sixty-eighth Street. The most technical section is on the southeast side, where horses are permitted to ride. This is also the only section with any drop in elevation. The nonequestrian trails,

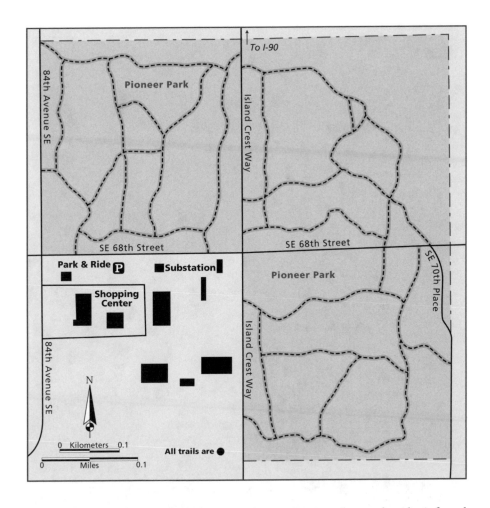

located in the northeast and northwest sections, are groomed smooth and reinforced with pea-sized crushed gravel.

The peaceful trails wind throughout the park with virtually zero climbing involved. The best plan is to ride the trails early in the morning, as they tend to be crowded with joggers and walkers later in the day. Ride in control, tread lightly, and be polite to the other trail users. If the residents can force the Department of Transportation to spend millions of dollars to build a road, they'll have no problems closing the trails to mountain bikers.

Miles and Directions

Simply explore the trails via the map provided. There are not enough miles in any one direction to provide a specific route. Cyclists will have to pick and choose from the various trails and ride them in different directions to pull together any significant mileage.

Native American art marks the park entrance.

Ride Information

Local Events

Shakespeare in the Park, July through August, Wooden O Theatre Productions, Luther Burbank Park Amphitheater, Luther Burbank Park (Lake)

Mostly Music in the Park, Sunday and Tuesday, July through mid-August; Mercerdale Park and Hillside

Restaurants

Chabela's Mexican, (206) 232-8934
Roberto's Pizza Pasta, (206) 232-7383
Islander Pub & Grill, (206) 232-0174
Thai Kitchen, (206) 232-2570
Mi Pueblo Grill, (206) 232-8750
Note: Above restaurants are all on Mercer Island.

2 Wilburton Hill Park and Kelsey Creek Farm

Start: Wilburton Hill Park
Length: 5 to 8 miles
Approximate riding time: 1 hour
Technical difficulty: Novice to intermediate
Trail surface: Pavement, gravel, and single-track
Trail contacts: City of Bellevue Parks and Communities Information, (425) 452-6881 or (425) 452-6855
Fees and permits: None
Schedule: Open year-round
Maps: *Washington Atlas and Gazetteer,* page 79, D7

Land status: Bellevue Parks Department
Nearest town: Bellevue
User density: Moderate to heavy
Other trail users: Joggers, hikers, parkgoers
Canine compatibility: Leashed dogs permitted
Wheels: Single-speed, BMX, hard-tail, and light suspension
Hazards: Automobiles, pedestrians, slick wooden bridges

Finding the Trailhead

From I-405 take the Northeast Eighth Street exit and head east. Turn right on 124th Northeast at the Lamps Plus store and then head south to the corner of Main Street. Wilburton Park is on the left.

The Ride

Wilburton Hill and Kelsey Creek Parks offer decent urban riding for mountain bikers who live in Bellevue and have minimal time to spend in the saddle. The ride is simply too short to consider it a destination ride unless it's to take a first-time cyclist off road. The Bellevue Parks Department maintains the trails constantly, making the area a safe and sane adventure. More experienced riders will want to add a few miles on the road in order to turn the ride into a real workout. Sixty percent of the trails are buffed-smooth soft-packed dirt; the rest of the route is over crushed gravel and pavement. Nearly all the trails drain extremely well, so even during Seattle's infamous rainy season Wilburton and Kelsey Creek are a good combination for riders who need a few quick strokes of the pedal.

Wilburton Park is one of many entrances to the small circuit of trails that wind throughout this urban forest on the east side of Bellevue. Completed in 1991, the 103-acre park is the largest in the city. It has soccer and ball fields and tennis and basketball courts and showcases a botanical garden of native Northwest plants. The trails are easily accessed behind the ball fields, and riders can connect several trails in any number of combinations to form loops of different sizes and shapes. The trails are almost completely nontechnical and velvety smooth as the terrain rolls up and down behind Wilburton Hill Park.

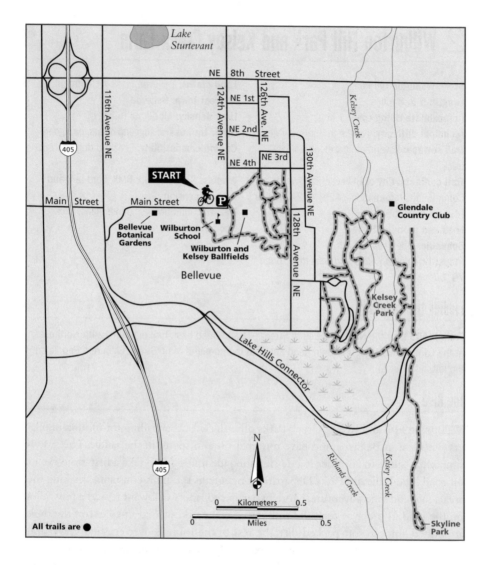

Lake
Sturtevant

NE 8th Street

116th Avenue NE

124th Avenue NE

126th Ave. NE

NE 1st

NE 2nd

NE 4th | NE 3rd

130th Avenue NE

128th Avenue NE

Kelsey Creek

405

Main Street

START

Main Street

P

Bellevue
Botanical
Gardens

Wilburton
School

**Wilburton and
Kelsey Ballfields**

Bellevue

■ Glendale
  Country Club

Kelsey
Creek
Park

Lake Hills Connector

405

N

Richards Creek

Kelsey Creek

0   Kilometers   0.5

0   Miles   0.5

All trails are ●

Skyline
Park

A quick coast down the hill leads cyclists to Kelsey Creek Park with its two historic barns, green pastures, grazing livestock, and jogging paths. The park receives more than 200,000 visits per year—mostly pedestrians with small children. Please act responsibly: be respectful to all nonmountain bikers, do not feed the animals, and ride slowly. Any irresponsible acts by mountain bikers are sure to shut down the park as fast as Anne-Caroline Chausson can rocket through any downhill course in the world.

On the backside of the park the gravel trail turns back into the forest and immediately crosses Kelsey Creek before turning into more satiny smooth soft-packed singletrack. The trail winds through the forest, over several wooden footbridges, and up and down the side of a small gully. Make a few loops in the area before climbing to the top and crossing all four lanes of the Lake Hills Connector Road.

The next section of the route takes riders back into the forest, over additional smooth singletrack, and down and then up several flights of wooden steps built by the Bellevue Parks Department before busting out underneath the power lines. The trail turns into a wide gravel swath that makes six quick climbs and descents as it heads north toward the residential area just below the Bellevue Community College. Upon reaching Sky Line Park, a tiny playground for young children, turn around and head back to Wilburton Hill Park via Kelsey Creek Farm.

▶ Anne-Caroline Chausson is the most dominating downhill racer the sport has ever seen. She is the only racer, male or female, to win the World Championship ten times. When asked who her fiercest competitors are, she calmly responds by naming male champions as opposed to her female counterparts with all the seriousness of a courtroom hearing.

Miles and Directions

0.0 Start from the parking lot and head east toward the baseball fields and the rest rooms along the blacktop path.

0.07 Turn left on the soft dirt/bark trail that climbs above the third base line of Field Number One. The trail is well maintained and follows the edge of the woods around the outfield.

0.2 Turn left into the woods on a wide dirt trail, roughly behind right center field. You can explore this area in about twenty minutes. When you've had enough, head east (away from Wilburton Park) and turn right when you hit 128th Street to reach Kelsey Creek Park.

(**Note:** The following are general directions to Kelsey Creek Farm and the other parts of this ride.)

Turn left on Northeast Fourth Place, drop down another hill, and ride through the main entrance to Kelsey Creek Farm at 130 Northeast Avenue and Northeast Fourth Place. Ride south around the park on the wide gravel trail. The trail follows the edge of the woods, a thick wall of blackberry bushes. Follow the gravel trail until you reach a well-constructed wooden bridge on the right. Turn right here to access another small circuit of well-maintained trails.

After exploring all the trails in this area, which shouldn't take more than twenty minutes, follow the main trail that heads east and up the ridge. Do not take any trail that is not well maintained and covered in the smooth dirt/woodchip surface. You will know you are on the main trail as it climbs up the hill over a series of wooden steps.

At the top of the steps, the trail reaches the westbound lanes of the Lake Hills Connector Road. Cross the road and then a large strip of land between the east and westbound lanes. Eastbound lanes head uphill; westbound lanes head downhill.

Cross the eastbound lanes and follow the gravel trail along the guardrail. Just a short distance down the hill, the trail turns into the smooth dirt/woodchip surface and heads back into the woods. The trail heads up and down a few more sets of stairs before coming out beneath the power lines. Once the forest opens up for the power lines, the trail follows them south over a wide gravel path.

The trail climbs and descends six different hills along this path as it heads north toward the residential area just below Bellevue Community College. Reach the end of the trail at Sky Ridge Park, and head back in the opposite direction to Kelsey Creek Farm and Wilburton Hill Park.

Ride Information

Restaurants

Chantanee Family Thai Restaurant, (425) 455-3226

California Pizza Kitchen, (425) 454-2545

3 Pigs Bar-B-Q, (425) 453-0888

Note: Above restaurants are all in Bellevue.

3 Willows Fjords

Start: NetLink and MetaWave parking lot—
10675 Willows Road
Length: 5.4-mile trail network
Approximate riding time: 1 hour
Technical difficulty: Intermediate to advanced
Trail surface: Singletrack
Trail contacts: Redmond Parks and Recreation, (425) 556-2300
Fees and permits: None
Schedule: Open year-round

Maps: *Washington Atlas and Gazetteer,* page 79, B–C8; USGS Bellevue North
Land status: Redmond Parks and Recreation
Nearest town: Redmond
User density: Light
Other trail users: Bikers, hikers, archers
Canine compatibility: Leashed dogs permitted
Wheels: Front and light dual suspension
Hazards: Stinging nettles, mosquitoes, archers

Finding the Trailhead

From Seattle take I–5 to State Route 520 or I–90 and head east. From both SR 520 and I–90 go north to the 124th Street exit and head east to Willows Road/142nd Avenue Northeast. Turn right onto Willows Road and follow it to 10675 Willows Road. Park on the road in front of MetaWave and NetLink, across from the golf course clubhouse.

Option: Trails are also accessible off 132 Avenue Northeast through various residential areas and power line easements. However, be aware the power line access roads are severely overgrown in many areas. Where the tall wild grass and blackberry bushes open up, the terrain is covered in uneven, teeth-chattering crushed rock. The only reason to access the trail from this side is if you live in the area.

The Ride

The city of Redmond is a bit of a mystery. There are more bike shops in the area than any other place in the region—probably since much of the populace considers their sleepy Microsoft-financed community the cycling capital of the state. There is Marymoor Park and its Velodrome; the Sammamish River Trail, which travels from the city all the way to Seattle via the Burke Gilman trail; a BMX park on Education Hill; the Redmond Puget Power Trail; and finally the city's annual Cycle Derby Days, an event that's sixty-plus years old.

All this is wonderful for roadies and their skinny tires. However, the city seemed to thumb its nose at fat-tire brethren when it closed some of the coolest riding in the Puget Sound area. Since most of the Redmond Watershed (Novelty Hill) was closed to mountain bikers, off-road riding in Redmond has been scarce. What little there is has been watered down with smooth gravel trails; all that is wonderful about technically challenging terrain has been destroyed. However, for mountain bikers living or working in Redmond and with little time to spare, Willows Fjords still retains an element of the muddy and gnarly terrain of Novelty Hill.

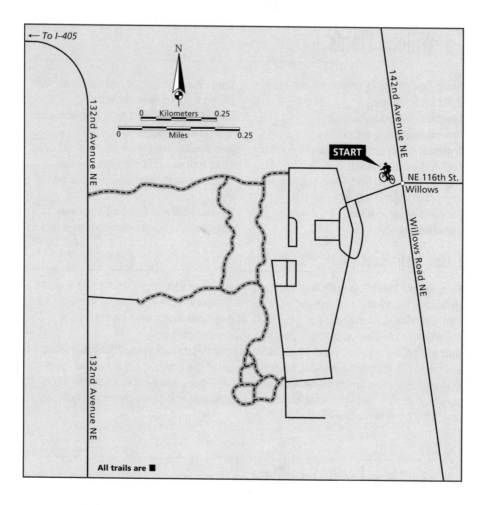

Located off Willows Road behind various office parks, the trail is cut through a dense forest of Douglas fir, big-leaf maple, alder, cedar, and a barricade of blackberry bushes. The trails ride up and down through the forest, with transitions and switchbacks that are too steep and too sharp for most riders to navigate. One section of smooth singletrack is a blast, but to accumulate any mileage the loop must be completed at least three or four times. By then most riders will want a little variety. Still, a short trek through the Fjords is better than not riding at all.

From the parking lot the trail begins to climb on hard-pack singletrack. The ascent is short and slightly steep. Be sure to commit the trail to memory, as this will be the descent as well. Don't worry about getting lost. The ride is too short and the trails too few to worry about losing track of time or direction. Simply head downhill to reach any of the parking lots that crawl up to the edge of the forest.

The rest of the ride follows the ridge of the Redmond Valley, rolling up and down the fjords formed millions of years ago. The route would be much more fun if the transitions were not so drastic and the switchbacks so tight. As it stands now, it is difficult to gain any kind of rhythm. However, this ride will help cyclists become more proficient at shifting during dramatic transitions between descents and ascents.

The trail crosses several creeks and winds through dense moss-covered trees before reaching a stretch of trail with three to four signs reading RING BELL LOUDLY. Why? The trail cuts along the back of an archery range. It's best to heed the advice of the signs, or sing at the top of your lungs. It's probably best not to dally either.

The last major section of the trail cuts through a seemingly impenetrable barricade of blackberry bushes—at least until someone willing to suffer for the rest of us went to work with a high powered weed-whacker. Most of this part of the trail is relatively new, and the shoulders of the trail are soft and crumble easily. Ride right down the middle of the trail, or you'll end up in blackberry brambles. Ouch! The intensity of growth of the biting bushes means that the best time to ride the trail is a little later in the season, when our erstwhile mystery trail maintenance man has again cut through the natural barricade.

Miles and Directions

Pedal through the parking lot heading west (away from the road) straight back to the rock wall—the trailhead is at the end of the rock wall on the left-hand side as you face the wall. Climb a small set of stairs cut into the ground. The trail begins to climb immediately. This is the south end of the ride, and you'll soon see several trails going in different directions. To log any mileage here, you've got to ride them all. The loops are too small to get lost, and you've always got the parking lot on the east side and the power lines on the west side to help you keep your bearings. Stay between the two and head north for roughly 2.2 miles. Turn around and head back to the south end of the trail.

Have fun exploring the short, intense climbs, narrow trails, creek crossings, the archery range (Mile 2.0—don't lollygag through this area, and make a lot of noise while pedaling through), and the unforgiving blackberry gauntlet.

Ride Information

Restaurants
Brown Bag Cafe, (425) 861-4099
Northwest Brew House & Grill, (425) 498-2337
Big Time Pizza, (425) 885-6425

Coho Cafe, (425) 885-2646
Thai Ginger, (425) 558-4044
Note: Above restaurants are all located in Redmond.

4 Redmond Puget Power Trail

Start: Marymoor Park
Length: 11-mile out-and-back
Approximate riding time: 2 hours
Technical difficulty: Novice to intermediate
Trail surface: Paved bike path, gravel and dirt roads, hard packed dirt and mud.
Trail contacts: Redmond Parks and Recreation, (425) 556–2300
Fees and permits: None
Schedule: Open year-round
Maps: *Washington Atlas and Gazetteer,* page 79, B–C8; USGS Bellevue North

Land status: Redmond Parks and Recreation
Nearest town: Redmond
User density: Heavy on the Sammamish River Trail and light on the Redmond Puget Power Trail.
Other trail users: Equestrians, joggers, skaters
Canine compatibility: Leashed dogs permitted
Wheels: Single speed, cross-country, light full suspension
Hazards: Mud, loose gravel on the descents

Finding the Trailhead

From the south end, take I-405 north to State Route 520. Head east on SR 520 and take the West Sammamish Parkway exit. At the end of the off ramp, turn right and drive about 100 yards to Marymoor Avenue and turn left. Park anywhere in the park.
From Seattle, head north or south to SR 520 and follow the directions above.

The Ride

Need an early-season ride to pedal the body back into shape? How about a ride to take a significant other on for a first mountain bike ride without killing him or her—or the relationship? Or how about a few quick miles in the saddle without having to drive to the outreaches of the Puget Sound region? The Redmond Puget Power Trail may be the answer. Easy access, a smooth, flat blacktop trail along the Sammamish River, a double lane–wide trail buffed smooth by construction crews and covered with crushed gravel the size of corn kernels, and a couple of climbs and drops to keep it interesting make this route a favorite among local area novice and intermediate mountain bikers. But after the legal battles over the Redmond Watershed that pitted equestrians and hikers against mountain bikers a few years back, this area of the East Side has fallen off the mountain bike radar.

Riders can access the Redmond Puget Power Trail from several points along the route outlined below, but the only way to log any decent mileage is to begin the ride at Marymoor Park or across town on Avondale Road. Without parking on Avondale, Marymoor is the logical choice. Besides, it gives riders the opportunity to loosen up while riding along the mellow, meandering Sammamish River. The ride is peaceful and the scenery pleasant as it cuts through the middle of a community

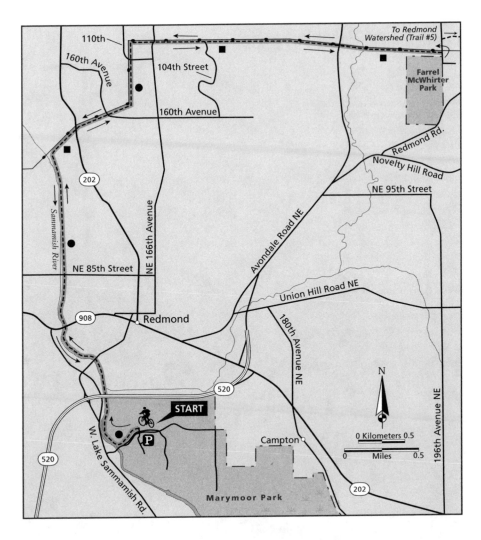

made affluent by the Microsoft money factory. Cyclists will notice sculptures of children playing leapfrog and salmon swimming upstream, and there are exercise areas along the trail.

The route then turns away from the river and heads east over one of the many hills in Redmond. Most riders with any degree of physical fitness, even first-time novices, can handle the climbs, although a few sections are quite steep. The entire trail is finely manicured and covered with tiny pieces of crushed gravel, plus most of the route is wide enough for a small bus. Technical obstacles do not exist on this trail. The only challenging part of the ride will be the short, steep downhills that are unstable because of the gravel. With a quick lessen in descending and breaking, 99.9 percent of riders will have no problem with these downhill sections. A day in the saddle couldn't be easier.

Safe and sane riding in Redmond

Miles and Directions

0.0 Start from the parking lot and pedal west toward West Lake Sammamish Parkway. Look for the blacktop trail just past the tennis courts and to the left. The trail immediately crosses the Sammamish River. Follow the trail to the right (north). This is the Sammamish River Trail. Stick to the bicycle path crossing under SR 520 and Leary Way. Follow the loop to the left and across the river to the other side, then to the left, and down the short hill. Ride under an overpass, pedal past Redmond City Hall on the right and go under one more underpass.

2.3 Turn right onto the Redmond Puget Power Trail, which loosely follows the power lines. The trail is wide enough for two bikes to ride side by side and covered in crushed gravel about the size of peas. Climb up the hill to Redmond Woodinville Road. Cross the road and keep climbing.

2.7 Stick to the main trail on the right.

2.9 Spur trail connects from the left. Ignore this trail and continue riding east. Continue pedaling east crossing 160th Avenue and Northeast 110th.

3.7 Cross a gravel road and drop down a shallow descent. **Option:** As the drop bottoms out you can follow the main gravel trail to the left or stay to the right and get in a little singletrack through a tract of grass that grows as high as 6 or 7 feet in the summer.

4.0 Climb out to 172 Avenue Northeast, cross the street, turn left and then back to the right, and start climbing the main trail. Stick to the main trail, ignoring the trail on the left. The trail becomes steep, and the ride to the bottom is fast and a bit unnerving due to the unstable gravel.

5.0 Reach the bottom of the hill and cross Avondale Road Northeast. On the other side of Avondale, the trail changes to dirt dual track. Cross the bridge shortly thereafter—and watch out for the horse droppings. After crossing the bridge, the trail turns back into wide singletrack but is muddier as it is not covered in gravel. Pass Farrel McWhirter Park; stick to the main trail and pass the horse arena on the right.

5.5 Stay to the left and climb back up under the power lines. Take the immediate next right-hand turn. Arrive at the road (the halfway point) and turn around to head back to the car. **Side trip:** To reach the Redmond Watershed, turn left from here (196th Avenue Northeast) and look for the power line trail on the right a short distance up the road. Turn right on the power line trail and follow all the way to the watershed (approximately 2 to 3 miles).

Options: For additional riding in the area, when returning back to 160th Avenue Northeast, turn right and follow the road. It will turn back to the left and change into Northeast 104th Street. Pedal to 166th Avenue Northeast and turn right. Ride down the road and turn left on Northeast 100th Street. Ride up the hill to the corner of 171st Avenue Northeast and Northeast 100th, which actually ends/turns to the right on 171st. You'll find another trail straight ahead. A short distance in, a BMX park on the right has at least twenty different jumps and some wicked banked turns. Feel free to explore and watch the BMXers catching air. Afterward, continue on down the trail; you'll notice a couple of dirt singletrack trails off to the right and one to the left. There is a little less than a mile of singletrack to be ridden in this area. Once you have explored them, go back out to the main trail and continue east. The trail quickly drops in elevation. Once you reach the bottom you can ride back to the top and retrace your steps to the Puget Power Trail or ride out to Avondale Road and turn right. Follow Avondale to Redmond Way, and then turn right again. Follow Redmond Way all the way to the Sammamish River Trail. Turn left and head back to Marymoor Park.

Ride Information

Restaurants
Brown Bag Cafe, (425) 861-4099
Northwest Brew House & Grill, (425) 498-2337
Big Time Pizza, (425) 885-6425

Coho Cafe, (425) 885-2646
Thai Ginger, (425) 558-4044
Note: Above restaurants are all located in Redmond.

5 Redmond Watershed

Start: Redmond Watershed Preserve
parking lot
Length: 7.9-mile out-and-back
Approximate riding time: 1 to 2 hours
Technical difficulty: Novice
Trail surface: Pea-sized crushed gravel, hard-pack dirt, and mud.
Trail contacts: Redmond Parks and Recreation, (425) 556–2300
Fees and permits: None

Schedule: Open year-round
Maps: *Washington Atlas and Gazetteer,* page 79, B–C8; USGS Bellevue North
Land status: Redmond Parks and Recreation
Nearest town: Redmond
User density: Medium
Other trail users: Equestrians, hikers
Canine compatibility: Dogs not permitted
Wheels: Cross-country or light full suspension
Hazards: Mud

Finding the Trailhead

Take State Route 520 east to Redmond. Cross SR 202 and bear right onto Avondale Road. Drive for 1.5 miles and stay to the right again on Novelty Hill Road. Proceed east for 2.4 miles. The park entrance is on the left-hand side across from 218th Northeast.

The Ride

The Redmond Watershed is excellent for folks who have not spent a lot of time in the saddle. Climbing is almost nonexistent, and the trails are buffed almost as smooth as blacktop. On the main trails there are no roots or rocks to navigate, just a wide, smooth trail covered in pea-sized gravel. The riding is completely nontechnical; the area is beautiful and full of wildlife. Deer, rabbits, black bears, woodpeckers, beavers, red-tailed hawks, great blue herons, chipmunks, and squirrels dwell in the forest and around the numerous creeks and swamps. Cougars and coyotes are occasionally spotted as well. Most wild animals will only attack if provoked or cornered; however, cougars have been known to attack small children who stray or are left alone.

Officially known as the Redmond Watershed Preserve, these 800 acres of forest, meadows, and wetland used to be known as Novelty Hill among off-road cyclists. However, after a bitter feud pitting hikers and equestrians against mountain bikers, most of the trails that attracted fat-tire fanatics have been closed or watered down so much that you can almost ride them with your eyes closed and your legs tied together. It just goes to show how important it is to ride responsibly and respectfully. Learn more about trail advocacy by joining the Back Country Bicycle Trails Club. Call (206) 283–2995, e-mail them at bbtc@cycling.org, or visit www.bbtc.org.

The fact that any trails are open to mountain bikers at all is a testament to the dedication of the Back Country Bicycle Trails Club. During the early to mid-1990s, the BBTC fought to keep the trails open. While the riding at Novelty Hill is not

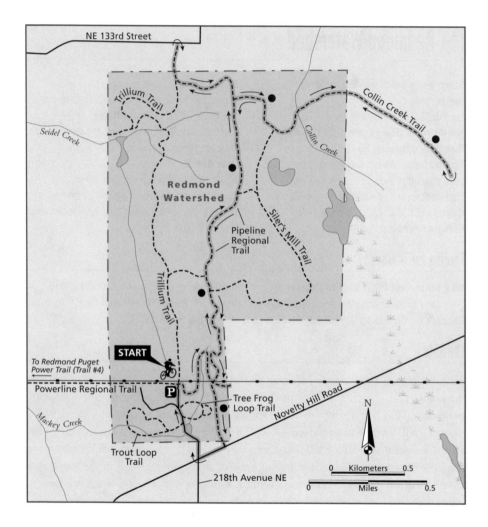

nearly as challenging as it used to be, the Redmond Parks Department has made considerable improvements to the trail circuit, ensuring long-term use and enjoyment by all kinds of outdoor enthusiasts.

Miles and Directions

0.0 Start by riding to the back of the parking lot (away from Novelty Hill Road) and look for the Trillium Connector Trail. Turn right and head down the short shallow hill to the Powerline Regional Trail. Turn right and take either trail, as the main trail splits and then reconnects at the fence. Continue straight if you are emerging from the woods after making a right, or turn left if you continued straight where the trail split. Cross the cement bridge and look for the four-way intersection. Turn left onto the Pipeline Regional Trail. Be sure to

An easy roll through the Watershed

respect the EQUESTRIAN and HIKER ONLY trail signs. Cross a couple more bridges and the Collin Creek Trail on the right at roughly 2.0 miles. Don't worry—you can hit this sweet little chunk of singletrack on the way back.

2.2 Pass the gravel storage site.

2.6 Reach Northeast 133rd, turn around, and head in the opposite direction.

2.8 Turn left on Collin Creek Trail, which narrows to less-manicured singletrack. (**Note:** The Collin Creek Trail is not buffed smooth and covered with the pea-sized gravel. It still contains roots, rocks, and mud.)

3.0 Pass the Siler's Mill Trail (a hiker's only trail) on the right, and stick to Collin Creek Trail. Cross the bridge and Collin Creek a third of a mile up the trail.

3.6 Cross the road and construction area. It will probably be developed by the time this book is in print.

3.9 Cross the dirt road and ride the narrow singletrack trail. The road will probably be completely developed by the time this book is on shelves. (Even in late June the trail is often covered in water and mud. This might be a good place to turn around unless you'd like to gunk up your bike.)

4.2 Reach another road, and turn around.

5.6 Turn left onto the Pipeline Regional Trail.

REDMOND BICYCLE DERBY DAYS

Redmond Bicycle Derby Days, now sixty-plus years young, is an annual community festival featuring a grand parade, kid's parade, bike safety rodeo, pancake breakfast, music festival, and food court. Held in mid-July, the festival hosts America's longest running race—the Criterium. Six races are held throughout the day, including local and national cyclists vying for a $10,000 purse.

The following events are all part of the Redmond Bicycle Derby Days:

- **Davis Amusements Carnival:** The carnival features amusement rides to thrill, games to test your skills, and carnival treats
- **TimberLake MusicFest:** A weekend of music ranging from local to regional acts, including jazz, blues, reggae, and pop
- **Kid's Bicycle Parade:** An extremely popular event, with all participants receiving a $2.00 bill at the finish line. Kid's Parade participants ride their decorated bikes along the Grande Parade route and finish at the Redmond Community Center. Entry is free and open to children of all ages
- **Derby Days Grande Parade:** A traditional family parade including marching bands, floats, cars, SEAFAIR clowns, Sea Fair Marshalls, and previous Miss Redmonds
- **Bike Safety Rodeo:** Organized by the Redmond Boys and Girls Club, this event offers kids an opportunity to learn about bicycle safety through an onsite safety course. Each child receives a free bicycle helmet upon completion of the safety course.
- **Criterium at Derby Days:** The Annual Saturn of Bellevue Criterium at Derby Days is America's longest-running bicycle race. Six races are presented throughout the day, including local and national cyclists. A total purse of $10,000 is divided among the top finishers.

For more information visit www.derbydays.net, call (425) 885–4014, or write The Greater Redmond Chamber of Commerce, 16210 Northeast Eightieth Street, Redmond, WA 98052.

7.3 Reach the four-way intersection (Power Line Trail and Pipeline Trail). You can turn right and head directly back to the car or go straight. (**FYI:** If you choose to go straight, hit the road and turn right.)

7.6 Turn right into the park.

7.9 Reach the parking lot.

Side trip: To connect the Watershed Trail with the Redmond Puget Power Trail, exit the park to the west on the Powerline Regional Trail and follow it all the way until you pass Redmond Road to 196th Northeast. Turn left and then right a short distance up the road and back underneath the power lines—the corner of Farrel McWhirter Park (approximately 2 to 3 miles).

Ride Information

Restaurants

Brown Bag Cafe, (425) 861–4099

Northwest Brew House & Grill, (425) 498–2337

Big Time Pizza, (425) 885–6425

Coho Cafe, (425) 885–2646

Thai Ginger, (425) 558–4044

Note: Above restaurants are all located in Redmond.

6 Saint Edwards State Park and Big Finn Hill King County Park

Start: Saint Edwards Park
Length: 1 to 2 hours
Approximate riding time: Varies on 10 miles of trails with countless combinations
Technical difficulty: Easy to advanced
Trail surface: Singletrack
Trail contacts: St. Edwards State Park, (425) 823-2992
Washington State Parks, (800) 233-0321
Backcountry Bicycle Trails Club, Activities Hotline, (206) 283-2995; www.bbtc.org
Fees and permits: None
Schedule: Open year-round

Maps: *Washington Atlas and Gazetteer,* page 79, 6B–C; USGS Bellevue North, Seattle North
Land status: King County Parks
Nearest town: Kenmore, Kirkland, Bothell
User density: Heavy
Other trail users: Hikers
Canine compatibility: Dogs permitted on a leash of no more than 8 feet. Pet lovers must clean up after their dogs.
Wheels: Single-speed, front, and light dual suspension
Hazards: Blackberry bushes, other mountain bikers, hikers, mosquitoes

Finding the Trailhead

From Seattle, take I-5 north to Lake City Way (State Route 522) to Kenmore. Turn right onto Juanita Drive Northeast (look for more visible Sixty-eighth Avenue Northeast sign at the same intersection). Follow Juanita Drive to Saint Edwards State Park on the right. Drive into the park; stay to the right at the fork, then turn right and park behind the building above the playfield.
From the East Side, take I-405 north or south to 116th Avenue Northeast and head west to bottom of hill. Cross intersection (Ninety-eighth Street Northeast) onto Juanita Drive Northeast; follow it up hill past QFC and pass Holmes Point Drive. Turn left into park.

The Ride

Side by side, Saint Edwards State and Big Finn Hill Parks provide fat-tire zealots with 372 acres of trails that twist, turn, roll, drop, and climb over roots, rocks, gravel, hard-pack singletrack, jumps, bumps, logs, man–made obstacles, dusty loose dirt in summer, and hub-deep clinging mud in winter. Although the mileage listed above is low compared with rides farther away from the megatropolis of the Emerald City, the area offers nearly as many combinations of trails as there are Starbucks in Seattle. Cyclists can spend hours in the saddle exploring all the different routes before becoming familiar with the seething snakepit–like maze of trails. However, the popularity of the two parks and their tremendously easy access are also the area's biggest downfall. It may see more traffic than any other ride in the region. Please respect the trail signs that read, NO BICYCLES in certain areas, or this park may suffer the fate of so many others that are now closed to cyclists.

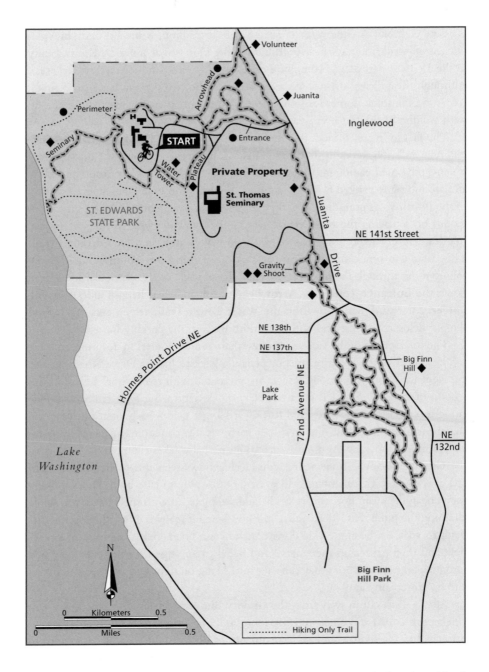

Located on the north end of Lake Washington between Bothell and Kirkland and less than thirty minutes from nearly anywhere north of Renton and south of Everett, Saint Edwards and Big Finn provide the most popular two-wheeled urban adventure in the Puget Sound region. Purchased by the state in 1977 from the

Roman Catholic Archdiocese of Seattle for $7 million, Saint Edwards provides wicked off-road riding for nearly all abilities. Big Finn was acquired by King County in the 1970s as part of a $110 million project to increase outdoor recreational areas. Although the mileage of any one route through the two parks is less than 3 miles, riders can combine numerous unnamed trails and ride them backward to come up with a different ride for every day of the week.

The first loop cuts though the northwest side of Saint Edwards and connects five different trails. The straight shot **Arrowhead** is up first and provides a smooth, easy warm-up before heading into **Juanita**—a rolling, twisting track over roots and rocks and around tight-banked turns. In summer, the trail is dusty dry, but after a few days of the Northwest's pounding rain, the trail becomes a quagmire of sticky, slick mud. Count on replacing the brake pads after one or two rides here in the wet season. **Juanita** deposits bikers at the top of two trails—**Volunteer** and the **Entrance Trail.** The latter is a quick straightaway back to the parking lot; **Volunteer** is a kinky rolling romp through the forest. To increase the mileage of this particular loop, head down the **Entrance Trail,** ride **Arrowhead** again, and then hang it all out in **Volunteer.** Afterward, wind down on the **Water Tower Trail,** which cuts out behind the playfields and picnic area and then heads back to the parking lot.

The total length of the ride so far is less than 5 miles. Riders up for more mileage can head over to the Big Finn area by pedaling back to Juanita Drive Northeast and cut right back into the woods. Riders are presented with two major choices in this section of the park. Stay left for a relatively quick trip to Big Finn Hill over undulating terrain and more twists and turns. Or hang a razor-sharp right just after the switchback, and head out into fresh-cut narrow trails containing man-made obstacles, jumps, bumps, and even more turns. This trail also takes riders to the bottom of the **Gravity Shoot**—an apt name, considering how steep this particular hill is. In fact, it is so steep that many pro riders may not be able to ride up it. Those looking for a cheap thrill can hop off the saddle and scramble up with their bikes. It is while climbing the pitch that riders realize just how steep it really is. Near the top it is difficult to walk up, let alone ride down. At the crest, bikers reach the back of a playfield and then gather up their nerve and pedal to an edge they can't see over and into the darkness of woods they can't see into. Hang on tight, stay off the front brake, and try to remain calm!

After a short climb away from the **Gravity Shoot** and back up to the main trail, riders cross a road and enter into Big Finn Hill. Big Finn is a maze of trails that cut through the forest in a multitude of directions. It will take days for any rider to explore the entire area. There are many different combinations to choose from as the wildly rolling terrain cuts through big-leaf maples, a dense field of blackberry bushes, Douglas fir, and sword fern. There are steep, short drops, banked turns, loose dirt, man-made jumps, washboard descents, and short, wide-open straightaways for out-of-the-saddle pounding-on-your-pedals riding.

However, due to their location, Saint Edwards and Big Finn probably see more traffic than any other off-road area in the state. And the traffic is taking its toll. Some of the trails are designated for hikers only, although hikers are allowed to use the bike trails. There is not much else more frightening to a hiker than the possibility of being run over by a mountain biker ripping down the trail. Be responsible; stay off the hiking-only trails, and be courteous to the hikers you see along the mountain bike trails. Slow down to pass, and always say thank-you when they step aside.

Miles and Directions

Start from the parking lot, ride back to the main entrance road, and enter the woods on the dirt trail across the road from the playfields. This trail accesses the Arrowhead, Juanita, Entrance, and Volunteer Trails.

All four of these trails are also accessible at the park entrance just off Juanita Drive Northeast. Juanita, Entrance, and Volunteer Trails all converge here, and directly across the park entrance riders will spot another trail. This trail cuts through the property of the Saint Thomas Center and transports riders south to Big Finn Hill and southwest to the Gravity Shoot.

Mountain bikers can also access the trail from Holmes Point Drive/141st Street, which runs perpendicular to Juanita Drive Northeast and parallel to the QFC Grocery store. Many riders park in the QFC parking lot and enter the trails from here. Just be sure to be responsible: Do not leave any garbage or play music too loud. Heading southwest (toward Lake Washington) on Holmes Point Drive and turning right onto the trails deposits riders into the Saint Thomas Center and back toward Saint Edwards Park.

Upon turning left, riders will enter a small section of trails located between Holmes Point Road, Seventy-second Avenue Northeast, and Northeast 138th Place. Take an immediate right after re-entering the trail, and drop down into a steep gully and *try* to climb back out. Or stay to your left and at each **Y** in the trail and you will quickly reach Seventy-second Avenue Northeast and Northeast 138th Place. Cross the road; pass the small kiosk, map, and garbage can; and you are officially in Big Finn Hill Park. Big Finn is loaded with tight-banked turns, narrow trails, steep drops, jumps, roots, rocks, and challenge after challenge that will keep any rider entertained for hours.

Ride Information

Restaurants

The Slip Restaurant & Bar, (425) 739-0033
Acropolis Pizza, (425) 827-3777
Rikki Rikki Sushi, (425) 828-0707

Taco Villa Señor (Home of the tastiest burritos on the West Coast), (425) 825-8128
Note: Above restaurants are all located in Kirkland.

In Addition

Keeping Trails Open

In August 1991 the fledgling BBTC became aware that Saint Edwards State Park was considering banning mountain bikes within its boundaries. BBTC, still new to advocacy issues but learning quickly, introduced themselves and offered help to the powers that be at Saint Edwards State Park. Soon after, the state parks manager for Saint Edwards approached BBTC asking their help to route and build a small network of mountain bike–friendly trails in Saint Edwards State Park.

In April 1991 the first of many work parties began at the park. Since 1991 BBTC has led an average of four work parties a year, including adding new trail, maintaining old trail, placing educational signage, and leading a mountain bike bootcamp at Saint Edwards. BBTC also pays for most of the materials needed for maintenance from their donation-maintained trail fund.

The successful intervention of BBTC and the forward-thinking state parks manager gives hope that with continued volunteer support BBTC can have a dramatic effect on the amount and quality of mountain bike trails close in to Seattle. The state parks manager has also made it clear that without BBTC's support there would be no mountain biking at the park because the park's limited resources are not enough to maintain the network of trails by themselves. Also, when complaints do come in, the park can point to the continued services BBTC performs both in trail maintenance and in educating riders to ride responsibly.

Mountain biking is still heavily opposed in many trail-user communities. There is a perception that mountain bikers are wild and unfriendly and ruin the trails. To help dispel these myths, follow the guidelines below.

Some common arguments are used by opponents of mountain biking to get trails closed to mountain bikers. By getting involved and following the common-sense suggestions below, you can make a difference in whether a trail stays open or is closed. To find out about trail work and advocacy meetings, contact your local mountain bike club or the IMBA.

Perception: We don't give back to the trails.
What you can do:

- If you ride more than once or twice a year, join your local bike club and the IMBA. Numbers equal political clout; membership dues help build trails.
- Volunteer at a trail work party or attend a meeting in support of mountain bikes.
- Call the land managers of your favorite trail and let them know you support mountain bikes on the trails.

Perception: We're crazed adrenaline junkies that don't care if we run over hikers and horses.

What you can do:

- Smile. Be friendly to everyone. It is amazing how much good a simple hello and smile can do to disarm a mountain bike versus non–mountain bike encounter.
- Be prepared to dismount for horses. Ask the equestrians what they would prefer you to do.

Perception: We cause more damage to trails than hikers.

What you can do:

- Don't skid, don't ride around obstacles, and don't ride in wet conditions unless the trail can handle it. Don't cut switchbacks. Ride in control. All trails require maintenance—the main difference between mountain bikes and hikers regarding trail damage is caused by skidding.

For more information contact:
Backcountry Bicycle Trails Club (BBTC)
P.O. Box 21288
Seattle, WA 98111-3288
(206) 283–2995
bbtc@cycling.org
www.bbtc.org

7 Beaver Lake

Start: Beaver Lake Road
Length: Up to a 6-mile circuit
Approximate riding time: 1 to 2 hours
Technical difficulty: Easy to moderate, depending on how fast the trails are ridden. There is little or no climbing, but there are a couple of tight technical sections.
Trail surface: Singletrack
Trail contacts: King County Parks Department, (206) 296–2966
Back Country Bicycle Trails Club, (206) 283–2995; www.bbtc.org
Fees and permits: None

Schedule: Open year-round
Maps: *Washington Atlas and Gazetteer*, pages 79 C–D8 and 80 C–D1; USGS Fall City and Bellevue South
Land status: King County Parks Department
Nearest town: Issaquah
User density: Moderate
Other trail users: Equestrians, hikers, joggers
Canine compatibility: Dogs permitted
Wheels: Single-speed, cross-country, and light dual suspension
Hazards: Stinging nettles, mud in winter, rickety footbridges, pedestrians, equestrians

Finding the Trailhead

From Seattle, go east on I-90 to Issaquah. Take the Front Street exit (second Issaquah exit). Turn left at the light onto East Lake Sammamish Parkway. Pass the McDonald's and Albertson's on your right, and then turn right onto Southeast Forty-third. Continue uphill; at the crest of the hill, the road turns into Southeast 228th. Pass the QFC grocery store and Wells Fargo Bank, and continue to Southeast Twenty-fourth; turn right. Follow this road for 1.4 miles, where road takes a sharp turn to the left and changes into Beaver Lake Road. Follow the road for 2.4 miles to an ultrasmall parking space/shoulder of the road on the right. The trail begins across the street.

The Ride

Located on the Issaquah Plateau, the Beaver Lake Trail System is microchip small but excellent for quick rides when you're pressed for time. Three to five small single-track loops connect to form a 3-to-6-mile surly circuit of rolling trails. Physically fit novice riders can probably handle Beaver Lake; intermediate and advanced riders will get a small jolt out of some of the more challenging technical problems scattered throughout the ride.

Beaver Lake is a fantastic fix for fat-tire junkies who need a midweek evening-ride destination. Located within thirty minutes of Seattle, and even less from most areas on the East Side, Beaver Lake is 100 percent singletrack and grade AAA fun.

From the road, the **Beaver Lake Trail** dives into the dense forest of mostly Douglas fir, Sitka spruce, vine maple, and a few patches of western red cedar, which provides shade in summer and shelter from the rain in winter. However, once the rainy season arrives, the circuit of connectable loops is monstrously muddy. During summer the tightly packed forest combined with the moisture in the air creates a mild sauna effect.

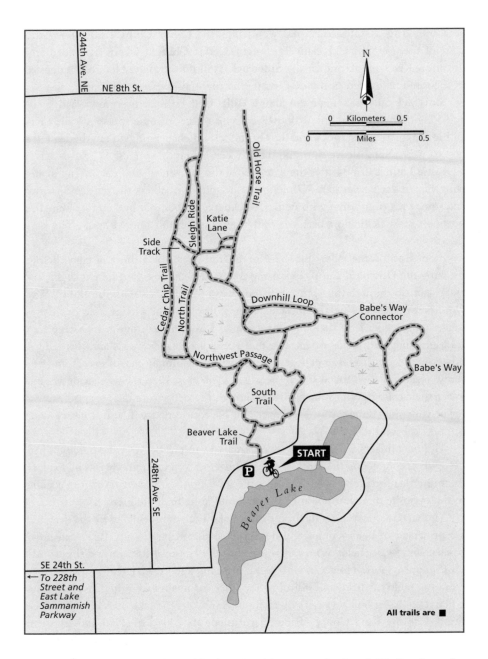

The **Beaver Lake Trail** quickly deposits riders onto the **South Trail,** where the real fun begins. The **South Trail** rolls with the relatively level terrain as it winds its way to the **Northwest Passage Trail.** The **Northwest Passage** and **North Trails** require more skills as the turns grow sharper and singletrack becomes spiked with roots, large logs, whoop-de-dos, rickety footbridges, mud bogs, and short, steep climbs.

Covered in dark brownish-red woodchips, the **Cedar Chips Trail** follows the edge of the golf course. Relatively straight, **Cedar Chips** descends in a northerly direction. Keep a look out for the **Sidetrack Trail** on the right. Due to the density of the forest and speed of the descent, the narrow trail is easy to miss.

Sidetrack quickly connects to **Sleigh Ride.** Both trails are overgrown with ferns and stinging nettles. The forest floor is difficult to see in some spots, making navigating the turns, roots, rocks, and dips in the terrain challenging, to say the least. It's best to wear a long-sleeve shirt and tights when riding these trails.

Katie Lane is named after the daughter of the local rider who voluntarily maintains the trails at Beaver Lake. While the name sounds harmless, the trails are narrow and somewhat overgrown with nettles, blackberry bushes, and broken tree branches waiting to tear flesh and fabric. You won't get through this one without a few battle scars.

From **Katie Lane** riders hit the **North Trail** again for a short distance before reaching the **Downhill Loop.** The name is a bit deceptive, as the slope is slight, but riders can rip through this section of straightaway. Combined with the **Babe's Way Connector,** this may be the most exciting portion of the circuit. The descent is longer and steeper here than anywhere else at Beaver Lake—but not so steep that it's frightening for novice riders. The trail is overgrown as it twists and turns, dives down, jumps up, crosses over logs and roots, and seemingly makes every effort to throw riders off their metal steeds. Because riders must keep their heads down and lower their riding position to navigate through the dense forest, it's a good idea to lower your seat. **Babe's Way** is an excellent adventure that will also improve your timing, skills, and stamina.

Mountain bikers will find only two drawbacks to the Beaver Lake Circuit. First, even when connecting the loops, the rides are short. You can remedy this by exploring more than one loop or riding the same loop frontward and backward. Pedaling in the opposite direction will turn the trail into an entirely different ride.

The second drawback is that the Beaver Lake Trails are shrinking by the year and are in danger of being completely destroyed so that King County Parks can build baseball and soccer fields. Who can argue with the National Pastime and the world's most popular sport? However, with some planning and creativity, the parks department can build the fields and still allow for killer mountain bike riding. As in all cases when it comes to trail access, it's up to mountain bikers to make our collective voice heard. Call the King County Parks Department at (206) 296-2966 and let them know you want to the trails to remain open for mountain biking. You can also learn more about trail advocacy by joining the Back Country Bicycle Trails Club. For more information call the BBTC at (206) 283-2995, send an e-mail to bbtc@cycling.org, or visit www.bbtc.org.

Miles and Directions

You'll never be farther than 1 mile from the road. The map is easy to read, and if you hit the golf course or the housing development, turn around and head back to the Beaver Lake Trail. It will take you back to the road with only a few pedal strokes.

Ride Information

Local Events

Issaquah Concert on the Green, early July through August
Issaquah Full Scale Music Festival, mid-August
Annual Issaquah Jazz Festival, late August. Reggae, rock, western, swing, dance, funk, salsa, and more. Visit www.ci.issaquah.wa.us, or call (425) 392-6342 for more information.

Issaquah Salmon Days, October. Visit the OFISHAL Salmon Days Web site at www.salmondays.org, or call (425) 392-0661 for more information.

Restaurants

Sushi Man, (425) 392-4295
Orchid Tree Restaurant, (425) 392-5262
Georgio's Subs, (425) 392-5624
Note: Above restaurants are all located in Issaquah.

8 Grand Ridge

Start: Gilman Boulevard, Issaquah
Length: 10 to 11.5 miles
Approximate riding time: 2 to 3 hours
Technical difficulty: Intermediate to advanced due to steep climb and descent and technical challenges
Trail surface: Pavement, gravel road, wood-chip road, hard-packed dirt singletrack
Trail contacts: King County Parks Department, (206) 296-2966 · Back Country Bicycle Trails Club, (206) 283-2995; www.bbtc.org
Fees and permits: None
Schedule: Open year-round

Maps: *Washington Atlas and Gazetteer,* pages 79, D8 and 80, D1; USGS Fall City and Belle-vue South
Land status: King County Parks
Nearest town: Issaquah
User density: Medium
Other trail users: Hikers, equestrians
Canine compatibility: Dogs permitted
Wheels: Cross-country and light dual suspension
Hazards: Automobile traffic, deep mud, steep descents covered with loose terrain, construction and development, thieves at the trailhead

Finding the Trailhead

Take I-90 east to the Issaquah Front Street exit (exit 17). At the end of the off-ramp, turn right and then take an immediate right onto Gilman Boulevard. Park in any of the larger shopping complex parking lots along Gilman. There is a small parking area located at the trailhead just off I-90 and farther east from Issaquah (High Point Way, exit 20). However, parking here is an invitation to have your vehicle broken into. The amount of theft from this tiny parking lot is staggering, so park here at your own risk.

The Ride

Grand Ridge may soon become one of the more disappointing mountain bike trail casualties of Seattle area development. Located just outside Issaquah, the Grand Ridge Loop continues to shrink and change every year as more and more homes are constructed on the plateau above the rapidly growing bedroom community. Cut through a forest of Douglas fir, western red cedar, alder, and sword fern, Grand Ridge offers challenging singletrack, technical climbs, and short, steep descents. Just a short distance from Seattle and even closer to the East Side, Grand Ridge is an excellent choice for quick evening rides and short adventures for riders with little time to hang out in the saddle.

Located just north of Tiger Mountain on the other side of I-90, the ride is accessible from two directions. Mountain bikers are free to park at the trailhead just off the High Point Way exit (exit 20), but do so at your own risk. Every year, double-digit numbers of mountain bikers' automobiles are victims of forced entry and theft. The best plan is to park along Gilman Boulevard in one of the many shopping center parking lots and access the trail from the opposite direction. Ride through the

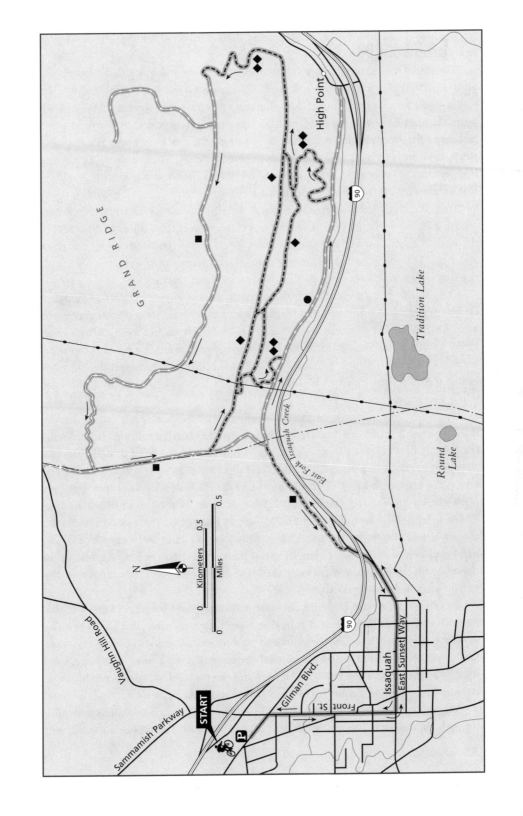

middle of old Issaquah on Front Street and then head west through the residential area on East Sunset Way.

The actual trail starts off with a short, mellow descent and quick dash underneath I–90. The trail also follows the east fork of Issaquah Creek for a short distance. Be sure to look for the small footbridge, which isn't much more than an 8-by-24-inch beam set high on two large boulders above the creek. It's located under the second section of the freeway. This is the only spot to ford the creek without taking a bath. Keep your head down, and watch for gigantic spiders while walking across the bridge. On the other side, riders will find a choice spot to watch spawning salmon make their way up the creek in September and October.

From the creek, the singletrack climbs to a well-maintained railroad grade, where mountain bikers will encounter more hikers and joggers than on any other part of the trail. The gravel-covered route gradually ascends as it heads east along the creek and I–90. This section of the ride is a good warm-up, because after roughly a mile the trail begins to climb up the ridge over rocky, loose terrain.

Even in the best of conditions, the ascent is nearly impossible to flash without dabbing. During summer the trail is riddled with ruts, large loose rocks, gravel, and roots. During fall it becomes even uglier as the trail becomes hidden by a thick blanket of giant maple leaves. Add in the Puget Sound area precipitation, and the route becomes a seriously slippery climb over avalanching terrain that even the strongest mountain biker may not be able to ride. Frankly, it can be a difficult climb even while walking and pushing a bike.

Upon reaching the crest of the first major climb, the trail levels out as it twists through a small grove of alders. The respite from the short, punishing climb doesn't last long. Riders continue to gain elevation while following a long straightaway that alternates between year-round mud bogs and three more steep climbs over loose terrain. After a thousand feet of climbing in less than 2 miles, the trail tops out on a small plateau high above a ravine and I–90, evidenced by the sound of automobiles whizzing by at 60-plus miles per hour. Mountain bikers find this a good spot to dismount, release bodily fluids, and recharge with a swig of H$_2$O and a chunk of energy bar. From here the real fun begins as speed freaks have two choices: Return in the opposite direction for a free fall over the loose and now treacherous terrain, or finish the loop by heading north.

Heading back in the opposite direction requires a cool head and nerves of titanium. Remember those steep climbs that were tough to even *walk* up? The long, straight shot of stair step–like descents and plateaus are dangerous because they contain some of the fastest sustained vertical drops on the East Side. The large, loose rocks look even larger, the ruts look deeper, and the trail feels steeper from this angle. Be sure to keep your weight back—and lay off the front brakes.

Mountain bikers who follow the loop are rewarded with a challenging romp through the forest as the trail gradually descends toward the woodchip road, with one exception where the route drops down nasty old dry creekbed full of large loose hunks of rock and gravel. If a rider is going to go over his or her bars during this ride, this is typically the spot. The vertically challenged will probably want to walk down this section, while riders who are willing to risk there necks should use their breaks gingerly and make sure to shift their weight way back behind their saddles. The singletrack finishes off by snaking its way through tight gaps in the trees, over blown-down logs and burly roots, and through banked turns and muddy quagmires.

The trail then breaks out of the forest onto the woodchip road, which follows the power lines for roughly a mile before heading back into the forest and down more full throttled, full tilt terrain. Possibly even steeper than every other descent in the ride, this last section is even more challenging because most riders are already feeling fatigued by the earlier punishing climbs and downhill sections. Throw in a few tight turns and the last couple of drops are big, bad, and ugly. The ride finishes by popping out onto the old railroad grade, whence riders can head back to town.

Miles and Directions

Ride east on Gilman Boulevard and turn right onto Front Street. Follow Front Street south for about 0.5 mile and then turn left onto East Sunset Way. The ride and mileage log begins on East Sunset Way right after it crosses the east fork of Issaquah Creek and right before it crosses over I–90. Look for the trail just on the other side of the steel guardrail, where it meets the cement barricade on the left-hand side of the road.

0.0 Follow the singletrack down toward the bridge and cross under the first underpass. While under the second underpass, look for the footbridge crossing the creek. The bridge is nothing more than an 8 x 24 beam set above the creek on a couple of large rocks. It often washes out early in the spring. Keep your head down and crawl out from under the bridge to your right. Follow the singletrack up the bank away from the freeway.

0.3 Turn right onto the old gravel railroad grade.

1.3 Turn left up the loose, rocky singletrack. The trail immediately splits into a Y. Take either route, as they reconnect just a short distance into the woods. However, the trail on the right is a much easier climb.

1.7 The trail plateaus for a brief respite from the climbing. A short distance up the trail you'll have to dismount to cross the creekbed. The trail bends to the left and begins a steep technical climb. Very few mountain bikers are able to flash the trail, which is littered with loose rock, sand, loads of leaves, and gnarly roots. Fortunately it is a short climb.

2.3 Turn right and cut through a section of young alders and smooth soft-dirt singletrack. Hit the wide pipeline trail and turn right. (**FYI:** In summer the trail is packed but soft, tacky dirt; in winter it is coated in slick, unforgiving, and often deep mud. You'll know it's the pipeline trail by all of the yellow danger/hazard signs. The trail continues to climb up three steep sections with short plateaus between them, all of which cross through year-round 10-to-30-foot mud holes.)

2.8 Cross the dirt road, another ugly sign of the development taking place in this area.

3.1 Cross a second dirt road.

3.2 Pass the trail on the left and arrive at the highest point of the climb and the end of the pipeline trail. Turn around and make an immediate right-hand turn. The singletrack begins to descend as it weaves throughout the thick garment of sword ferns and other low-lying foliage.

3.4 Cross the road, take a soft right then a soft left, and go back into the woods.

3.5 Cross the small clearcut, and ride the edge on the east side (to your right).

3.6 Drop down a steep technical section. Look for the trail on the left, and start climbing again.

4.2 Exit the woods on a high bank above the blacktop road. Turn left, and ride for less than 50 feet until the bank is safe enough to ride down. Cross the road, and look for the trail heading back into the woods. The trail descends a steep, nasty section covered in large jagged rocks that tend to throw both riders and bikes back and forth across the trail.

4.9 Make a hard left and enjoy the slight descent; blast through twisting banked turns and roller-coaster terrain.

5.3 Turn left onto the woodchip road, and follow the power lines.

6.3 Turn left and head into the clearcut. (**FYI:** A good landmark is the singletrack trail on the other side of the road that heads downhill.)

6.4 Turn right in between two tall stumps, which are roughly 20 feet apart. The trail is difficult to follow through the clearcut, but follow the left edge of it and you'll run into the trail at the back. Head back into the woods and begin to descend back toward the old railroad grade.

6.7 Stay to your left at the Y, and drop down a steep, rocky section.

7.0 Reach the old railroad grade; turn right and head back to the bridge and underpass.

8.0 Turn left and descend over the singletrack. Reach the underpass, cross the bridge, turn right, and pedal back toward East Sunset Way.

8.2 Reach East Sunset Way, and ride back toward town. Turn right on Front Street then left on Gilman Boulevard, and pedal back to your car.

Ride Information

Local Information

Issaquah Visitor Information Center, (425) 392-7024; www.issaquah.org or www.ci.issaquah.wa.us

Local Events

Issaquah Concert on the Green, early July through August

Issaquah Full Scale Music Festival, mid-August

Annual Issaquah Jazz Festival, late August. Reggae, rock, western, swing, dance, funk, salsa, and more. Visit www.ci.issaquah.wa.us, or call (425) 392-6342 for more information

Issaquah Salmon Days, October. Visit the OFISHAL Salmon Days Web site at www.salmondays.org, or call (425) 392-0661 for more information.

Restaurants

Sushi Man, (425) 392-4295

Orchid Tree Restaurant, (425) 392-5262

Georgio's Subs, (425) 392-5624

Note: Above restaurants are all located in Issaquah.

9 Carey Creek

Start: Issaquah Hobart Road and Highway 18 intersection
Length: 9.5-mile circuit
Approximate riding time: 2 to 3 hours
Technical difficulty: Novice to advanced due to the undeveloped trail network
Trail surface: Gravel road, sand, hard-pack singletrack, mud, and loose rock
Trail contacts: King County Parks Department, (206) 296-2966 · Back Country Bicycle Trails Club, (206) 283-2995; www.bbtc.org
Fees and permits: None
Schedule: Open year-round but best May through October (the trails tend to be muddy in spots even in late August).

Maps: *Washington Atlas and Gazetteer*, page 64, A1; USGS Hobart
Land status: King County Parks
Nearest town: Issaquah
User density: Light
Other trail users: Equestrians
Canine compatibility: Leashed dogs permitted
Wheels: Front and light dual suspension
Hazards: Sticker bushes, slugs, automobiles along Issaquah Hobart Road

Finding the Trailhead

From anywhere north of Highway 18 in the South End, drive to I-90 and head east to Issaquah. Take the Front Street exit and head south through town. Follow Front Street for about 7.5 miles to Highway 18. Pass under Highway 18, and look for a small turnout area just past the traffic signal. The turnout is on the left-hand side of the road; park here.
From south of Highway 18, follow I-5 to Highway 18 and head north. Take Highway 18 all the way to the Issaquah Hobart Road exit. Turn right at the end of the off-ramp, and look for the pull-out area on the left-hand side of the road; park here.

The Ride

Carey Creek is uncrowded, unspoiled, undeveloped, and full of tremendous potential. Almost completely unknown in the mountain bike community, the Carey Creek trails are overgrown, sketchy, muddy, and scattered with such loose debris as sticks, logs, sand, and rocks. Located just 7 miles southwest of Tiger Mountain, the terrain here is nearly identical to this popular mountain bike destination. Once discovered by cyclists, the trails at Carey Creek are only going to improve.

King County owns several acres of land between south of Highway 18 and the tiny community of Hobart, Washington. Currently the main trail, an old railroad grade, cuts through the south end of the park. With minimal elevation gain, the biggest challenge along this trail is negotiating the mud holes. Even in late August, a day or two of rain turns sections of the trail into a thick morass of dark, sticky mud. Novice to intermediate riders will probably want to bypass the rest of the trails at Carey Creek and stick to the railroad grade. From the parking area, head south

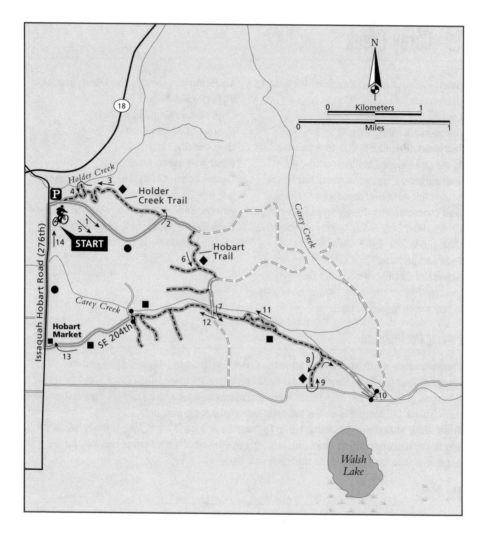

on the Issaquah Hobart Road (276th) and turn left onto 204th. Follow to the end of the road and go around the gate.

The railroad grade is lined with red alder, salmonberry, cottonwood, and maple. The forest is also filled with bald eagles, red tailed hawks, beavers, black-tail deer, elk, and woodpeckers. While the trail is not exactly challenging, the area is beautiful and peaceful.

For more of a challenge and gain in elevation, follow the directions outlined in the mileage log. Once off the main access road, your obstacle-clearing skills will become a necessity. Several logs cross the trail at various points and angles. With a dense forest canopy, moss and mold cover nearly everything, making all the obstacles slick and difficult to clear. Many are over 2 feet high; if you can clear even half of them, consider yourself an off-road stud.

Today the trails tend to be muddy and chewed up. To realize its full potential as a mountain bike destination, Carey Creek needs the same type of attention that Tiger Mountain has received. The Back Country Bicycle Trails Club has spent hundreds of hours working with the King County Parks Department to upgrade and maintain the trails at Tiger Mountain. Let the county know you'd like to see more mountain bike trails developed in the area, and join the BBTC trail maintenance work parties.

Miles and Directions

0.0 Start from the pullout area on Issaquah Hobart Road; pedal to the south end of the parking area, looking for the trail on the left. Follow the trail to the gravel access road. (**Note:** You can also ride a short distance down the road (20 to 30 feet) and look for the gravel access road on the left.) Go around the gate and pedal east, passing a couple of dirt roads and climbing up the hill.

0.9 Turn left on the trail that climbs up on the ridge above the road. The trail is narrow and lined with nettles and sticker bushes. For the next 0.75 mile the road rolls up and down before coming to a Y.

1.7 Reach the Y in the trail. To the right is the **Holder Creek Trail,** which dead-ends at Holder Creek (1.8 miles). Most riders will want to walk this short, steep section. The creek is a good place for dogs to get a drink of water, but there isn't much more reason to take the trail. Stay to the left on the main trail, and drop back down to the road.

2.0 Reach the road and turn left, climbing back up the road. The trail is almost completely overgrown here, which is why you couldn't see it on the way up the first time. Another landmark is the 20-to-30-foot-tall rotten stump with burn marks on it. The trail cuts between this stump and the road.

2.7 Pass the trail on the left (the first trail you took from the road) and turn right, just a short distance down the road on the **Hobart Trail.** (**FYI:** The first 0.25 mile is sketchy due to the mud and the trail being chewed up by horses' hoofs.)

3.4 The trail makes a bend to the right. After the curve, continue past the trail on the right. Arrive at the gravel road and turn right. Pedal down the road (pass the Holder Creek Trail on the right), and look for the old railroad grade intersection.

3.6 Reach the old railroad grade and turn left. The trail is nearly smooth and flat as it rides the ridge above Carey Creek.

4.3 Drop down and cross the dry creekbed, then climb up the hill. Pass two trails on the left, and cross a creekbed.

4.9 Turn right at the large rusty pipes, and begin climbing up the hill. Turn around at the road and enjoy the descent!

5.8 Continue past the rusty pipes and follow the trail as it changes into a dual-track dirt-and-gravel road. Turn right onto the gravel road, and reach the gate. Turn around and head back in the opposite direction.

7.4 Cross the gravel road and follow the railroad grade for the next 0.5 mile. You'll cross another creekbed with a few trails to the left and the right. Stay on the main trail, and then turn left after going down a short, steep descent to reach gravel road.

Holder Creek

8.0 Hit the pavement (Southeast 204th Street), and continue moving west. Pass the Foothills Farm on the left.

8.6 Reach the Issaquah Hobart Road (276th), and turn right. Pass the Hobart Market on the right.

9.5 Reach the car.

Ride Information

Local Information

Issaquah Visitor Information Center, (425) 392-7024; www.issaquah.org or www.ci.issaquah.wa.us

Local Events

Issaquah Concert on the Green, early July through August

Issaquah Full Scale Music Festival, mid-August

Annual Issaquah Jazz Festival, late August. Reggae, rock, western, swing, dance, funk, salsa, and more. Visit www.ci.issaquah.wa.us, or call (425) 392-6342 for more information

Issaquah Salmon Days, October. Visit the OFISHAL Salmon Days Web site at www.salmondays.org, or call (425) 392-0661 for more information.

Restaurants

Sushi Man, (425) 392-4295

Orchid Tree Restaurant, (425) 392-5262

Georgio's Subs, (425) 392-5624

Note: Above restaurants are all located in Issaquah.

10 Rattlesnake Lake

Start: Rattlesnake Lake Park Trailhead

Length: 13.2 miles

Approximate riding time: Advanced riders, 1 hour; novice to intermediate, 2 hours

Technical difficulty: Easy

Trail surface: Gravel wide track on old railroad grade, minimal singletrack, and dirt road

Trail contacts: Washington State Parks, (800) 233-0321

Fees and permits: None

Schedule: Open year-round

Maps: *Washington Atlas and Gazetteer,* page 64, A-B2-3; USGS North Bend

Land status: Washington State Park

Nearest town: North Bend

User density: Heavy

Other trail users: Hikers, climbers, equestrians, family bikers

Canine compatibility: Leashed dogs are permitted

Wheels: Safe and sane enough for baby trailers; no suspension necessary

Hazards: Bridge crossings (it's a long way dowwwwwnnnnn!), snow in winter

Finding the Trailhead

Head east on I-90 to exit 32. Turn right on to 436th Avenue Southeast, which becomes Cedar Falls Road Southeast. Follow Cedar Falls Road to Rattle Snake Lake. Park in the gravel parking lot.

The Ride

The old railroad grade is extremely popular among Seattle area residents due to its easy access, scenic views, and nontechnical riding. Climbing is minimal, and technical skills are not required in the least. The surrounding area is dotted with daisies, dandelions, and blue prairie lupines; several waterfalls and streams fall from high on the ridge and run below the trail to the south fork of the Snoqualmie River.

Located in Iron Horse State Park, the Rattlesnake Lake route follows the Old Milwaukee railroad grade, which has been renamed the John Wayne Pioneer Trail. With the exception of a short stretch of singletrack, the entire two-wheeled adventure consists of well-maintained gravel trails. The result is a perfect ride for novice mountain bikers and families.

From the parking lot the ride follows Cedar Falls Road down a wide track of gravel. A short distance down the trail, the only challenging section and the only singletrack on the entire ride cuts through a thick growth of lush trees and underbrush. Most novice riders will be able to clean the short climb. For parents with trailers or baby seats, this may be a bit tricky, though. This section of the trail is less than 0.25 mile, and once onto the old railroad grade, the trail is nearly as wide and smooth as a two-lane road.

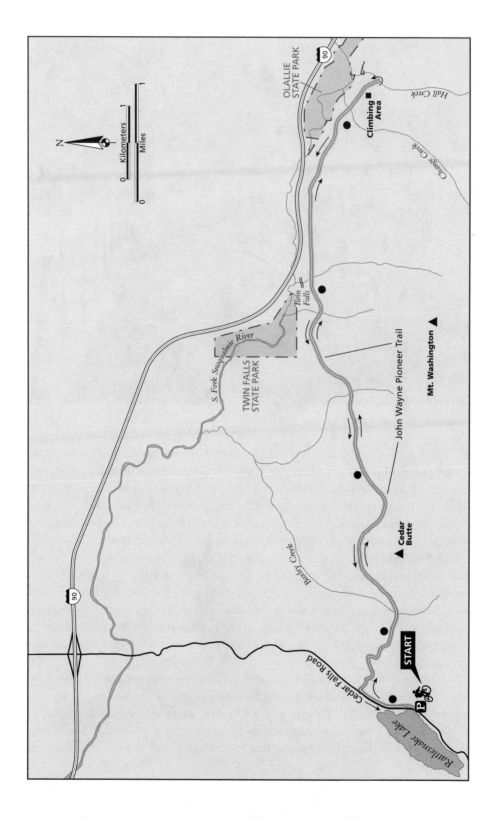

Stay away from the edge! There are no guardrails.

Once at the top, the remainder of the ride follows the tame terrain of the wide gravel covered **John Wayne Pioneer Trail.** The forest canopy provides some shade for the first couple of miles. Clear-cutting has wiped out most of the forest below the ridge, but it does provide scenic views of the Snoqualmie River Valley below and the North Cascades. Mountain bikers will enjoy the relaxing trek past numerous waterfalls and small meadows speckled with bright white, yellow, and blue wildflowers.

Shortly before the halfway point, riders will find a group of sanicans on the left side of the trail and another egress to the main railroad grade. Congregations of rock climbers scramble up and down various routes in the summer, making this a fun spot to have lunch and watch them dangle from the cliffs above the trail. For the next 0.5 mile, climbers hang from several routes up the mountain faces. This is also the only dangerous part of the ride, as the trail crosses an old railroad trestle without guardrails. Stay away from the edge—and don't look down!

The new bridge that crosses Hall Creek is the turnaround point in the ride. Riders also have the option of continuing on to Snoqualmie Pass through the old railroad tunnel, which is 3.2 miles long and 13 miles farther up the trail.

Rattlesnake Lake is as gentle a mountain bike ride as is possible without riding on pavement. Advanced riders will find themselves bored, but the trail does cut through a beautiful forest and is the perfect ride for families with baby carriages and inexperienced riders who need to build confidence before hitting the singletrack.

Miles and Directions

0.0 Start from the Rattlesnake Lake State Park parking lot. Cross the road to the wide, well-maintained gravel trail, and follow Cedar Falls Road back toward I-90.

0.2 Turn right onto gravel road and go around gate. (**Note:** The trail parallels the Seattle Watershed.)

0.5 The gravel road begins a gradual turn to the right. Follow the singletrack straight and to the left. **Note:** The sign reads IRON HORSE STATE PARK AND JOHN WAYNE PIONEER TRAIL. The singletrack is overgrown with dense foliage for a short distance.

0.8 Turn left where the singletrack reaches the crest of the climb and the John Wayne Pioneer Trail. Continue following the power lines. Over the next mile you'll cross Bo' Ey, Weeks, and Boetze Creeks.

4.6 Pass the small transformer station on the left side of the trail and the Twin Falls pedestrian trail on the left just a short distance farther.

5.2 Stay high on the ridge, passing the access road/trail on the left that drops down the hill.

5.9 Pass the portable toilets on the left-hand side of the trail. The remainder of the ride is usually crowded with climbers on the weekend. This is a great spot to have lunch and watch the climbers as they dangle from the rocks above the trail.

6.0 Cross the old railroad trestle. (**Warning:** Be careful; it's a long way down, and there is nothing to prevent riders from going over the edge. This is the only dangerous spot in the entire ride.)

6.2 Cross the new cement bridge over Change Creek.

6.4 Reach the new bridge over Hall Creek. Turn around and head back to the car.

12.1 Turn right, back down the singletrack.

12.6 Reach the gravel road and continue straight.

12.9 Turn left, back onto well-maintained gravel wide track returning to the parking lot.

13.2 Cross the road and reach the parking lot.

Ride Information

Local Information

Issaquah Visitor Information Center, (425) 392-7024; www.issaquah.org or www.ci.issaquah.wa.us

Local Events

Issaquah Concert on the Green, early July through August

Issaquah Full Scale Music Festival, mid-August

Annual Issaquah Jazz Festival, late August. Reggae, rock, western, swing, dance, funk, salsa, and more. Visit www.ci.issaquah.wa.us, or call (425) 392-6342 for more information

Issaquah Salmon Days, October. Visit the OFISHAL Salmon Days Web site at www.salmondays.org, or call (425) 392-0661 for more information.

Restaurants

Sushi Man, (425) 392-4295

Orchid Tree Restaurant, (425) 392-5262

Georgio's Subs, (425) 392-5624

Note: Above restaurants are all located in Issaquah.

11 Tiger Mountain

Option 1. Preston Railroad Trail and Northwest Timber Trail

Option 2. Iverson Railroad Trail

Option 3. Poo Poo Point

Option 4. Crossover Road

Start: Tiger Mountain parking lot on State Route 18

Trail contacts: Back Country Bicycle Trails Club, (206) 283-2995; www.bbtc.org

Fees and permits: None

Schedule: Open April 16 through October 14

Maps: *Washington Atlas and Gazetteer,* page 64, A1; USGS Hobart; Tiger Mountain State Forest; Washington State Department of Natural Resources

Land status: State forest

Nearest town: Issaquah

User density: High

Other trail users: Hikers, joggers, equestrians

Canine compatibility: Dogs permitted on a leash

Wheels: Cross-country and dual suspension

Hazards: Occasional automobiles and logging trucks on the gravel access road; equestrians on the trails; extremely technical sections full of rocks, roots, drop-offs, and so much more

Finding the Trailhead

Take I-90 east to exit 25. Head southwest on SR 18 for 4.5 miles to Tiger Mountain parking lot on the right-hand side of the road.

The Ride

Located in the middle of 1,300 acres of state forest, Tiger Mountain is one of the most popular mountain bike areas in the Puget Sound region. Only forty minutes from downtown, Tiger is home to more than 30 miles of off-road adventure on five different trails, three of which will challenge nearly every rider who isn't a professional mountain bike racer. Right from the start, each ride throws down the gauntlet and says, "I am going to beat you into submission." All of them—**Preston Railroad Trail, Iverson Railroad Trail,** and **Northwest Timber Trail**—contain steep climbs, technical descents littered with small boulders, constant twisting masses of slippery roots, deep ruts, mud, nasty switchbacks, more mud, and deceptively deep puddles that require strength, stamina, and superior skills to survive without broken bike parts, gashes, gouges, and aching muscles.

For more reasonable individuals, **Poo Poo Point** and the **Crossover Trail** offer safer and saner alternatives. While parts of the climb to Poo Poo are steep, the entire route is on well-maintained gravel roads. At the top, riders are rewarded with outstanding views of Mount Rainier; the community of Issaquah; and the Cedar, White, and Green River valleys. Best of all, Poo Poo Point serves as a launching pad for local

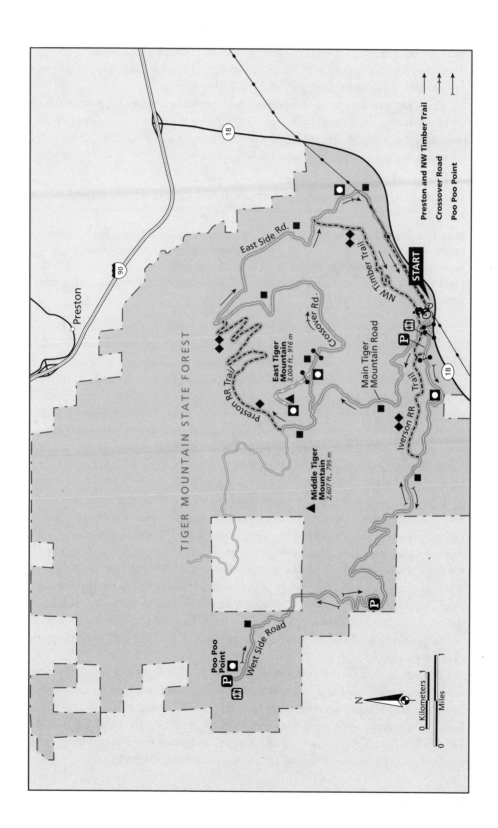

TIGER MOUNTAIN STATE FOREST

Preston

East Side Rd.

Crossover Rd.

Preston RR Trail

East Tiger Mountain
3,004 ft., 916 m

Middle Tiger Mountain
2,607 ft., 795 m

Main Tiger Mountain Road

Iverson RR Trail

MN Timber Trail

START

Poo Poo Point

West Side Road

N

0   Kilometers   1

0   1
Miles

Preston and NW Timber Trail

Crossover Road

Poo Poo Point

hang gliders. Trouble is, if you are riding this route, it's because Iverson, Preston, and Northwest Timber are closed (October 15 to April 15)—the same time of year that Seattle earns its reputation for gray skies and rain.

The Crossover Trail is much like Poo Poo Point but without the potential payoff of a stunning view. When the three singletrack trails are open, it is pointless to ride the Crossover Trail. But when the other trails are closed and you need the miles, Crossover is a good alternative to riding on the pavement.

Option 1: Preston Railroad Trail and Northwest Timber Trail

Start: Tiger Mountain parking lot
Length: 11.0 miles
Approximate riding time: 1 to 2 hours for expert riders, 2 to 3 hours for advanced riders
Technical difficulty: Advanced

Trail surface: Gravel logging roads, crushed gravel singletrack, hard-packed dirt singletrack, and mud.
Wheels: Cross-country and full suspension

Constructed and opened in the early 1990s by the BBTC (Backcountry Bicycle Trails Club) the combination of the **Preston Railroad** and **Northwest Timber Trails** makes for one of the most technically challenging rides in the region.

The route begins with a steep 3-mile climb up a logging access road. At the crest of the climb, riders are rewarded with buttery smooth, rolling, twisting singletrack through a dense forest of Douglas fir. Every year this section of the trail grows longer as BBTC volunteers spend their free time maintaining and improving the trail. If you encounter a member, be sure to thank him or her profusely for the backbreaking work—not to mention the fact that they continually fight to keep the trail open to mountain bikers.

Enjoy the smooth singletrack while it lasts. Once it is gone, the remainder of the ride is a rowdy washboard of wicked terrain that challenges even the most skilled riders. Cyclists will encounter long straightaways loaded with mud, roots, rocks, drops, puddles, and even running water at times. Speed is your friend here. Lay off the front brakes, and let the momentum carry you over the brutal terrain. As always, when in doubt keep pedaling. Most of the problems out here can be overcome if a rider's momentum keeps the bike moving forward. Be sure to keep your weight off the front wheel when jamming through the mud bogs and puddles. Many of them are deeper than they look, and they will eat up front wheels and throw riders up and over the handlebars.

The last section of the ride, the Northwest Timber Trail, is a couple of miles down the access road. The NTT cuts back into the forest and rolls up and down a ravine, over two bridges, and through an eerily quiet section of alders covered in long lime-green hanging moss. This section of the trail is no less forgiving than the Preston Railroad Trail; it also contains tangled masses of roots, rocks, mud, more mud, drops, tight turns, sections of slick clay, and nasty switchbacks.

Miles and Directions

0.0 From the parking lot walk around the gate to the Main Tiger Mountain Road, on the right. The road immediately turns to the right and then back to the left at the crest of the first incline.

0.3 Pass the Northwest Timber Trail on the right and the Iverson Trail on the left.

1.4 Reach a scenic viewpoint. (**FYI:** On clear days, Mount Rainier is visible, as are the Cedar, White, and Green River valleys. The toughest part of the climb is complete.)

2.63 Come to a T in the road. Turn left onto Main Tiger Vista Road. To the right is Crossover Road 5500. (**Note:** The Crossover connects with the east end of the Preston Railroad Trail.)

3.1 The Preston Railroad Trail is on the right-hand side of the road, marked by a gate and sign. Enjoy the singletrack while you can!

4.4–6.6 Six switchbacks, tangled masses of roots, drop-offs, ruts, mud, more mud, twists, and turns. Hang on!

6.6 Reach the Crossover Road 5500. Turn left to reach the Northwest Timber Trail. (**Note:** Turning right takes riders back to the T in the road and the Main Tiger Mountain Vista Road, which is 4 miles west and then another 2.63 miles to the parking lot. The Connector Road is covered with loose gravel and contains a fast descent and a short steep climb.)

6.8 Make a hard right at bottom of the hill onto East Side Road.

8.9 Turn right onto the Northwest Timber Trail.

10.6 Reach Main Tiger Mountain Road. Turn left and head back to parking lot.

11.0 Reach the gate.

Option 2: Iverson Railroad Trail

Start: Tiger Mountain parking lot
Length: 3.8 miles
Approximate riding time: 45 to 90 minutes

Technical difficulty: Advanced
Trail surface: Singletrack and gravel road
Wheels: Cross-country and full suspension

While the **Iverson Railroad Trail** lacks the long climb and pounding descent of its neighbor, the **Preston Railroad Trail,** it does serve up seriously challenging terrain. Yard for yard, it may be one of the toughest rides you'll ever experience. Brutal drops, big ugly roots, jagged rocks, and rapidly changing transitions are sure to test any rider's ability. And at just under 4 miles, Iverson is a deceptively inviting ride. After a mild warm-up on a rolling gravel road, the trail begins in earnest as it jogs up a steep hillside and through a clearcut that is showing signs of rejuvenation.

Ducking back into the woods, the singletrack gets downright dangerous as it transports riders over drops that are routinely 3 feet high and through a creekbed that is full of rocks the size of basketballs. Cleaning the creek is just the start of a short,

Speed is your friend on the Preston Railroad Trail.

punishing descent over rocks and roots that can bash bikes and mountain bikers to pieces. Make it through the minefield and you're rewarded with an eerie but cool ride through another grove of alders covered in moss and smooth, gravel-covered singletrack that is maintained by the BBTC. Upon reaching the road, riders have two choices: Head back to the parking lot and call it a day, or cross the road to ride the Northwest Timber Trail. Hardcore riders, however, save Iverson for last after riding the Preston Railroad Trail and the Northwest Timber Trail. After exiting the Northwest Timber Trail, cross the road and dive into Iverson, riding it in the opposite direction.

Miles and Directions

0.0 From the parking lot pedal up the West Side Road (on the left), which immediately begins to climb.

0.7 Ride to the top of the hill and coast down to the trail, which will be on the right.

1.8 Turn right onto singletrack and begin to climb up through the clearcut.

2.2 The trail reaches its highest point and begins to traverse east, back toward the parking lot.

3.7 Take the right fork in the trail, and turn right at the road to reach the parking lot. Or cross the trail to ride the Northwest Timber Trail.

3.8 Reach the parking lot.

Options 3 and 4: Poo Poo Point and The Crossover Road

Odds are, if you have chosen either of these two rides, it's because the other three are closed. Besides the view at Poo Poo Point and from the top of East Tiger Mountain, neither ride is nearly as fun as the other options. While the gravel roads are well maintained year-round, the crushed chunks of rock are large and jagged, making the climbing more difficult—which makes this ride a no-go for families and first-time rides with inexperienced friends or significant others. The climbing is tough, and the descent over the unstable surface can be dangerous. Still, for experienced riders who need some training miles and want to get off the pavement, there are worse choices.

Option 3: Poo Poo Point

Start: Tiger Mountain parking lot
Length: 15 miles
Approximate riding time: 2 to 4 hours

Technical difficulty: Easy to moderate
Trail surface: Dirt and gravel road
Wheels: Front suspension and hybrids

Miles and Directions

0.0 From the parking lot pedal up the West Side Road (on the left), which immediately begins to climb.

0.7 The road tops out and then descends for a short distance past the **Fat Hand Trail** entrance at 1.8 miles. The road curves back up, following Holder Creek for less than a quarter mile.

2.0 Pass **South Tiger Loop Trail,** an equestrian- and hiking-only trail.

2.4 Reach the second crest and then drop back down into lush green forest. Continue descending for the next 2 to 3 miles. Be careful to watch for the gate at about 5.0 miles.

5.0 Reach the gate after the blind corner.

5.4 Stay right at the fork of the road, and get ready to climb just over 500 feet in the next 2 miles.

7.2 Take the right fork again, and pedal toward the vantage point.

7.5 Reach Poo Poo Point. Turn around and head back to the parking lot.

7.8 Stay left.

9.6 Stay left again.

10.0 Arrive at the gate. (Watch for riders coming around the corner from the opposite direction.)

15.0 Reach the parking lot.

Option 4: The Crossover Road

Start: Tiger Mountain parking lot
Length: 11 miles
Approximate riding time: 2 to 4 hours

Technical difficulty: Easy to moderate
Trail surface: Dirt and gravel road
Wheels: Front suspension and hybrids

Miles and Directions

0.0 From the parking lot walk around the gate to the Main Tiger Mountain Road, on the right. The road immediately turns to the right and then back to the left at the crest of the first incline.

0.3 Pass the Northwest Timber Trail on the right and the Iverson Trail on the left.

1.4 Reach a scenic viewpoint. (**FYI:** On clear days Mount Rainier is visible, as are the Cedar, White, and Green River valleys. The toughest part of the climb is complete.)

2.6 Come to a T in the road. Turn right onto the Crossover Road 5500.

3.2 The road forks, and you can reach the top of Tiger Mountain by hanging a hard left and pedaling for just under a mile. The right fork continues to the east side of the mountain.

3.3 Reach the top of the climb. (It's not the last climb, but at 2,600 feet it is the highest point in the ride without going all the way to the top.)

6.0 Pass the east end of the Preston Railroad Trail after a steep descent and a slow traverse.

6.1 Drop down the short hill and make a hard right onto East Side Road heading south.

7.6 Hang on for the steep downhill over unstable gravel as the road crosses Trout Hatchery Creek.

8.1 The East Side Road climbs back up to the east end of the Northwest Timber Trail. Continue straight.

8.8 After two climbs and two descents, the road reaches the power lines. Pass under the power lines and follow the road to the right as it parallels them.

9.4 Take the right fork in the road, and begin the steep climb. (**Note:** If you reach SR 18, you have gone too far. You can ride back to the car on SR 18, but it is not recommended.)

9.7 Take the left fork that bends around and below the left-hand tower. The road continues under the power lines, rolling up and down with the terrain.

10.5 Turn right onto singletrack that crosses under the power lines and enters a section of dense woods.

10.7 Reach the Main Tiger Mountain Road. Turn left.

11.0 Reach the parking lot.

THE BACKCOUNTRY BICYCLE TRAILS CLUB

What is the BBTC?

The BBTC is a bunch of tread heads who joined together in the late 1980s to both ride and maintain and lobby for our gorgeous trails here in western Washington. If you have ever hit the trails out at Tiger Mountain or Saint Edwards State Park, you have benefited from the BBTC's work. In the early '90s the founders of the BBTC fought to keep trails open on Tiger Mountain. Today they are still organizing work parties to improve the trails at Tiger and Saint Edwards. In addition they organize rides so that you can discover new areas and meet new people, have work parties to keep the trails in good shape, and lobby for you to keep and increase our access on Washington lands. They also educate the public on mountain biking's impact, have a good time, and will help introduce anyone to the fun sport of mountain biking. Riders of all skill levels and backgrounds can join the BBTC, and everyone is welcome to their rides and socials. To learn more, visit their Web site at www.bbtc.org, or call their hot line at (206) 283-2995.

Ride Information

Local Information

Issaquah Visitor Information Center, (425) 392-7024; www.issaquah.org, www.ci.issaquah.wa.us

Local Events

Issaquah Concert on the Green, early July through August

Issaquah Full Scale Music Festival, mid-August

Annual Issaquah Jazz Festival, late August. Reggae, rock, western, swing, dance, funk, salsa, and more. Visit www.ci.issaquah.wa.us, or call (425) 392-6342 for more information

Issaquah Salmon Days, October. Visit the OFISHAL Salmon Days Web site at www.salmondays.org, or call (425) 392-0661 for more information.

Restaurants

Sushi Man, (425) 392-4295

Orchid Tree Restaurant, (425) 392-5262

Georgio's Subs, (425) 392-5624. Note: Above restaurants are all located in Issaquah.

12 Tokul Creek

Start: Fall City Community Park
Length: Up to 30 miles of trails
Approximate riding time: 2 to 3 hours
Technical difficulty: Intermediate to advanced due to technically challenging descents
Trail surface: Forest roads, dual track, and singletrack
Trail contacts: King County Parks, (206) 296-2966
Fees and permits: None
Schedule: Open year-round, but best June through October

Maps: *Washington Atlas and Gazetteer,* page 80, C1; USGS: Fall City and Snoqualmie
Land status: King County Park and Weyerhaeuser
Nearest town: Fall City
User density: Moderate
Other trail users: Hikers, equestrians
Canine compatibility: Dogs permitted on a leash
Wheels: Front to light dual suspension
Hazards: Horse manure, mosquitoes, loose rocky descents

Finding the Trailhead

Drive east on I-90 to the Preston Fall City exit (exit 22). Turn left at the end of the off-ramp, and then turn right onto Preston Fall City Road Southeast. Follow to Preston Fall City (notice the Small Fries burger joint on the left as you drive into town—a delicious pit stop after a hard day in the saddle). Turn right onto Southeast Fall City Snoqualmie Road and drive over the bridge. Immediately turn left onto Fall City Carnation Road Southeast (State Route 203). The highway will bend back to the right and straighten out. Turn left onto Neil Road Southeast, and park in the gravel parking lot of the Fall City Community Park, across the street from the Fall City Grill and Fall City Fire Arms.

The Ride

Moderate climbs and more joy-inducing descents than Starbucks has brews and blends, Tokul Creek is a sweet area for after-school/work riding. Cyclists departing from Seattle and the East Side can reach the parking lot in forty-five minutes and the trailhead in an hour by driving out on I-90. Originally constructed by local equestrians the Tokul Creek Trail network cuts through a thick canopy of second-growth fir, cedar, cottonwood, and big-leaf and vine maples, blackberries, huckleberries, and spring gold. The only downside to this area is that the descents are short, requiring riders to make the same climb more than once. In addition, on the more popular equestrian routes, the singletrack can be a bit chewed up at times.

The Tokul Creek Trail circuit has existed in relative obscurity for years. Never before has it been published in a book, and the few mountain bikers who knew of the area's existence guarded their secret jealously. After a long, hard negotiation session (three sixpacks of Fat Tire Ale, a water bottle, and a Clif Bar) and a bit of espionage, the trails are being shared publicly for the first time. And, yes, the author feels a bit guilty about it.

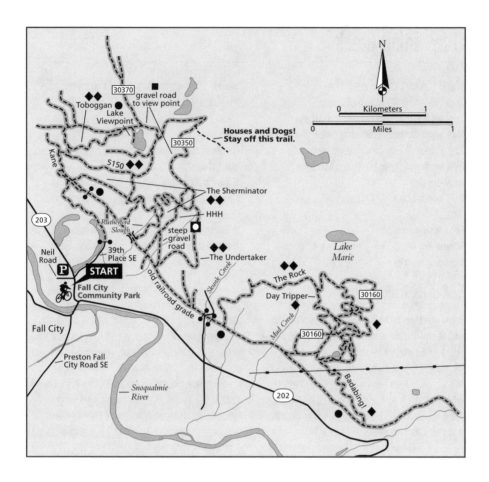

It's important to realize that the relationship between mountain bikers and Weyerhaeuser (owners of much of the land) is tenuous at best. Ride responsibly, and respect the equestrians, who have been using the area for years with Weyerhaeuser's blessing. Always dismount when encountering a horse, and let equestrians pass without incident. It's even wise to chat calmly and politely to help keep the horse at ease. Riding responsibly will ensure that the trails are kept open to cyclists for years to come.

Tokul Creek is crammed tight with demanding descents and groovy singletrack. Your first few rides in the area may leave you confused because there are simply so many trails, with new ones being cut all the time. Part of Tokul Creek's appeal is exploring the area and determining your own route. If you become lost, simply head south (downhill) to the old railroad grade. From here it's simply a matter of heading back to the access road off Thirty-ninth Place.

Mountain bikers will find two main areas to explore—the northwest side of the access road and the southeast side. The northwest side contains shorter climbs and fewer trails but is fun in its own right. **The Toboggan Trail** (TT) is a relatively short descent that starts off smooth and velvety and ends with taxing drops, loose dirt, debris, and five or six banked turns. While TT is short compared with many of the other trails at Tokul Creek, it is a solid warm-up for the adventures still to come.

From here riders have several choices. Cyclists can continue down to the old rail-road grade and head east to find more trails, or they can climb back up to the view-point, which is worth the effort. On clear days the view from this 800-foot perch of Fall City (see your car in the parking lot below) and the Bellevue and Seattle sky-lines, while not stunning, is worth the trip to the top. Advanced to expert riders will want to try **The Undertaker,** which falls off the top of the ridge and viewpoint. One look down, and the name will make perfect sense. It's best not to attempt this one alone. It is steep and so choked with rocks that it feels like riding on marbles. Plus the narrow trail is lined with blackberry bushes.

For safe and sane riders, the first major descent of this route is on **The Shermi-nator,** a long stretch of singletrack that follows the ridgeline back to the west before plunging down over sections of roots, rocks, loose dirt, and more debris. Between the obstacles, the singletrack is fast, carpet smooth, and virtually guaranteed to produce oxygen deprivation and adrenaline overload! Lay off the brakes, position your tail behind your saddle, and enjoy the ride.

Now follow the route out to the next climb and, of course, wicked descent. Again, the gain in elevation is consistent and taxing. The reward (massive adrenalin surge), however, is as strong a return as investing in Microsoft during the late '80s and early '90s. Fall into **The Rock,** a short brutal descent covered in a moving layer of rocks, dirt, sand, and roots. Most cyclists will not ride this section of trail. Fortunately it's short, but if you go down, it

► THE BEAR FACTS

Did you know that there are nearly 25,000 black bears in Washington State? The average male weighs 225 pounds; is 5 to 6 feet long and 2 to 3 feet tall at the shoulder; and eats grass, berries, nuts, tubers, insects, and small mammals, including deer fawns, elk calves, and fish. They are the smallest member of the bear family and are not always black. In fact, they are often brown, cin-namon, or reddish blonde. The average black bear lives twenty-five years in the wild and thirty in captivity.

will be painful. You can always bypass The Rock and ride the road back to **BadaBing!** BB follows the ridgeline through a grove of small alders before descend-ing back under a thick forest canopy. The trail is narrow, and the turns are quick. There are sections filled with more burly drops and loose rocks the size of grapefruits.

Miles and Directions

0.0 Exit the parking lot onto Neil Road and pedal the short distance to State Route 203. Cross SR 203 and turn left heading north.

0.1 Take a right onto Southeast Thirty-ninth Place as it splits to the right. It is marked as a dead-end street, and it follows the Rutherford Slough, a pond/marshy lake.

0.6 Ride around the gates and start up the gravel access road as it follows the Rutherford Slough and SR 203. Stay on the main access road, ignoring all the trails at this level—they all lead to the old railroad grade.

1.3 Reach the crest of the first climb and the old railroad grade. (**Note:** To the left, riders will find the trails *Kane, Toboggan, The Undertaker, The Sherminator,* and more. Enjoy exploring the area, and don't worry about following a specific route. Always remember which direction is southwest (back to the old railroad grade) and it is easy to find your way back to the parking lot. To the right, riders will find numerous spur trails heading up the ridge to the left. Ignore them, and cross the bridge over the 100-foot-deep ravine (roughly a mile out the access road); continue for 2 miles. Find Day Tripper on the left, and shoot back into the forest. Let the exploring begin on trails like BadaBing! Mountain bikers will find miles and miles of singletrack on this side of the main access road. Again, if you become lost head back down to the old railroad grade and head back to the parking lot.)

Ride Information

Restaurants

Fall City Grill, (425) 222-5622

Small Fries, (425) 222-7688. Note: Both restaurants are located in Fall City.

13 Tolt MacDonald Park

Start: John MacDonald Park parking lot
Length: 7-to-15-mile circuit, depending on the trails chosen and how they are combined
Approximate riding time: 2 to 3 hours
Technical difficulty: Difficult due to immature nature of the freshly cut trails, tight turns, and undulating terrain
Trail surface: Singletrack and gravel road
Trail contacts: King County Parks, (206) 296-2966
Fees and permits: $15.00 per campsite, $6.00 per extra vehicle; 38 campsites available March 19 through October 31. Each site contains a fire pit and a picnic table.

Schedule: Open year-round, 8:00 A.M. to 10:00 P.M.
Maps: *Washington Atlas and Gazetteer,* page 80, C1; USGS Carnation
Land status: King County Parks
Nearest town: Carnation
User density: Moderate
Other trail users: Hikers, campers
Canine compatibility: Dogs permitted on a leash
Wheels: Cross-country and full suspension
Hazards: Rocks, high ridgelines, slippery roots, technical sections

Finding the Trailhead

Drive east on I-90 to the Preston Fall City exit (exit 22). Turn left at the end of the off-ramp, and then turn right onto Preston Fall City Road Southeast. Follow to Preston Fall City (notice the Small Fries burger joint on the left as you drive into town—a delicious pit stop after a hard day in the saddle). Turn right onto Southeast Fall City Snoqualmie Road and drive over the bridge. Immediately turn left onto Fall City Carnation Road Southeast (State Route 203). Drive for fifteen minutes, and turn left onto Northeast and Fortieth and the Tolt River John MacDonald Park just before entering the main drag through Carnation. Follow road to parking lot, and park.

The Ride

Owned by King County Parks, the Tolt MacDonald area is quickly becoming a Seattle favorite among fat-tire enthusiasts. The Tolt is an old, well-known ride with a reputation for being an unexciting gravel access road waste of time. In the past couple of years, however, miles of new trails have been cut through the dense, dark Snoqualmie Forest. In fact, if you haven't been there in the past eighteen months, you'll hardly recognize the place. The entire ridge above the Tolt and Snoqualmie Rivers has been injected with sharp turns, gun barrel–narrow singletrack, and rolling terrain. This book describes several of the most popular trails, but feel free to explore any of the trails shown on the map.

Located on the plateau above the sleepy community of Carnation and the Snoqualmie and Tolt Rivers, the Tolt MacDonald area is one of the few mountain bike locations that is growing rather than withering under the brutal disease of development. King County Parks owns 450 acres on both sides of the river, which hopefully means that development is a long way off. Meanwhile, a secret society of

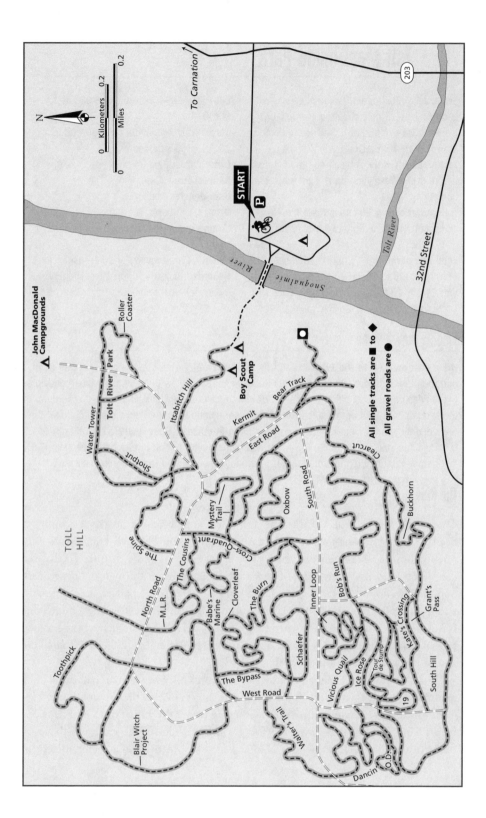

mountain bikers has quietly cut miles of new singletrack. At press time there were more than thirty trails weaving through 200-plus acres of luscious emerald-colored forest. Bright green moss cloaks many of the trees in the area, creating an eerie lime-green haze. Members of the society won't give you their names, but they do troll through the area handing out rough handcrafted maps. The mileage log below details how to access the area, but it is up to each mountain biker to determine his or her own route. With so many trails to choose from, it's part of the adventure. No two rides in the area will be the same.

Itsabitch is the only steep, sustained pitch on the entire ride. It's a hell of a warm-up, climbing nearly 1,000 feet in less than a mile. Enjoy the views of the valley below while

▶ **NOT INTERESTED IN FROG LEGS?**

Then call Small Fries, Preston Fall City's tasty burger joint as you leave the park. Order a greasy but tasty bacon cheeseburger, a fish sandwich, curly fries or onion rings, and a strawberry-banana or peanut butter-and-chocolate milkshake. It will be ready by the time you drive back through town. Small Fries is located at 4225 Preston Fall City Road, across from the Exxon Station; (425) 222-7688.

climbing up the ridge, but pay particular attention to the actual trail and its surface. The only way back down is through Itsabitch, and most riders will open it up and let their bikes run through this section. Be prepared—it's a long way down if you go over the edge.

Kermit is a fresh-cut trail that is barely wide enough to pedal through. Branches constantly poke and grab at mountain bikers, tearing jerseys and skin. Froglegs for lunch? Halfway through, a choir of frogs begins a symphony of croaking. You'll be amazed by how loud they are.

Bear Track is a short but sweet romp out to a viewpoint above the park. A slight descent and several turns make it a worthwhile trip to the edge of the cliff above the Snoqualmie River. There are no signs marking the edge of the ridge. Decrease your speed when you see the trees opening up—it's a long, long way down.

Bob's Run follows the South Road and heads west to an area that is packed with several trails, but not before weaving and bobbing back and forth and up and down like Muhammad Ali through one of the less dense areas of the forest. The **Inner Loop, Ice Rose, Vicious Quail, Tour de Stump, Dancin',** and **19** are all super-model-slim trails that from above would look like a tangled extension chord. Most of the turn radiuses are almost too small for a bike. They come at riders one after another, and they keep coming and coming. Even combining all the trails this area has to offer makes up little more than a couple miles of riding. However, there is simply no place to relax, and, once finished, most mountain bikers feel as though they have had a truly hard day in the saddle.

On the north side of the South Road lie more climbing—and therefore more descents! Trails like **Oxbow, Mystery Trail, Cross-Quadrant, Babe's Marine,**

Chasing "Vicious Quail"

M.L.R., The Cousins, and **The Bypass** are more wide open with fewer turns. They do, however, deliver riders to the tip-top of the plateau, not that there is a view, rewarding them with short, quick drops to any of the main roads. Mystery and Oxbow cross by the frog swamp for another great spot to listen to the spotted green orchestra.

Finally, **The Burn** is one of the longer trails that combine a fast straightaway, the **Cloverleaf,** wicked turns, and a blissfully sweet descent, making it an area favorite. Following the East Road to the South Road and then heading north into the forest most easily accesses it.

Miles and Directions

0.0 From the parking lot ride over the Tolt River on a 500-foot wooden suspension bridge. (**Warning:** Pay attention when the bridge is wet. The wood becomes slick, and more than one mountain biker has toppled over when his or her rubber tires slipped out from underneath.) Follow the main trail, Itsabitch, up into the hills and past the cabins. The trail turns into steep singletrack and follows the ridge just after the second cabin.

0.3 Looking off to the right (east), riders can enjoy limited views of the Cascade Mountains, the Tolt River, and the tiny community of Carnation in the valley below.

0.49 Turn left at the T and climb through a forest of maple, cedar, and Douglas fir, many of which are covered with moss. Continue climbing, and look to the left for views of the Cascades and Carnation. The trail turns from narrow singletrack to rocky wide-track trail.

0.9 Pass a trail on the right (it has two side-by-side entrances, so it looks like two trails), and continue down the wide track for a short distance. Hit the jeep road, and make a soft left onto the East Road. Take the immediate next left. Pass the trail on the right, and ignore the straightaway as well. Make a short climb through a section of bamboo. East Road now becomes an actual gravel road. From here mountain bikers can access any of the trails on the map. Mileage will vary depending on which trails are combined, but count on two solid hours of riding being available.

Ride Information

Restaurants

Fall City Grill, (425) 222-5622

Small Fries, (425) 222-7688.

Note: Both restaurants are located in Fall City.

14 The Summit Biking Center

Start: Bottom of Central Express High Speed Quad at Summit Central
Length: Up to 35 miles of trails
Approximate riding time: 2 to 6 hours
Technical difficulty: Advanced to expert
Trail surface: Singletrack and fire roads
Trail contact: The Summit at Snoqualmie, (425) 434–7669; www.summit-at-snoqualmie.com
Fees and permits: Lift ticket prices for biking 9:00 A.M. to 4:30 P.M.: adults $15, kids (six and under) $10; biking 1:00 P.M. to 4:30 P.M.: adults $12, kids (six and under) $10; Summer Seasons Pass, $90
Schedule: Late May to early September, depending on the snow levels. Friday through

Sunday and holidays, 9:00 A.M.–6:00 P.M. for the chairlift. You can ride trails all week, but no chairlift running on weekdays.
Maps: *Washington Atlas and Gazetteer,* page 65, A5; USGS Snoqualmie Pass
Land status: National forest and private property
Nearest town: North Bend
User density: Heavy
Other trail users: Hikers
Canine compatibility: Dogs not permitted
Wheels: Cross-country, full-suspension, and full-on downhill bikes
Hazards: Rocky terrain

Finding the Trailhead

From Seattle, take I–90 east to exit 53 for Summit Central. Turn right at the end of the off-ramp and then left at the stop sign or T in the road. Biking Center is a few hundred yards down on the right.
From South Puget Sound area, take I–5 north to I–90, and follow above directions.
From North Puget Sound, take I–5 south to I–405. Go south to I–90, and follow above directions.

The Ride

Billed by the Summit ownership as the mountain bike center with something for everyone, local off-road cyclists know the area is Washington's mecca for downhill riders. True, there are miles of trails around the beautiful Twin Lakes and Mount Catherine. And for cross-country riders in search of a strenuous workout, there is plenty of napalm-burning, lung-busting climbing. The main attraction, however, is the DH circuit of trails that are punishing and unforgiving to flesh, bone, aluminum, carbon fiber, chrome moly, steal, titanium, and anything else bicycle engineers can throw at the mountain.

Former home to previous NORBA and World Cup downhill events, **The Summit** was considered one of the most vicious courses in the world. The pros and local riders know it isn't an exaggeration. Although the ride up the chairlift is relaxing, for the average mountain biker there is no easy way down. Even the gravel access roads are littered with large chunks of granite and loose unstable debris. The major

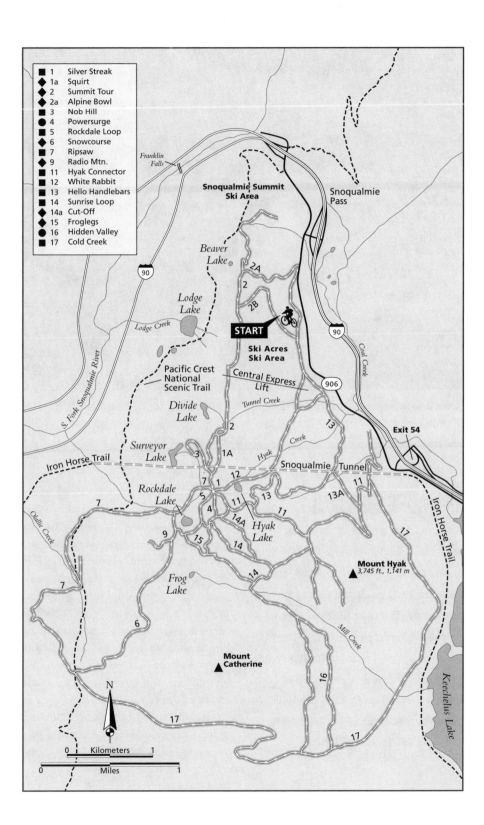

■	1	Silver Streak
◆	1a	Squirt
◆	2	Summit Tour
◆	2a	Alpine Bowl
■	3	Nob Hill
●	4	Powersurge
◆	5	Rockdale Loop
◆	6	Snowcourse
■	7	Ripsaw
◆	9	Radio Mtn.
■	11	Hyak Connector
■	12	White Rabbit
■	13	Hello Handlebars
■	14	Sunrise Loop
◆	14a	Cut-Off
◆	15	Froglegs
●	16	Hidden Valley
■	17	Cold Creek

Franklin Falls

Snoqualmie Summit Ski Area

Snoqualmie Pass

90

Beaver Lake

2A

2

2B

Lodge Lake

Lodge Creek

START

Ski Acres Ski Area

906

Central Express Lift

90

S. Fork Snoqualmie River

Pacific Crest National Scenic Trail

Divide Lake

Tunnel Creek

2

Creek

13

Exit 54

Surveyor Lake

3

1A

Hyak Creek

Iron Horse Trail

Snoqualmie Tunnel

Rockdale Lake

7

1

12

Oldilie Creek

7

5

4

11

13

13A

11

11

14A

Hyak Lake

13

9

15

14

Mount Hyak
3,745 ft., 1,141 m

17

Frog Lake

14

Iron Horse Trail

6

N

Mount Catherine

Mill Creek

16

Keechelus Lake

17

0 Kilometers 1

17

0 Miles 1

17

Double back diamonds from top to bottom

downhill runs are full of angry, jagged boulders, elevator chute–like steeps, and drops as high as 15 feet.

Hello Handlebars offers up the best singletrack on the mountain. It was originally constructed for a NORBA event in 1997 and later acted as the World Cup Cross Country course. The top section is relatively flat as it wiggles and worms its way through the forest before dropping 500 feet over terrain as complex as 4,000 lines of Microsoft SQL code in a matter of seconds. The Summit map lists it as a blue-square "more difficult" ride, but intermediate riders will be freaked by the terrain, and novices will probably have to walk much of this trail.

If you happen to pick up a Summit map at the base, note that the trail ratings are slightly inaccurate. Many of the

► THE PACIFIC CREST TRAIL

Feel like walking to Mexico? Or maybe you are in the mood for a shorter jaunt to Canada? Then catch the Pacific Crest Trail, which can be accessed from the Summit West parking lot. Running from Canada to Mexico, the trail is one of the most popular in North America. Follow it north to reach Steven's Pass (67 miles) as the trail travels through the North Cascades, around alpine lakes and meadows. Ninety-seven miles south, hikers can take in the view of the mighty Columbia River, Mount Rainier, and Mount Saint Helens.

single black diamonds should be double black diamonds, and the blue squares should be single black diamonds. Also be sure to factor in the length of the trail and the elevation gain. **Hidden Valley** and **Cold Creek** are both beautiful and scenic rides over well-maintained access roads. Factor in the length of each and the climbing, and novice and intermediate riders with average physical abilities and fitness will be seriously tested.

Miles and Directions

Ride the chairlift up and pick a trail down. Ride the chairlift up, and pick a different trail down—again, and again, and again.

Ride Information

Restaurants

Bob's Barbecue, Friday through Sundays and holidays, 10:00 A.M.–6:00 P.M.

Family Pancake House, open twenty-four hours.

Note: Restaurants are located at the mountain bike center.

The South End

Cyclists will find two types of trails in the South End: short, watered-down rails-to-trails or short, punishing technical labyrinths packed with turns and singletrack. **Lake Wilderness** and **Lake Youngs** are ideal for first-time cyclists and family outings with young children. The trails are wide, safe, and sane.

Renton's **Tapeworm,** on the other wheel, is loaded with constricting curves and slender singletrack that spanks even experienced riders. Add in **The Parasite,** and after 5 miles on the trail most cyclists are ready to call it a day. The constant barrage of turns, twists, kinks, and bends and riding up and down the sides of a small gully require quick, controlled bursts of power and a considerable amount of time out of the saddle.

Victor Falls is just as challenging. Because the trails are changing on a regular basis as the area's trees are harvested and new trails are cut every season, riders never know what they'll find. Plus, the terrain has been tattooed with deep scars from years of off-road vehicle use. The **Black Diamond Coal Mine,** while similar to the Tapeworm, is even tougher. The turns are tight, but there are more of them, and there are simply more miles of trails in the area and fewer places to bail out and head back to the car.

The upside to riding the lopsided loony terrain is substantial improvement in steering and bike handling skills. Riders must learn how to finesse their rides through these trails. Choosing the correct line, negotiating speed, and energy output and timing shifts properly will all determine just how abused a rider will feel at the end of a day.

15 Phillip Arnold Park

The Tapeworm and Parasite Trails

Start: Phillip Arnold Park
Length: 5.8-mile circuit
Approximate riding time: 60 to 90 minutes
Technical difficulty: Advanced due to technically challenging terrain and tight, twisting turns
Trail surface: Singletrack
Trail contacts: Renton Community Center, (425) 235–2560, www.ci.renton.wa.us
Fees and permits: None
Schedule: Open year-round
Maps: *Washington Atlas and Gazetteer,* page 63, A7; USGS Renton

Land status: Renton Parks Department and Puget Power
Nearest town: Renton
User density: Heavy
Other trail users: Bikers, hikers
Canine compatibility: Dogs permitted on a leash
Wheels: Cross-country and light dual suspension
Hazards: Low-hanging trees and tree branches, trash, and glass; extremely technical sections of trail

Finding the Trailhead

From I-405 North, take exit 4B onto Sunset Boulevard. Follow to second large intersection, and turn right onto Bronson Way. Pass the baseball fields and tennis courts on the left, and move into the left lane. Cross the Cedar River, and immediately turn left onto Mill Avenue. Cross Second Avenue South, and come to light on Houser Avenue South. The Renton Historical Museum is on the right-hand corner, and across the intersection is a large cement retaining wall and I-405. Cross Houser onto Renton Avenue South, which turns to the left and begins to climb up the hill. Follow Renton Avenue South to South Seventh Street, and turn left. Cross Grant Avenue South and High Avenue South. Seventh intersects Jones Avenue South and becomes Beacon Way. The corner of the Phillip Arnold Park begins here. Follow Beacon for a short distance, and park in the lot on the right.

From I-405 South, take exit 4 (Renton–Enumclaw), and turn left at the end of the off-ramp. Cross Sunset Boulevard onto Bronson Way and follow above directions.

The Ride

Located in Royal Hills just above the old mining town turned Boeing industrial park, Renton's Phillip Arnold Park is home to the infamous **Tapeworm** and **Parasite Trails.** Mountain bikers here ride through some of the most deceptively technical and physically challenging terrain in the area. Despite the fact that the Tapeworm and Parasite combine for less than 6 miles of trails and minimal elevation gain, this ride gives new meaning to the words *tight, twisting,* and *narrow.* Packed

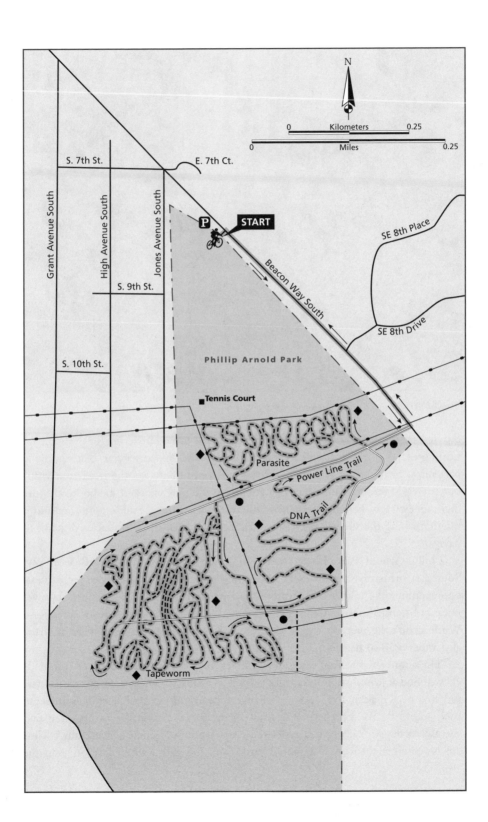

N

0   Kilometers   0.25
0   Miles   0.25

S. 7th St.

E. 7th Ct.

SE 8th Place

P **START**

Beacon Way South

SE 8th Drive

Grant Avenue South

High Avenue South

Jones Avenue South

S. 9th St.

S. 10th St.

Phillip Arnold Park

■ **Tennis Court**

Parasite

Power Line Trail

DNA Trail

◆ Tapeworm

One of 108 turns on the Tapeworm and Parasite

into less than a couple of acres, the turns are almost too constricting for the standard turning radius of most mountain bikes, and the trails are so narrow that removing bar ends is a must—the average handlebar may not fit between the trees even without bar ends. Riders who don't pay attention will get whacked in the head more than once by low-hanging branches. Due to the tight turns, building momentum is tough, making the short climbs, tangled roots, and man-made obstacles difficult to navigate.

Phillip Arnold Park, nestled between Jones Avenue South and Beacon Way Southeast, primarily serves the neighborhood residents with a variety of recreational opportunities like softball and tennis. Directly behind the park, a junction of power lines and transformers cut through the area heading in a multitude of directions. While it isn't the prettiest riding location in Seattle, the power lines make it virtually impervious to development.

The entire Parasite Trail is less than 2 miles long, but don't let that fool you. Riders will find at least forty to fifty tight turns and fifteen to twenty logs of various sizes to climb over, making the route a challenge for most mountain bikers. The turns cut back and forth like a bizarre maze through the forest. First-time visitors often find themselves directionally challenged and lost in a matter of minutes. Thankfully, cyclists are never more than a few hundred yards from the park and civilization. Add the amusement park terrain and obstacles across the trails, and Parasite is a seriously fun challenge for any rider.

The Tapeworm is a masterpiece of efficient land use and the main reason Phillip Arnold Park has become such a popular place to ride. According to the maps posted on various trees in the area, aliens constructed the Tapeworm. More than fifty turns of odd shapes, sizes, and angles cut back and forth across a narrow gravel road rolling up and down the banks of a shallow gully. The conniving curves conspire with rocks, roots, man-made obstacles, and mud to push riders to their limits. Establishing a rhythm is difficult, to say the least. So much so that most riders will average less than 7 miles per hour on either trail. Any rider who can average over 12 miles per hour might want to think about a career in racing.

Cyclists usually find themselves banged up by the low-hanging branches and with bloody knuckles from bashing their hands on the trees as they try to navigate the narrow gashes that substitute for trails in the Worm. During the summer months, when the trails are overgrown, it gets even worse.

Miles and Directions

0.0   From the parking lot head south on Beacon Way around the gate. (**Note:** The baseball field will be on the right side of the road, which makes a short climb up to a residential area on the left.)

0.3   Turn right between the chain link fence, the rusty green gate, and the large cement barricades. The trail is a narrow gravel road. Take the first next right at Mile 0.34 onto the singletrack. Take the next left at Mile 0.4, and then turn right at Mile 0.46. Welcome to the Parasite.

0.6   Stay to the right and then stay to the right again.

0.7   Turn right over the log marked with chain-ring teeth.

0.8   Return to the chain-ring-chewed log (on your left). It almost looks as though you can continue straight, but to finish the Parasite follow the trail to the right around the tree.

1.7   Escape from the Parasite . . . come out underneath the power lines at a four-way intersection and turn right. Follow the trail as it bends to the left.

1.8   Come to a five-way intersection and turn right; then make the immediate left.

1.82 Pass the Tapeworm exit.

1.84 Turn right into the Tapeworm. A few hundred yards in, the trail will begin to drop into and climb out of a small gully several times. Down the middle is a small gravel access road. Simply follow the singletrack back and forth across the road.

4.0   Pass the teeter-totter and reach the end of the Tapeworm. Turn right and pass the entrance on your left. Climb the hill looking for the DNA Trail on your left. If you reach the gravel road you've gone too far.

4.2   Veer to the left on DNA Trail.

5.2   Reach Power Line Trail and turn right.

5.5   Reach the green rusty gate, and turn left onto the road.

5.8   Return to the parking lot.

Ride Information

Local Information

City of Renton, (425) 430-6400;
www.ci.renton.wa.us

Seattle/King County Convention and Visitors Bureau, (206) 461-5840

Restaurants

Foody Goody Chinese Buffet, (425) 227-8898

Vince's Italian Restaurant & Pizzeria, (425) 226-8180

Angelo's Pizza & Pasta House, (425) 228-7415

Note: Above restaurants are all located in Renton.

16 South Sea Tac

Des Moines Creek Park Trail

Start: Des Moines Park Creek Trail
Length: Up to 10 miles of trails
Approximate riding time: 1 to 2 hours
Technical difficulty: Intermediate
Trail surface: Hard-packed dirt, pavement, and sand
Trail contacts: Des Moines Parks and Recreation, (206) 870-6527; www.ci.des-moines.wa.us/recreation
Fees and permits: None
Schedule: Open year-round
Maps: *Washington Atlas and Gazetteer,* page 63, A6; USGS Des Moines

Land status: Port Authority
Nearest town: SeaTac International Airport
User density: Medium
Other trail users: Joggers, BMX-ers, cyclocross racers
Canine compatibility: Leashed dogs permitted
Wheels: Single-speed, cyclocross, cross-country, and full suspension
Hazards: Glass and other garbage

Finding the Trailhead

From Interstate 5, take the South 200th Street exit (exit 51). Head west on South 200th and cross International Boulevard/State Highway 99. Follow 200th for 0.25 mile, and turn left into the small gravel parking lot across from the golf course. Park here.

The Ride

Set aside as an audio buffer zone for SeaTac International Airport, and later turned into a park, Des Moines Creek Park offers several miles of smooth, rolling, and twisting singletrack. The trails crisscross back and forth through an abandoned neighborhood surrounded by chain-link fencing and locked gates. The remaining landscaping has been left unkempt for all these years, creating an eerie, apocalyptic atmosphere. The overgrown streets are completely devoid of cars and houses. Some of the trails ride through what is left of the foundations of the many homes destroyed when the airport was built.

The park is directly in the path that pilots use for takeoff. Despite the noise produced by the jets, the riding is big-time fun for any level of ability. The terrain lacks serious climbing or hardcore technical sections, but it is loaded with banked turns, hairpin curves, dips, drops, and jumps. There is even a BMX zone, **Fun House,** created by local riders. Young baggy-pants-hanging-below-the-hip-wearing punks are constantly launching themselves into the air from man-made kickers (jumps) and flashing various tricks and stunts. The park may be known best for hosting the Seattle Metro Cup cyclocross racing series (one event of the National Super Cup series

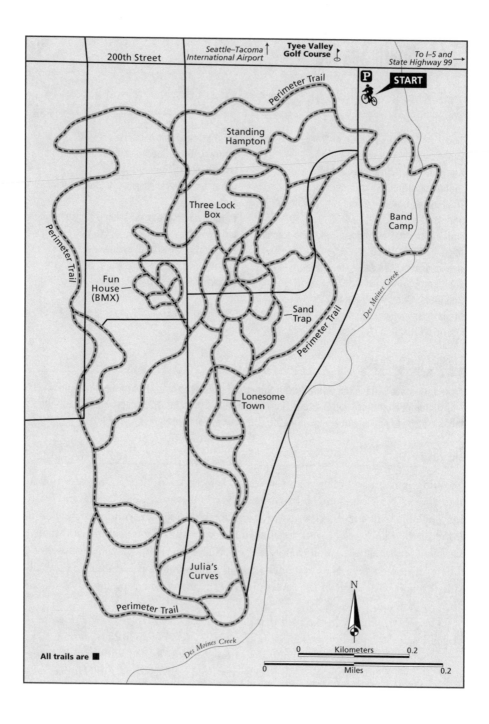

200th Street

Seattle–Tacoma
International Airport ↑

**Tyee Valley
Golf Course** ⛳

To I–5 and
State Highway 99 →

Ⓟ

START
🚴

Perimeter Trail

Standing
Hampton

Three Lock
Box

Band
Camp

Perimeter Trail

Fun
House
(BMX)

Sand
Trap

Des Moines Creek

Perimeter Trail

Lonesome
Town

Julia's
Curves

Perimeter Trail

N

Des Moines Creek

All trails are ■

0   Kilometers   0.2

0   Miles   0.2

that is held every fall) and the summer night weekly mountain bike race series hosted by Stif Wick Productions.

Except for the occasional crossing or the abandoned streets, the entire ride consists of singletrack buffed smooth by years of use. The lack of climbing and serious technical riding make the park a great place for novice riders to gain time in the saddle. The velvety singletrack is also super-attractive to those advanced riders who like to ride hard and fast through turn after turn after turn.

The **Perimeter Trail,** winds back toward South 200 Street and passes by a cemetery before exploring nearly 75 percent of the buffer zone boundary. In the northwest corner the trees are packed tight, and so are the turns. For a short distance the trail is like a tunnel cut through a solid wall of bark, branches, moss, and ivy. In general, however, the forest opens up, and the Perimeter Trail is the longest sustained trail in the park. Perimeter Trail rolls with the mild terrain changes, and all of its turns are mild compared with the rest of the trails.

Located in the center of the park, the **Sand Trap** and **Lonesome Town** are separated by a large, open, grassy field, which usually serves as the staging area for the local cyclocross and mountain bike races. The Sand Trap is just like it sounds. Several trails crisscross the area, and the depth of the sand is difficult to determine. Many a front wheel has been sucked in to the sand causing more than its share of endos and face plants. Most riders carry their bikes up the hills cyclocross style.

Lonesome Town contains two short, steep descents with semitechnical entrances at the top. A couple of 2-to-3-foot drops onto a steep fall line keep trails interesting. After that, the singletrack mellows out and rips through the forest toward the grass field.

Across the street and west of the grass field, riders will find the **Fun House.** Young trials and BMX riders have built five to ten kickers, banked turns, and other obstacles in order to cop air and attempt tricks. Many of them make it look easy as they maneuver their smaller bikes around the turns, over the jumps, and through the air to Grandmother's house they go.

Located on the south end of the park **Julia's Curves** comprise an inner circle of trails that twist and turn through a nasty patch of blackberry bushes that can lash out at unsuspecting cyclists. Expect to earn a few gashes. Ahh but the sweet **S** turns are almost perfectly round and as sexy as the hips on a supermodel, hence the name. Best of all, the singletrack is hard and fast, making it worth every burning scratch.

Unless they build a third runway on the buffer zone, it is unlikely that the park will ever be closed to mountain biking. Horses will be spooked by the constant noise of the jets taking off overhead, and the bike community is firmly established. Des Moines Creek Park is open year-round. During the rainy season the trails become choked with mud, as do most Northwest area rides. By midsummer the trails are dry, packed hard, and lightning quick. Have fun—and remember to duck as the 747s buzz the tree tops.

How does he do that?

Miles and Directions

Due to its size and the number of trails, no mileage log is provided. It would drive you nuts trying to follow all the various turns and possible route combinations. The best plan is to simply explore the area on your own. If you get lost, simply head east until you reach the paved bike path. Then turn left (north), and you'll end up back at the parking lot.

Ride Information

Local Events

Seattle Metro Cyclocross Race Series and Super Cup, September through December; www.nwcycling.com

Summer Weeknight Mountain Bike Series, Stif Wik Productions; www.dirtworld.com for up-to-date race information

CYCLOCROSS DEFINED

Cyclocross is roughly the equivalent of cross-country running for bicyclists. The sport, which originated in Europe more than seventy-five years ago, was intended as off-season (October–January) training for road riders. Riders practiced in parks and on forest trails, soccer fields, etc. This often meant crossing streams, climbing over fallen trees, and carrying their bikes through unridable sections.

The typical 'cross course consists of a 1-to-2-mile loop of varied terrain, including dirt, pavement, steep run-ups, and off-camber turns. Natural and artificial barriers are often used to force riders to dismount and remount their bicycles at speed. The races are timed events that last between thirty and sixty minutes each, depending on riders' age and/or ability level.

The classic image of cyclocross is the high-speed dismount-remount maneuver—when the bike is to be carried on the shoulder up a particularly steep or muddy incline or when an obstacle on the course cannot be ridden. In terms of technique, cyclocross is one of the most difficult forms of cycle racing. The bicycle resembles the road machine, with its dropped handlebars, 700C wheels, and relatively narrow tires. Yet the conditions for these two disciplines could hardly be more different. For a start, cyclocross is a wintertime sport. Woodland trails, open meadows, and short, steep hills are the main features of a cyclocross course.

The sport held its first world championship in Paris in 1950. In the early years, cyclocross was thought of only as an accessory to road racing. The intense work of the one-hour race and the use of narrow tires on muddy hills made a good combination to hone both fitness and handling skills. Gradually cyclocross specialists emerged, and the sport became dominated by riders who were little known in road racing. Apart from some notable exceptions—led by Adri Van der Poel—this remains the case today. Yet cyclocross stars do feature prominently at the top level of mountain bike racing—a sport far closer related to cyclocross than to road riding.

Where cyclocross and mountain bike racing differ in ideology is in-race technical support. In mountain biking the rider must be fully self-sufficient to carry out in-race repair work should his or her machine malfunction. In contrast, a cyclocross racer is allowed to use up to three bicycles in a race. Since this is a winter sport and the tracks are often very muddy, a clean cyclocross bike can weigh in excess of 10 kg less than a muddy one! The handicaps of excess weight and clogging mud have resulted in a highly organized pit stop system. Trained teams of mechanics work quickly throughout the race to ensure that the rider may have a clean, oiled bike once each lap. Normally two machines are in the use/cleaning cycle, while a third is kept in reserve in case of mechanical failure.

17 Lake Wilderness

Start: Lake Wilderness Park
Length: 8.0-mile circuit
Approximate riding time: 1 to 1½ hours
Technical difficulty: Novice
Trail surface: Gravel access road, dual track
Trail contact: King County Parks, (206) 296-4232
Fees and permits: None
Schedule: Open year-round but best May through October
Maps: *Washington Atlas and Gazetteer,* page 63, 8A; USGS Maple Valley and Black Diamond

Land status: Department of Natural Resources
Nearest town: Maple Valley
User density: Heavy
Other trail users: Hikers, equestrians
Canine compatibility: Leashed dogs permitted
Wheels: Cross-country
Hazards: Virtually none; the trail is flat, smooth, and nearly as tame as can be.

Finding the Trailhead

From Seattle, head south on I-5. Take the Renton/I-405 exit north at South Center in Tukwila. Take the Maple Valley Enumclaw exit (Highway 169). Drive through Maple Valley (roughly 8 miles), and turn right onto Witte Road Southeast after passing through a retail area. Drive a little less than a mile, pass the Lake Wilderness Elementary on the left, and turn left onto 248th Street. Follow for a little less than 0.5 mile, and turn left into Lake Wilderness Park.
From the East Side, head south on I-405 to the Renton/Sunset Boulevard exit. Follow Sunset for several blocks, turn left on the Maple Valley Enumclaw exit, and then follow directions above.

The Ride

Lake Wilderness is a slow, easy Sunday-stroll-through-the-park type of ride. Almost completely flat and nontechnical, it is the perfect trail for novices and family outings with a bike trailer. The trails can be slightly crowded on weekends, but locals are friendly and accommodating.

The majority of the Lake Wilderness rail-trail ride skirts the east side of the lake. However, in spring and summer the nearly seventy-acre lake is difficult to see due to the trees and brush growing densely on the shores and bank above the lake. The ride is pleasant even in summer heat, as most of it is in the shade.

King County's Lake Wilderness Park is not your average park. Not only can you obtain a marriage license there, but you can also hold the wedding ceremony and the reception and, for good measure, do a little fishing. The park also contains a Wilderness Center, an arboretum, tennis courts, softball field, soccer field, and beach with dock and swimming area. Lake Wilderness Trail cuts through the park, following the edge of the shoreline and connecting with the **Cedar River Trail,** which can be ridden all the way to Renton.

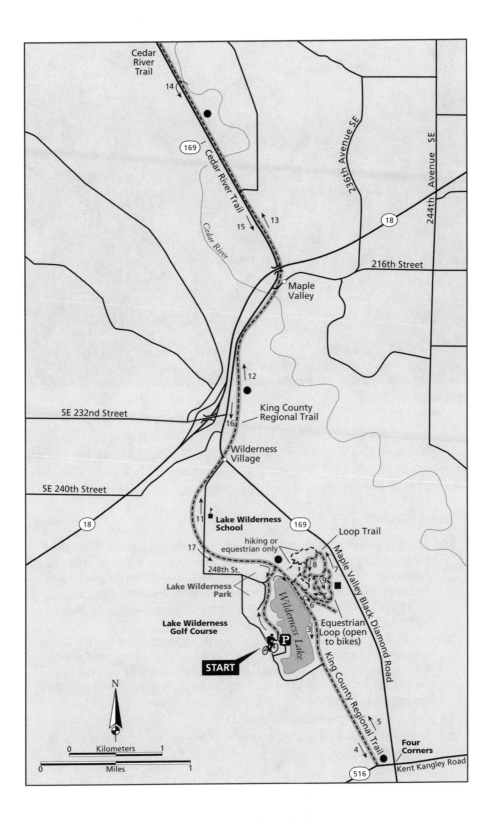

Lake Wilderness

Running through the middle of Lake Wilderness Park is Jenkins Creek, a tributary of Big Shoos Creek, which empties into the Green River. The park also includes three wetlands. A variety of birds and animals make their home in Lake Wilderness Park, including deer, beaver, raccoon, hawks, wrens, and ruffed grouse.

Miles and Directions

0.0 Start from the parking lot; ride to the northeast corner of the lot, and look for the paved path that quickly turns to gravel. Follow the trail northeast to the wide gravel parking lot. Pass through the parking lot gate and turn left downhill (paved), then make an immediate right into the parking lot. (**Note:** Look for the trail at the back of the paved parking lot. The trail is just to the right of a large boulder with a plaque reading SMITH MOSSMAN WESTERN AZALEA GARDEN.)

0.3 Stay on the main trail (wide dirt path), and pass the singletrack trail on the right. Reach a four-way intersection and turn right up the short, steep hill. At the top, turn right onto the Lake Wilderness Rails-to-Trails route. (**FYI:** The trail is a wide gravel path that parallels the east side of the lake. Stick to the main trail for the next 1.5 miles, ignoring all intersections and spur trails.)

1.8 Stick to the right of the Y as the trail drops down.

2.0 Reach Four Corners retail area and Kent Kangley Road. Turn around and head back in the opposite direction.

MAPLE VALLEY DAYS

For fifty years Maple Valley Days have been organized and operated by volunteers from throughout the greater Maple Valley area—a community coming together to serve one another. Held every year in June at Lake Wilderness Park, the festival includes a parade, live entertainment, vendor booths, and a carnival attracting some 25,000 people over a three-day period, complete with a grand parade scheduled at 10 A.M.

Over the years this community event has grown and changed. In 1950 a group of citizens gathered at Gaffney's Lake Wilderness Lodge to celebrate and raise funds in order to purchase the area's first fire engine. Firemen sold tickets for $1.00 each in their efforts to raise $1,000. They succeeded, and Maple Valley Days were born.

If you want to be part of the Maple Valley Days volunteer team or wish to participate in the festival, call (425) 961–2100, ext. 2398. You can find additional information on the Maple Valley Days Web page: maplevalleydays.webjump.com.

3.5 Reach a split in the trail and the kiosk. **Side trip:** For a quick singletrack adventure, turn right and head uphill. There is a small loop in the gully, but pay attention to trails that are open to bicycles. Trails 3, 5, and 10 are for foot access only. For more mileage, continue south on the main path out to Cedar River Trail. Pass all spur trails, and ride through two tunnels.

6.0 Reach the Cedar River Trail. Turn around and head back to the parking lot.

7.6 Turn right down a short, steep hill. Make an immediate left at the bottom, and head back to the parking lot.

8.0 Reach the parking lot.

Ride Information

Local Information
City of Maple Valley, (425) 413–8800

Restaurants
Taco Time, Maple Valley, (425) 413–4477

18 Lake Youngs

Start: Lake Youngs Trailhead parking lot
Length: 9.9-mile loop
Approximate riding time: 1½ to 2½ hours
Technical difficulty: Novice
Trail surface: Gravel access road and dual track
Trail contact: King County Parks, (206) 296-4232
Fees and permits: None
Schedule: Open year-round but best May through October
Maps: *Washington Atlas and Gazetteer*, pages 637–38, A–B; USGS Maple Valley and Black Diamond

Land status: City of Seattle, King County Parks
Nearest town: Renton
User density: Moderate
Other trail users: Hikers, equestrians
Canine compatibility: Leashed dogs permitted
Wheels: Cross-country
Hazards: Horse dung

Finding the Trailhead

From Seattle, head south on I-5. At South Center in Tukwila, head north on I-405. Take the Maple Valley Enumclaw exit (Highway 169). Head south on Highway 169 to 140th Way Southeast. Turn right and head up the hill to Fairwood. Turn left on Southeast Petrovitsky Road. Drive about 0.5 mile, and turn right onto Old Petrovitsky Road. Follow for a short distance, and park in the Lake Youngs Trailhead parking lot.

The Ride

With more than 9 miles of chain-link fence lining the trail and numerous KEEP OUT and NO TRESPASSING signs posted, Lake Youngs might feel like something out of an *X Files* episode. However, the mellow, perfectly mannered terrain is excellent for first-time off-road cyclists. Climbing is minimal, and nearly all the gravel and dirt trails are smooth and easy to navigate.

Riding next to a chain-link fence for 9 miles sort of defeats the purpose of getting back to nature, but this trail will not be destroyed by development like its neighbor, Lake Desire. Lake Youngs is part of the Seattle water system, which keeps it protected from urban sprawl. It also means, however, that the lake is completely fenced in and hidden behind a wall of thick, lush sword ferns, cedar trees and other evergreens, huckleberries, and big-leaf maples. Riders never get the slightest view of the lake, but deer are common behind the fence.

The trail is mostly dual track/access roads over relatively smooth crushed gravel. There are a few spots with large-chunk loose gravel, but a quick lesson in positioning the glutes over the tail end of the bike is usually sufficient enough to get most

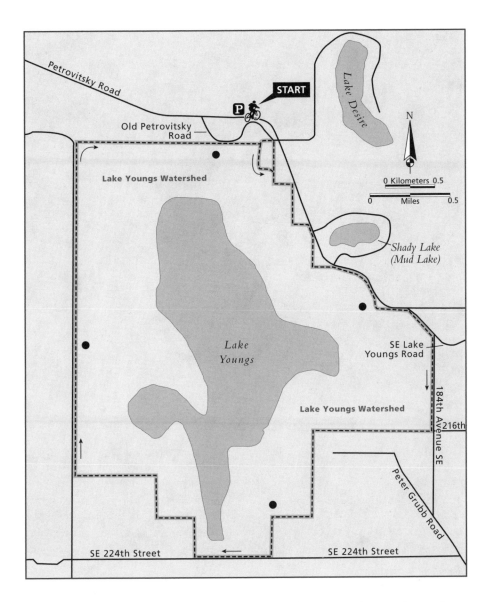

beginners through this ride. The easy terrain is also great for bringing your four-legged friends.

Miles and Directions

0.0 Start from the parking lot. Looking into the woods and away from Old Petrovitsky Road, find the trail to your right. This trail connects with the loop around Lake Youngs.

0.15 Turn left onto the Lake Youngs Loop Trail. The dual track follows the fenceline around the lake.

Patrolling the perimeter

2.3 Arrive at the intersection of Southeast Lake Youngs Road and 184th Avenue Southeast. Cross over the water pipe on the road, and continue following the trail alongside the fence.

6.5 Arrive at the corner of 184th Avenue Southeast and Southeast 216th Street. Turn right and follow the fenceline.

9.6 Reach the bottom of a short but steep descent. Climb to the top and the loop is complete.

9.75 Turn left and pedal back to the parking lot.

9.9 Arrive at the parking lot.

19 Victor Falls

Start: Hillside Christmas Tree Farm parking lot
Length: More than 30 miles of trails
Approximate riding time: 1 to 4 hours
Technical difficulty: Novice to advanced
Trail surface: Gravel, dirt, sand, and mud
Trail contacts: None
Fees and permits: None
Schedule: Open year-round
Maps: *Washington Atlas and Gazetteer,* page 63, C–D7; USGS Orting and Sumner

Land status: Privately owned
Nearest town: Bonney Lake, Sumner, Orting
User density: Heavy
Other trail users: ORVs
Canine compatibility: Dogs permitted but not recommended due to all the ORV riders in the area.
Wheels: Front to light dual suspension
Hazards: ORVs and logging equipment

Finding the Trailhead

From South Puget Sound (Tacoma area), head north on I-5 and take exit 127 to State Route 512; head east to Puyallup (about 12 miles). Just past Puyallup take Highway 410 east to Enumclaw. Drive 7 miles and turn right onto 214th Avenue East (Bonney Lake shopping plaza—there is a Safeway on the right). Drive 1.4 miles on 214th Avenue East to the first stop sign (there's a fire station just across the street). Turn right onto 120th Street East and drive 1 mile to 198th Ave East. Turn left and drive .07 mile to the Hillside Christmas Tree Farm. Park in the dirt parking lot on the right.
From North Puget Sound, head south on I-5 to Highway 410, and then head east. Follow above directions.

(**Note:** From Thanksgiving to Christmas, do not park at the tree farm. Instead take a right onto 198th Avenue East and drive until you pass the sign for the Victor Falls Elementary School. Park on the large shoulder just down the road. Be aware of the no parking signs. Please be respectful in this neighborhood.)

The Ride

Despite the constant logging and ORV use, the massive circuit of trails known as Victor Falls is one of Puget Sound's most frequented mountain biking areas. Located on the ridge above the Puyallup River, more than thirty named routes and countless others combine to form a maze of twisting, winding, turning, rolling trails totaling some 40-plus miles. Motocross riders have been gouging these trails into the landscape for decades. The result is an intermediate to advanced mountain bike paradise of banked turns, kinky singletrack, and tricky technical topography. Today nonmotorized knobbular Samaritans cut new singletrack on a regular basis. Not only are riders able to explore these new trails but the trails are usually narrow enough to keep ORV riders from using them. The same goes for equestrians.

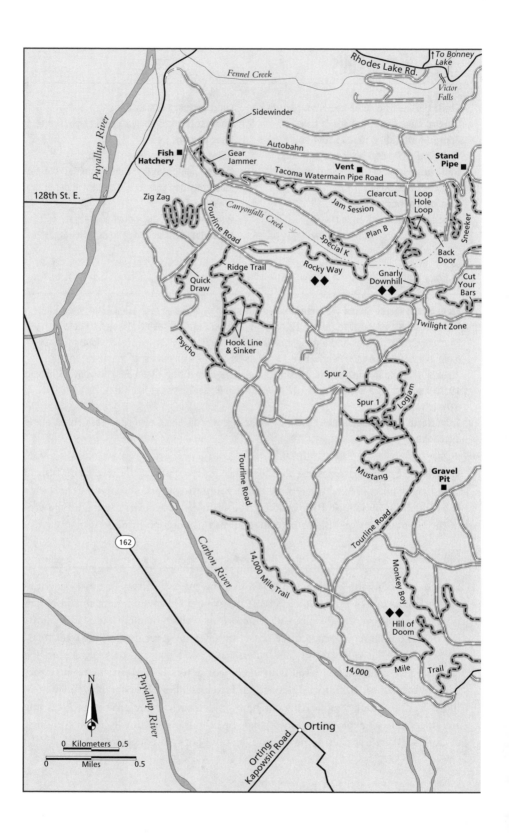

To Bonney Lake

Rhodes Lake Rd.

Fennel Creek

Victor Falls

Sidewinder

Autobahn

Fish Hatchery ■

Gear Jammer

Tacoma Watermain Pipe Road

Vent ■

Stand Pipe ■

128th St. E.

Zig Zag

Canyonfalls Creek

Tourline Road

Clearcut

Jam Session

Loop Hole Loop

Sneeker

Special K

Plan B

Back Door

Ridge Trail

Rocky Way

Gnarly Downhill

Cut Your Bars

Quick Draw

◆◆

◆◆

Puyallup River

Psycho

Hook Line & Sinker

Twilight Zone

Spur 2

Spur 1

Log Jam

Tourline Road

Mustang

Gravel Pit ■

162

Carbon River

14,000 Mile Trail

Tourline Road

Monkey Boy

N

◆◆

Hill of Doom

Puyallup River

14,000 Mile Trail

Orting

Orting-Kapowsin Road

0 Kilometers 0.5

0 Miles 0.5

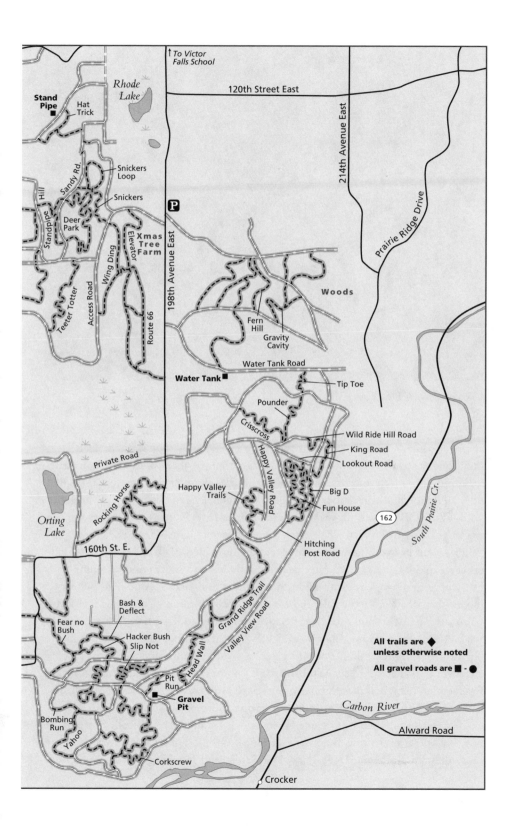

Cruising through Deer Park

Novice riders will find plenty of trails on which to learn the basics, while advanced riders can grab gears on the more challenging routes. Victor Falls lacks only long sustained descents. Still, riders can improve their skills and stamina by sprinting down any one of a hundred combinations of trails. Granted, the ORV noise pollution and continuous logging are possible black marks against the area. But without the ORVs the trails would lack the blessed banked turns and velvety smooth singletrack that make Victor Falls such a sweet place to ride.

Pick your poison. Victor Falls has something for riders of all abilities. Novice riders can explore the area on the access roads and dive into short nonthreatening trails like **Cut Your Bars, The Autobahn, Sidewinder,** and **Jam Session.** All four are in the northern half of Victor Falls and are easily accessible and close to the tree farm. Cut Your Bars twists and turns over relatively even ground and nontechnical singletrack. AutoBahn is a long, smooth straightaway that's perfect for hammering in the big ring or simply chillin' out and catching your breath. Sidewinder is a quick crossover trail that connects Autobahn with Jam Session, a local favorite. JS makes several blind turns as it cuts through a thick wall of ferns, trees, and low-lying shrubs. Other easy routes include **Route 66** and **Hook, Line & Sinker.**

The rest of the trails can be rated intermediate or advanced. It really depends on how fast you want to ride. Increase your speed, and the tight, narrow turns become more difficult. **Snickers, Deer Park, Hat Trick,** and **Rocking Horse** are all such trails. The terrain lacks long climbs and seriously challenging problems, but all four trails are a blast. Snickers is full of tight turns and has one fast section. Deer Park provides a needed rest over a flat section after bombing through Snickers. Hat Trick is another short, relatively straight shot, while Rocking Horse is an excellent spot to get up out of the saddle on a long straightaway before heading into a series of sharp turns.

Technically adept riders will eat up **Rocky Way,** an old creekbed full of rocks of all shapes and sizes polished smooth by years of erosion. Even more challenging, the forest cover is thick and the air moist, creating the perfect environment for slimy mold to grow on the rocks. Betcha can't do it without dabbing at least once! Mountain bikers who want to test their trials-riding skills can check out **Teeter-totter** and the **Twilight Zone.** They'll find man-made elevated trails and an actual teeter-totter that you ride. More technical terrain can be found in the **Fun House** and on the **Gnarly Downhill, Corkscrew,** and **Bombing Run.** Both the Fun House and Corkscrew are loaded with turns, dips, and drops; the Gnarly Downhill and Bombing Run should be self-explanatory.

Miles and Directions

New trails are constantly being cut, old trails are constantly being rerouted, and there are simply too many trails and too many possible combinations to choose from to develop an accurate or unrestrictive route. The adventure of Victor Falls is discovering each trail and possible combination ride after ride. Most mountain bikers still find new trails and thrills even after exploring the area for years.

20 Black Diamond Coal Mine

Start: Maple Valley Highway, gravel pull out just past 288th Street
Length: Up to 20 miles of trails
Approximate riding time: 2 to 3 hours
Technical difficulty: Intermediate to advanced
Trail surface: Old railroad grade, singletrack, roots, rocks, and logs
Trail contact: King County Parks, (206) 296-4232
Fees and permits: None
Schedule: Open year-round
Maps: *Washington Atlas and Gazetteer,* page 63, A8; USGS Black Diamond

Land status: County park
Nearest town: Black Diamond
User density: Light
Other trail users: Hikers, equestrians; no motorized vehicles!
Canine compatibility: Dogs permitted on a leash.
Wheels: Front, light dual suspension and single speed
Hazards: Lots of broken glass on one area of the trail

Finding the Trailhead

From the East Side, head south on I-405 to Renton. Take exit 4 (Renton Enumclaw), which deposits vehicles onto Sunset Boulevard. Follow Sunset Boulevard to Maple Valley Highway (State Route 169) and turn left. Pass through Maple Valley and Four Corners (intersection between Kent Kangley Road and Maple Valley Highway—Exxon, Union 76, Starbucks, Safeway, and Dairy Queen on the corners). Drive 0.3 mile past 288th, or 1.7 miles past Four Corners, and park in the small gravel turnout on the right-hand side. Or you can park 2 miles past Four Corners at the turnoff in front of the sign that reads WELCOME TO HISTORIC BLACK DIAMOND—VILLAGE WITH A VIEW.

From Seattle, head south on I-5, then take I-405 north to Renton. Take the Maple Valley/Enumclaw exit, and go south on Maple Valley Highway (SR 169); follow the directions above.

From the South End (South of Kent), take I-5 to State Route 18 and head north. Follow SR 18 to Maple Valley and take the Maple Valley exit. At end of off-ramp turn right, and then make another right onto Maple Valley Highway and head south. Follow above directions.

The Ride

Located on the edge of the historical town of Black Diamond, the Coal Mine trails weave and bob around the south end of Lake Sawyer, Frog Lake, and Ravensdale Creek. Mountain bikers will find a circuit of trails rambling through clearcuts, a thick forest of Douglas fir, vine and big-leaf maple, alder, thistle, spring gold, western yew, mountain ash, blackberry bramble, cedar, spruce, and more blackberries. The turns are plentiful, the singletrack is creamy smooth, and the terrain is mild. Open year-round and relatively dry compared with Victor Falls after several days of rain, the Coal Mine trails are excellent for improving steering skills and building stamina.

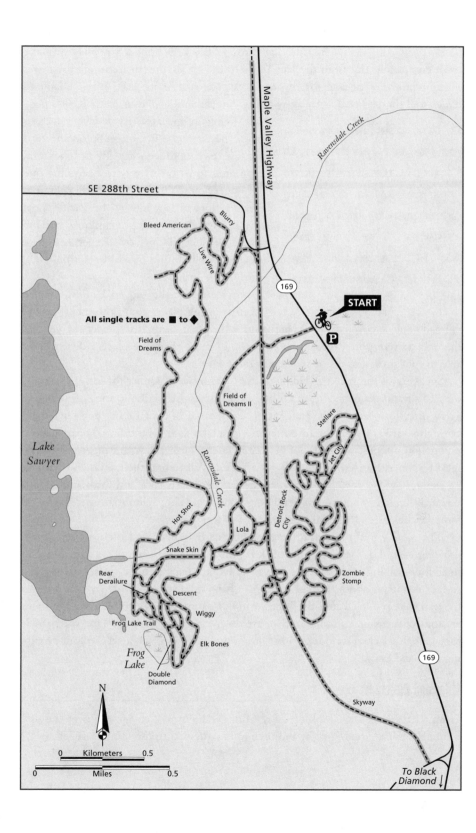

Today if you blink while driving through Black Diamond, you may miss the town completely. But from the late 1880s to the 1920s, the small mining town was a major producer of coal for the entire West Coast. At its peak, Black Diamond mined and shipped coal as far away as Los Angeles and had as many as 10,000 people living in the area. By today's standards these numbers are not huge, but at the turn of the twentieth century, Black Diamond appeared to be on its way to becoming one of Puget Sound's major cities. The coal mines were reopened in 1986 by the Pacific Coal Company when mining techniques became more efficient and lucrative. Experts estimate that 600 million tons of coal lie within 6,000 feet of the surface.

▶ **The Black Diamond Bakery opened in 1902, and today the old brick oven is still fueled by wood. The current owner has also established a deli and ice cream/coffee shop/art gallery along Railroad Avenue. Open seven days a week, the bakery (360-886-2741) is famous among Puget Sound natives for delicious muffins, bread, and hot coffee.**

Evidence of the old coal mines can be seen in many places along the trail. The old railroad grade is covered with charcoal-gray dust that accumulated over the years as the railroad transported coal from the area. In more than one place, riders will be able to spot small chunks of coal along the trail.

Speaking of the trail, the riding at the Coal Mine is perfect for lower intermediate to advanced riders. The area is like an ant farm, with trails shooting off in nearly every direction. Ninety-five percent of the ride consists of freshly cut singletrack through a variety of terrain. Intermediates can take their time riding the undulating topography and not worry about getting in over their heads with dangerously technical terrain. Advanced riders will get a kick out of testing their skills and stamina by seeing how fast they can negotiate the trail as it darts back and forth and up and down; around curves; through bends, dips, drops and short climbs; over roots, rocks, jumps and elevated logs; and through narrow forest alleys.

The route winds through three clearcuts that have been replanted and are slowly growing back. The clearcut singletrack is probably the least smooth in the area due to all the small logs and branches on the trail. Once back into the trees, however, the surface is sultry smooth throughout most of the ride. Some cyclists say that parts of the trail were modeled after the Tapeworm in Renton (see Ride 15). Although there are tons of turns in a small area, they are not nearly as tight as the Tapeworm. Still, for a ride that lacks a serious gain in elevation, riders can get a great workout by riding hard and fast.

Miles and Directions

From the parking area (looking away from the highway), go up and over the dirt mound/barricade on the right and then follow the trail to the immediate left. Pedal away from the highway on the wide, rocky, overgrown access road. Watch for broken glass in this area. The entire area is accessible from this point. Cyclists will find so many different combinations that the best plan is simply to ride in a direction and explore.

Ride Information

Local Information

City of Maple Valley, (425) 413-8800

Restaurants

CJ's Bakery, (360) 886-0855. CJ's is located in Black Diamond.

The North End

The North End is quickly becoming one of the most popular fat-tire playgrounds in the western part of the state, attracting mountain bikers from as far south as Tacoma and even drawing our cousins from north of the border. Exceptional views of Mount Baker, northern Puget Sound, the Olympic Mountains, Lake Sammish, and hundreds of rivers, streams, and smaller lakes make the North End a riding Shangri-la. But although the scenery is spectacular, it is the miles upon miles of singletrack that keep cyclists coming back again and again to areas like Galbraith Mountain, Walker Valley, and the Pilchuck Tree Farm.

Between these three rides there are more than a hundred trails to choose from, covering more than 200 miles of terrain. With so many choices and so many miles of trails to explore, riders of all abilities will find something to keep them interested for weeks. Whether on the silky singletrack of the Pilchuck Tree Farm, the rowdy ruts and banked turns of Walker Valley, or the constricting curves and roller-coaster terrain of Galbraith Mountain, cyclists will need more than a season to ride everything.

21 Paradise Lake

Start: Paradise Lake Road
Length: Up to 10 miles
Approximate riding time: 1 to 2 hours
Technical difficulty: Intermediate
Trail surface: Gravel, sand, hard-pack single-track, mud, and loose rock
Trail contacts: None
Fees and permits: None
Schedule: Open year-round but best April to October
Maps: *Washington Atlas and Gazetteer,* page 79, B7; USGS Maltby

Land status: Snohomish County
Nearest town: Woodinville
User density: Medium
Other trail users: Equestrians, hikers, ORVs
Canine compatibility: Dogs are permitted
Wheels: Cross-country to light dual suspension
Hazards: Automobiles and logging trucks on Paradise Lake Road

Finding the Trailhead

From the South End, head north on I-405. Take exit 3 for State Route 522 and U.S. Highway 2 (Wenatchee exit). Follow for about 6 miles to the first light, which is Paradise Lake Road to the south (right) and Maltby Road (left). Turn right. There are a Chevron and a Texaco on the corners. Follow Paradise Lake Road for about 1.4 miles. Just as the road drops down a short hill, look for a large pullout area with a row of old mailboxes just past the private road. Park here.

The Ride

Despite the name and the proximity to Paradise Lake and Paradise Valley, there is nothing utopian about mountain biking in the area. The small network of trails is damp most of the year, garbage is scattered about the trail entrance, motocross riders frequent the area, serious descents are nonexistent, and the locals are not exactly mountain-bike friendly. But if you live north of Bothell or out toward Monroe and are short on time, Paradise Lake is a viable alternative to not riding at all.

Paradise Lake consists of two distinct areas: North and South, as in north or south of Paradise Lake Road. The **North Trail** is an out-and-back mud fest just over a mile long. It provides a decent warm-up as it gradually descends, but if you prefer to stay dry don't bother. Even in later summer the trail can be moist and muddy.

The south side offers a respite from the Northwest muck and a variety of trails that are entertaining for at least a couple of hours. The outer trails tend to be wider and drier due to their exposure to sunlight. Most of them are relatively flat with mild descents. However, some of the trails are freshly cut or lead cyclists across rock gardens. Either way, the trails can be technical.

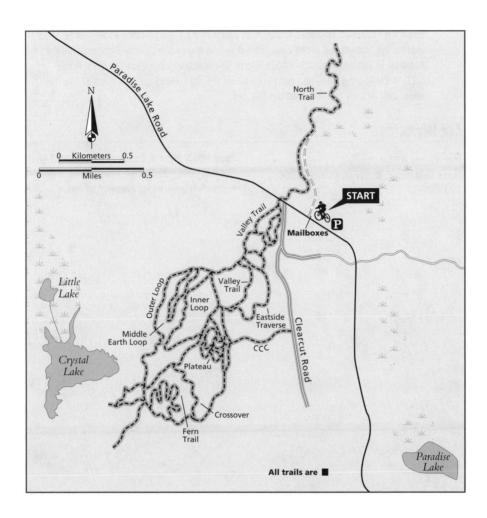

The inner trails consist of narrow singletrack cut through a dense forest. The turns are tightly overgrown and slippery nearly year-round due to the lack of light penetrating the forest canopy. However, motocross riders shy away from these skinny slits in the woods.

It's important to understand that the local residents are not crazy about mountain bikers. Pack out any garbage, do not blast music while loading or unloading bikes, and be polite to hikers and equestrians.

Miles and Directions

0.0 From Paradise Lake Road, head south around the cement-block barricades and begin to explore. One option is to follow the outer trails first **(Valley Trail, Outer Loop, Clearcut**

Road, and **Eastside Traverse)** to put in as much mileage as possible as well as to explore the boundaries of the area. Then dive into any of the trails within the perimeter. **Sidetrip:** To explore the north side, ride past the mailboxes back toward State Route 522. Duck into the trees and onto the trail on the right. Head straight out until the trail ends. Turn around and return to the car.

Ride Information

Restaurants

Jenos Restaurant & Italian Cuisine, (360) 794-5990

Papa MIAS Pizza & Pasta, (360) 794-9144

Sailfish Grill, (360) 794-4056. Note: Above restaurants are all located in Monroe.

22 Lord Hill Regional Park

Start: Lord Hill Regional Park parking lot

Length: 5.9-mile circuit

Approximate riding time: 1 to 1½ hours

Technical difficulty: Intermediate

Trail surface: Maintained gravel trails; hard-pack dirt with roughly a mile of technical riding over roots, rocks, and slippery obstacles.

Trail contacts: Snohomish County Parks and Recreation, (425) 388–6600; parks.department@co.snohomish.wa.us

Fees and permits: None

Schedule: Open year-round, with seasonal closures on some trails

Maps: *Washington Atlas and Gazetteer,* pages 79, A8, and 80, A1; USGS Snohomish and Lake Roesinger

Land status: Snohomish County Park

Nearest town: Monroe

User density: Moderate to heavy

Other trail users: Hikers, equestrians

Canine compatibility: Leashed dogs permitted

Wheels: Front to light dual suspension

Hazards: Wooden bridges, horse manure

Finding the Trailhead

From Seattle, cross Lake Washington on State Route 520 or I–90, and then head north on I–405. A few miles past Kirkland and near Bothell, take State Route 522 east toward Monroe. Drive roughly 12 miles, and then take the first Monroe exit (164th Southeast). At the end of the off-ramp, go north (to the left) on the Old Snohomish-Monroe Highway. Follow the highway for roughly 4 miles before turning left onto 127th. The park entrance is 2 miles up the road on the left. Park in the gravel parking lot for automobiles. Do not park in the area designated for horse trailers.

The Ride

Located south of the Old Monroe–Snohomish Road and north of the Snohomish River, Lord Hill Regional Park is a relatively unknown circuit of intermediate trails. The 1,300-acre park is crisscrossed with more than 10 miles of hiking, biking, and equestrian trails. Most of them are old logging roads wide enough for as many as four bikes to ride comfortably side by side. Unfortunately, not all of them are open to mountain biking, and some of the bike trails are closed during winter to protect the trail surface.

The majority of trails in Lord Hill Park are veiled by a thick canopy forest that keeps them moist and tacky, providing slot car–like traction. However, after a short burst of rain, the trails can become wet and muddy even mid- to late summer. Please pay attention to seasonal closures (November to April) of various trails. The 3 or 4 miles of singletrack reserved, although not exclusively, for fat-tire folks are challenging due to rocks, roots, and routinely slippery conditions. The lack of serious climbing makes the ride ideal for lower intermediate cyclists who want to improve their skills.

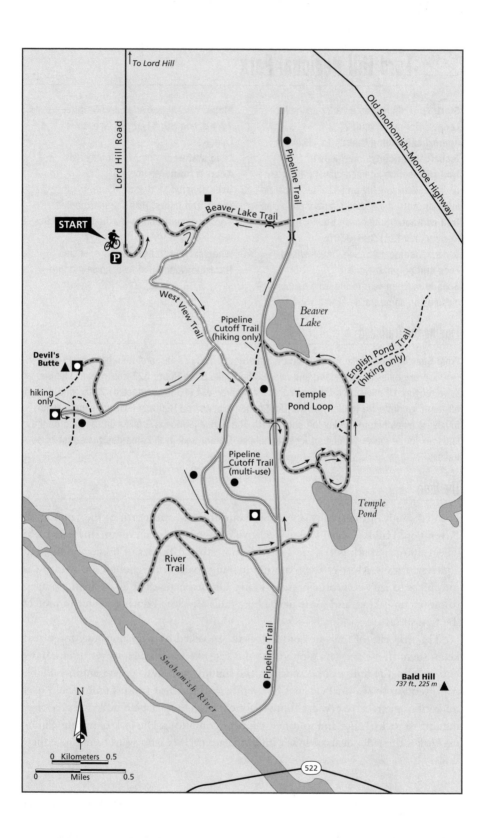

To Lord Hill

Lord Hill Road

Old Snohomish–Monroe Highway

Pipeline Trail

Beaver Lake Trail

START

P

West View Trail

Pipeline
Cutoff Trail
(hiking only)

Beaver
Lake

English Pond Trail
(hiking only)

Devil's
Butte

hiking
only

Temple
Pond Loop

Pipeline
Cutoff Trail
(multi-use)

Temple
Pond

River
Trail

Pipeline Trail

Snohomish River

Bald Hill
737 ft., 225 m

N

0   Kilometers   0.5

0   Miles   0.5

522

Even advanced riders will enjoy the short jaunt around the park's nine ponds. The largest are Beaver Lake and Temple Pond. The first's namesake is readily evident by all the beaver dams in the area. But our bucktooth friends are not the only wildlife in the area. A small herd of deer roams the park, as do the occasional bear and bobcat.

Novice riders will also enjoy the park, provided they stick to the well-maintained gravel jeep trails and the dual track of the **Pipeline Trail.** The singletrack is simply too technical for riders without any serious time in the saddle.

Miles and Directions

0.0 To begin, go to the back of the parking lot and pedal to the left of the kiosk/map, between the two large boulders, and down the short, steep hill.

0.4 Reach a T in the trail after crossing a series of footbridges through some low-lying wetlands, and turn right. (**FYI:** To the left is the Beaver Lake Trail.)

0.5 Follow the main trail to the left and up the hill.

0.8 Turn right and head up the hill toward Devil's Butte.

1.3 Cyclists have two choices here—continue straight on the West View Trail, passing the trail on the right, or turn right and pedal up the Devil's Butte Trail. This route continues straight, but the Devil's Butte Trail adds only 0.5 mile to the ride.

1.4 Pass the loop trail on the right; it is open to hikers only.

1.5 Reach the top of the trail and an open grassy area. The Loop Trail comes into the spot on the right, and there is another trail on the left. Both are closed to bikes. The view of the Snohomish Valley is merely OK during the midsummer. The trees are thick and healthy, obstructing the views. Early spring and late fall, the views are much better. Turn around and head back to the main trail.

2.2 Turn right at the bottom of the hill.

2.4 Turn right at the four-way intersection. (**FYI:** On the left is the Pipeline Cutoff Trail—for hikers only. On the right and straight ahead, the trails remain the same—wide maintained gravel road/jeep trails.)

2.7 Reach another part of the Pipeline Cutoff Trail and turn left onto the singletrack. The route makes a short climb and then traverses along the hillside.

2.9 Continue straight on singletrack, ignoring the trail on the right.

3.1 Reach the Pipeline Trail, a wide doubletrack road that breaks out of the forest. Turn left and climb up the slight hill.

3.3 Reach a four-way intersection and turn right onto the **Temple Pond Loop**—wide singletrack.

3.5 The trail splits for about 50 feet and then reconnects, forming a loop. On the left is a small pond.

3.7 The trail splits again. Head to the left for a short loop. You'll be back to this spot in a couple of minutes.

3.8 Turn right and loop back around to the last split in the trail.

4.3 Continue straight, ignoring trail on the right.

Always bring protection—wear your helmet!

4.5 Cross the bridge and pass Beaver Lake on the right.

4.7 Reach the Pipeline Trail and turn right. Drop down the hill. Ignore the spur trails on the left. Cross one creek.

5.1 Cross the bridge, reach a four-way intersection, and turn left; then cross another bridge. The trail begins to climb up more singletrack.

5.2 Continue straight, ignoring trails on the left. The trail widens into a jeep trail.

5.3 Stay on the main road and ignore the trail on the right.

5.5 Reach the main park entrance road and turn right. Cross the bridges; pedal up the ascent and back to the parking lot.

5.9 Arrive at the parking lot.

Ride Information

Local Events

The Evergreen State Fair, late August to early September; www.evergreenfair.org, twenty-four-hour events hot line, (425) 339-3309. Concerts, carnival, rodeo events, exhibits, and more.

Restaurants

Jenos Restaurant & Italian Cuisine, (360) 794-5990
Papa MIAS Pizza & Pasta, (360) 794-9144
Sailfish Grill, (360) 794-4056
Note: Above restaurants are all located in Monroe.

23 Wallace Falls State Park

Start: Wallace Falls State Park Trailhead
Length: Short ride, 13.6-mile out-and-back;
long ride, 19.1-mile out-and-back
Approximate riding time: Intermediate riders,
4 to 5 hours; advanced riders, 3 to 4 hours
Technical difficulty: Intermediate to advanced
Trail surface: Gravel trails and roads, dirt
roads, wide and narrow singletrack (Note: Singletrack is semismooth but contains a few
rocky sections and becomes slick when wet.)
Trail contacts: Wallace Falls State Park, (360)
793-0420
Fees and permits: None
Schedule: Open year-round from dawn to
dusk; best March through September

Maps: *Washington Atlas and Gazetteer,* page
80, A3; USGS Wallace Lake
Land status: State park, Washington State
Department of Natural Resources
Nearest town: Gold Bar
User density: High
Other trail users: Hikers, joggers
Canine compatibility: Leashed dogs permit-
ted
Wheels: Cross-country and full suspension
Hazards: Pedestrians, hidden obstacles under
the leaves in fall, cliffs above the falls. Traffic
on U.S. Highway 2 is maddening in the after-
noon!

Finding the Trailhead

From Seattle, take I-90 or State Route 520 east to I-405. Drive north to exit 194. Follow U.S. 2
east to the town of Gold Bar. Turn left onto First Street, just past the Serpentine Museum. Follow
First Street to May Creek Road and turn right. Follow signs to Wallace Falls State Park.

The Ride

Wallace Falls' easy access and nontechnical biking and hiking trails make the state
park a popular destination for Puget Sound outdoor enthusiasts. The trail contains a
variety of terrain that nearly any weekend warrior can handle. The climb to the falls
is long and steady, but the singletrack is smooth with only a couple of technical sections. Most of the trails are wide and fairly straight. Once up on the ridge, the views
of the Skykomish River Valley are fantastic and the view of Wallace Lake is serene.

Steeped in history, Wallace Falls State Park sits on the edge of the tiny town of
Gold Bar and right in the middle of the Mount Baker Snoqualmie National Forest.
The name "Wallace" after which the falls, lake, and mountain are named, is Native
American in origin and takes its name from Sarah Kwayaylsh, a member of the
Skykomish (*sky-KOH-mish*) Tribe. Sarah and her husband, Joe, were the first home-
steaders in an area now known as the town Start Up, which still exists today. Gold
Bar, now the closest town to the park, was named after the gravel bars that Chinese
railroad workers used to pan for gold in the early 1900s.

Established in 1977, the park's main attraction is the accessibility to hikers and
bikers of the 265-foot cataract, where thousands of gallons of water per minute rush

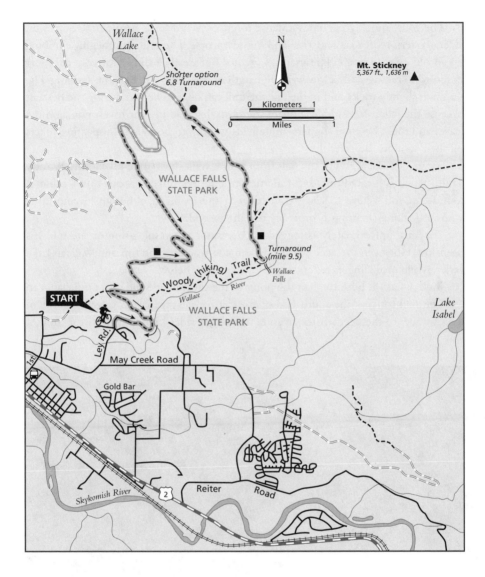

to the valley below. Standing at the top of the falls provides stunning views of the Skykomish Valley below.

Wallace Falls is a fantastic trail for nearly any rider with a decent amount of cardiovascular stamina and basic riding skills. The trail contains only a few technical sections, which are all relatively short and hikable/bikable. Don't be afraid to try and ride the challenging terrain—the trail is wide and relatively safe, as long as you maintain your speed and stay in control.

From the parking lot, the trail is wide and covered in loose gravel. The first couple of miles have the most pedestrian traffic, so be sure to ride responsibly, especially on the downhills.

The route quickly becomes a dense forest of sword ferns hemlock, Douglas fir, alder, western red cedar, and vine and big-leaf maple. The trail then begins climbing up an old railroad grade. The grade is gradual but steady, making for easy climbing in regard to biking skills. However, the length of the climb can be a bit draining. The terrain is slightly rocky, and in the fall, the trail can be treacherous during the descent because the fallen leaves hide most of the obstacles. Add in Northwest rain, and the leaves and rocks become slippery minefields waiting to bounce unsuspecting bikers off their mounts. Be careful!

For spectacular views of the falls from below, walk the 1-mile hiker-only **Woody Trail,** which is located only 0.5 mile up the trail. The hike is about thirty minutes round-trip. You'll have to leave your bikes at the trailhead, although leaving bikes without locking them up is probably not the best idea.

The area, unfortunately, is logged on occasion; as a result some of the trail has been lost. However, the access roads have made reaching the top and Wallace Lake easier, while providing excellent views of the valley below.

Wallace Lake is both the halfway point of the shorter ride and a stunning sight to see. The trail touches the south end of the calm, clear-green lake, offering views of the Cascades to the north. After crossing the bridge, riders will find a short section of

Wallace River just above the falls

singletrack that is often under a few inches of water. The trail disappears again due to logging, but the access roads are well marked and it is easy to pick up the last stretch of trail to the falls.

The view from the top of the falls is awesome, but is just the beginning of the real fun. What goes up must come down, and for most of the 9.5 miles to the falls, the trail has been gaining elevation. Advanced riders have reached speeds in excess of 45 miles an hour on the gravel roads on their way back down. Once back into the forest, speeds decrease, and the long, wide sections of the trail are easy to navigate. Be wary of hikers near the bottom of the route.

Wallace Falls is a tremendous off-road bicycle ride. However, the best part of the adventure may be the wonderfully delicious pastries, soup, and sandwiches baked daily at the Gold Bar Bakery. Syrupy sweet Apple Cups (glazed muffins with chunks of real apple), gigantic Big Foots (maple bars in the shape of a Sasquatch footprint), huge chocolate chip cookies, peanut butter cookies, apple pie, cherry pie, cinnamon rolls dripping with sweet frosting, and crème brulée to satisfy even the most extreme sweet tooth are all a part of Gold Bar Bakery's mouthwatering menu. After the long ride, however, you might want to try one of their mammoth-sized sandwiches on your choice of Dutch-crust or eight-grain bread. Light and nearly as fluffy as angel food cake, the bread is the foundation for sandwiches with fresh vegetables, smoked meats, and cheeses. The smoked turkey with thick bacon and avocado is a local favorite. The bakery is open daily and is a must for any hungry rider.

Miles and Directions

0.0 Start from the parking lot, and follow the wide gravel trail underneath the power lines.

0.3 The trail veers to the left and into the woods.

0.4 Pass the hiker-only Woody Trail on the right, a 1-mile trail leading to views of Wallace Falls. The bike trail climbs steadily on an old railroad grade.

1.5 Turn left toward Wallace Falls, where a park map and picnic table are located. The trail begins a steep, narrow climb over rocky terrain.

1.8 The trail makes a sharp turn to the right. Ignore the trail on the left.

2.5 The trail deposits riders onto a logging road. Go right up the hill.

4.1 Pass a road on the right and continue.

4.5 Take the right fork in the road.

6.3 Turn left and head back into woods on Wallace Lake Trail. A sign is on right hand side of the road.

6.8 Arrival at Wallace Lake. **Options:** For a shorter ride, turn around and head back to the parking lot. To reach the falls and finish the longer ride, turn right across the wooden bridge and head toward the falls (2.6 miles).

7.3 Logging has wiped out a portion of the trail here.

7.6 Follow the logging road to left. Look for a sign on the right. The logging road continues for about 1 mile and leads back into singletrack.

9.1 Pass a sign that reads WALK ZONE. (It's a good idea to pay attention here; otherwise you could end up riding over the cliffs, into the river, and over the falls. You probably don't want to do this without at least a barrel.)

9.5 Reach the end of the trail, the ride's halfway point, and the edge of the cliff overlooking the falls. Turn around and head back to Wallace Lake.

12.1 Take left at Wallace Lake.

12.6 Reach the gravel road and take a right. Follow the road down to the original singletrack trail.

16.4 Turn left and head back into the woods. Watch for pedestrians while headed downhill. It is at this point that the trail becomes more crowded.

17.6 Turn right at the kiosk, map, and picnic table.

18.8 Turn right onto a wide gravel trail under the power lines.

19.1 Reach the parking lot.

Ride Information

Local Information

Monroe Chamber of Commerce, (360) 794-5488

Washington Serpentarium, (360) 793-2000

Restaurants

Gold Bar Bakery, Gold Bar, (360) 793-7996

24 Pilchuck Tree Farm

Start:
Victoria Tract—Trailhead at the end of 316th Street Northeast
Armstrong Tract—Parking lot underneath the power lines, Seventy-first Avenue Northeast
Pilchuck Tract—Parking area underneath the power lines, Fifty-ninth Avenue Northeast
Length: Up to 30 miles of trails
Approximate riding time: 2 to 4 hours
Technical difficulty: Novice to advanced
Trail surface: Gravel access roads, hard-packed dirt trails, and muddy trails
Trail contacts: Tree Farm Office, (360) 652-7565
Fees and permits: None
Schedule: Pilchuck and Victoria Tracts have seasonal closures (November 1 to May 1); the Armstrong Tract is open year-round.

Maps: *Washington Atlas and Gazetteer,* page 95, B6–7 and C6–7; USGS Arlington East, McMurray
Land status: Private land (owned by Pilchuck Tree Farm)
Nearest town: Bryant, Smokey Point, Marysville
User density: Medium to heavy
Other trail users: Equestrians
Canine compatibility: Leashed dogs permitted
Wheels: Cross-country and light full suspension
Hazards: Bears, bobcats; mud, fine dirt and sand mixture

Finding the Trailheads

Victoria Tract
From Everett, go north on I-5 about twenty-five minutes to exit 215 (300th Street Northwest). Turn right onto 300th Street and follow for almost a mile to English Grade Road. Turn left and follow for 1.3 miles to 316th Street Northeast. Turn right, drive for 1.7 miles, and turn left onto a gravel road. Drive to the gate; park here but do not block gate! The trail begins up the road on the other side of the gate.

Armstrong Tract
From Everett, go north on I-5 to the Stanwood Camano Island exit. Head east on State Route 532/Bryant/Standwood Road, which turns into Grandview Road as it turns north. Shortly after the bend in the road, turn right onto Seventy-first Avenue Northeast and look for the parking area on the right underneath the power lines. A small red sign reads PILCHUCK TREE FARM FIRE GATE #4. There should be plenty of parking for both mountain bikers and equestrian trailers.

Pilchuck Tract
From Everett, go north on I-5 to the Stanwood Camano Island exit. Head east on State Route 532/Bryant/Standwood Road. Follow to Fifty-ninth Avenue Northeast and turn left. Follow until reaching the parking area just underneath the power lines.

The Ride

Minimal climbing and a massive matrix of suede-smooth singletrack over rolling terrain make the Pilchuck Tree Farm a definite must-ride for any Puget Sound area

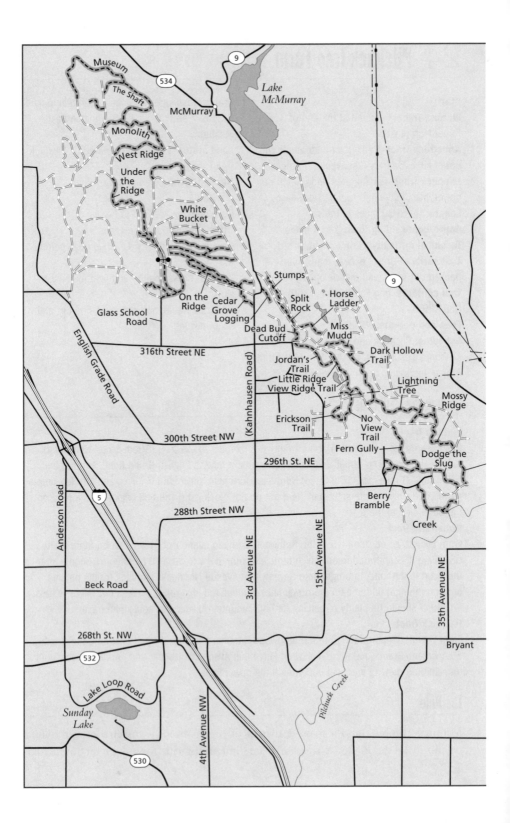

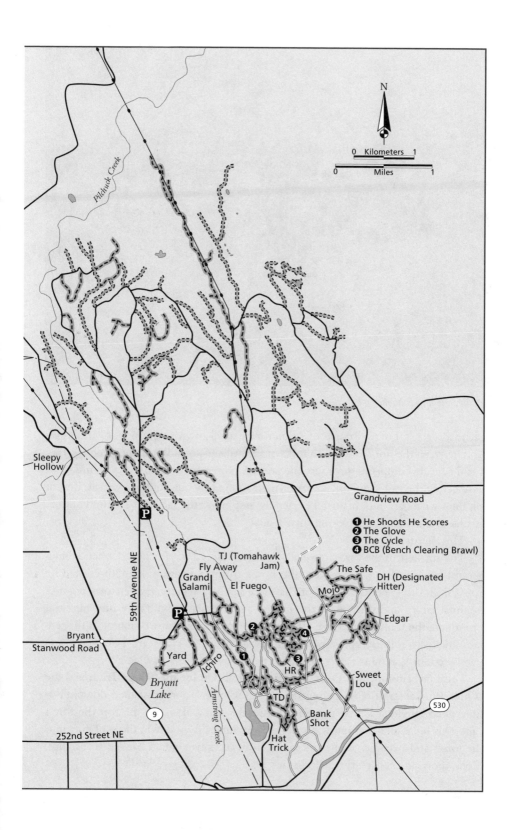

A modern-day Stonehenge?

off-road cyclist. Located north of Arlington, a small town sitting next to the junction between the north and south forks of the Stillaquamish River, the Pilchuck Tree Farm actually comprises three separate areas. All three are crisscrossed with fire roads connecting the miles and miles of well-used and freshly cut singletrack trails. Best of all, the owners are mountain-bike friendly and enjoy the fact that fat-tire enthusiasts have so much fun exploring their land.

The Victoria Tract

The smallest of the three, is usually the area riders are referring to when talking about the "Tree Farm." Victoria is also home to the futuristic monolith created by artists from the Pilchuck School of Glass (see sidebar). Climbing at Victoria requires minimal effort, and the top of the climb can be reached within twenty minutes. From here the trails cut through clearcuts and young new-growth forests as the terrain gradually rolls up and down small elevation gains. There are, however, a few steep sections that most riders may want to or have to walk.

Local favorites include **Over the Ridge Trail, Under the Ridge Trail,** and the **White Bucket Trail.** Combining the three produces a long sustained downhill of superplush singletrack that is tattooed into the forest floor. At the top the forest canopy is light, and the trail is usually dry. About halfway down, the trail cuts into the forest and becomes moist and tacky. Both sections contain banked turns, dips, drops, roots, and rollers for catching air.

Most of the trails in the Victoria Tract are closed November 1 through May 1. Please obey all closures signs. Although the land manager is friendly to mountain bikers, he doesn't have to be. Respect his wishes and we'll be able to ride here for years to come. The Armstrong Tract, on the other hand, is open year-round and, quite frankly, contains more trails and better riding than either of the other two tracts. The dirt and gravel roads of the Victoria Tract remain open throughout the year, even when its trails are closed. Although it isn't singletrack, it's still better than lounging on the couch with the remote control.

The Armstrong Tract

Open year-round, the Armstrong Tract might be the least well known but is without a doubt the best of the three areas on which to ride at the Tree Farm. Larger than the Victoria Tract, Armstrong is loaded with miles and miles of trails so buffed that you'd think they have their own professional manicurist. And compared with the Pilchuck Tract's brutal and unforgiving trails, Armstrong's are fast and graceful.

► PILCHUCK SCHOOL OF GLASS

Upon reaching the crest of the Victoria Tract climb, riders break out into a large clearing overlooking the Skagit River Valley, Skagit Bay, and Whidbey Island. In the center of the clearing, a lone sentinel of stainless steel greets riders and may cause some to ask, "Have aliens landed here?" "Is this a futuristic Stonehenge?" The truth is not nearly as strange as fiction in this case. The monolith is roughly 10 feet tall and was constructed by artists attending the Pilchuck Glass School. Founded by world-famous artist Dale Chihuly, the school is a retreat bringing artists together to work with and learn about glass amid the spectacular beauty of the Pacific Northwest. The fifty-four-acre wooded campus is the world's largest and most comprehensive education center for artists working in glass. The architectural award–winning studios include two hot-glass shops, a kiln shop, a cold-working studio, a flat shop for torch work, a wood and metal shop, a glass plate print-making shop, a gallery, and a library.

Climbing is minimal at the Armstrong Tract and dictated by the rolling terrain. The luxuriously plush singletrack cuts through second-generation forests of spruce, lombardy poplar, cedar, ponderosa pine, Douglas fir, sword fern, black hawthorne, willow, blackberry, and huckleberry, as well as clearcuts that have been replanted and are slowly filling in. Despite the constant logging in the area, wildlife is abundant. It is not uncommon to see black bear, fox, elk, deer, and beaver roaming about.

The only serious challenges at the Armstrong Tract are riding through some of the sandy trails and figuring out how to ride every last trail in the area. There are so many trails that finding them all will take several adventures. Things could be worse.

The Pilchuck Tract

The Pilchuck Tract has earned mixed reviews from local riders. The crux of the debate is this: If you like log riding, big drops, dangerously steep descents, man-made obstacles, and North Shore–type adventures, then you will probably like this section of the Tree Farm. If you prefer long twisting singletrack with smooth banked turns, then you're better off trying one of the other two tracts.

The trails in the Pilchuck Tract are difficult to find and even more difficult to negotiate. Crash here on the small section of granite slick rock and you'll leave behind a deposit of skin and blood. Eat it on **Smackdown** and you'll feel as though the Undertaker, Stone Cold Steve Austin, and the Rock have whipped your ass in a three-on-one submission match. These trails are meant only for serious mountain bikers who enjoy drops, turns, and jumps. No one really rides these trails without beefy dual-suspension bikes with at least 4 inches of front and rear travel.

Miles and Directions

The three tracts contain so many trails, twists, and turns that following a mileage log is more of a headache than anything else. Use the maps to access the areas, keep track of your general location, and then go thrill hunting. Part of the adventure at Pilchuck is discovering new routes, loops, and combinations. Enjoy!

Victoria Tract: Walk around the gate and pedal up the hill. Upon reaching the top, begin exploring trails on the left or the right. The monolith is located west (left) of the road.

Armstrong Tract: Follow the main trail south underneath the power lines. Drop down and cross Harvey Creek, then climb back up the short hill before diving into the forest on the right. Alternatively, stay to the left and explore to the west. In either direction, cyclists will find a maze of trails and several adventures.

Pilchuck Tract: Walk around the gate and pedal up the gravel access road. Take a right at the second major intersection, and begin exploring.

Ride Information

Restaurants
Alligator Soul, (425) 259-6311
Scuttlebutt Brewing Company, (425) 257-9414

Karl's Bakery & Coffee Shoppe, (425) 252-1774 or (800) 607-0003
Note: Above establishments are all located in Everett.

25 Walker Valley

Start: Walker Valley ORV parking lot
Length: 9.8 miles
Approximate riding time: 2 to 3 hours
Technical difficulty: Moderate to advanced due to the length and supertechnical terrain
Trail surface: Hard-packed dirt, roots, and rocks in the dry months; slippery mud and large, deep puddles in the rainy season
Trail contacts: Department of Natural Resources, Northwest Region, Sedro Woolley, (360) 856-3500 or (800) 527-3305
Fees and permits: None
Schedule: Open year-round
Maps: *Washington Atlas and Gazetteer,* page 95, A7; USGS McMurray, Sedro Woolley South

Land status: Department of Natural Resources
Nearest town: Mount Vernon
User density: Heavy
Other trail users: ORVs
Canine compatibility: Dogs permitted but not recommended; too many ORVs.
Wheels: Light dual suspension to full-on downhill rigs. During the rainy season it's best to have tires that shed mud.
Hazards: ORV riders, ruts, ticktacktoe cinder blocks, mud, high muddy bridges

Finding the Trailhead

From Seattle, take I-5 north to exit 221 (Lake McMurray/La Conner/Conway), about 50 miles north of Seattle. Turn right at the stop sign and head east on State Route 534 until it ends (approximately 5 miles). Turn left onto State Route 9, and head north toward Sedro-Woolley. Drive through the S turns, and pass Lake McMurray on the right. Continue north, passing Lake Cavanaugh Road. Pass Big Lake on the left, and turn right onto Walker Valley Road a mile later (just past the Big Lake Bar and Grill). Look for the trailhead sign and Fire Mountain Scout Reservation at Milepost 46. Drive 2.2 miles and turn right at the ORV park gravel road. Stay on the main road for about 1.0 mile, and park in the Walker Valley ORV parking lot.
From the East Side, take I-405 north to I-5, then follow the directions above.

The Ride

What do you get when you cross more than 10,000 acres of working forest with years upon years of ORV riders tattooing their signatures into the landscape? It's simple: 30-plus miles of singletrack riddled with ruts deep enough to swallow entire bikes, mud as thick and slick as raw brownie mix, wild whoop-de-dos, dangerous descents, zigzagging switchbacks, and big banked turns as tall as the average NBA player. Sounds fun doesn't it! Welcome to the Walker Valley ORV Park, located just 10 miles south of Mount Vernon, Washington.

Despite being home to some of the Puget Sound's coolest trails, Walker Valley is rarely mentioned by fat-tire folks during discussions on the region's best rides. The reason? Walker is extremely popular with the ORV riders. And while they are the

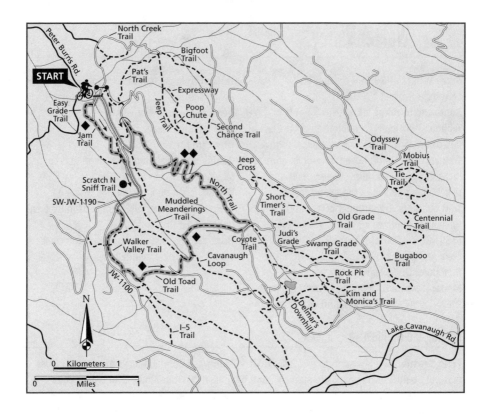

reason for the trails being so conducive to our beloved sport, they are also the reason many cyclists shy away from Walker Valley. By midmorning on the weekends, the parking lot is full of noise-polluting, gasoline fume–producing four-wheelers and motorcycles. The best plan is to ride Walker Valley midweek or early, early morning on the weekends. This usually keeps contact with our motorized cousins to a bare minimum.

Walker Valley is really a circuit of trails crisscrossing up and down foothills of the North Cascades and the east side of the Walker Valley. Since 1970 the forest has generated more than $4 billion in revenue. The money is used to protect fish and wildlife and to maintain the trail system. However, recreational use is at risk due to vandalism and abuse of the park. Each year, careless and irresponsible trail riders cost taxpayers thousands of dollars. It's a shame that only a few could cost the rest of the fat-tire community such a fantastic place to ride. For more information about how to help protect Walker Valley, call (360) 856–3500.

Although the trails are wacky and wicked, Walker Valley is a good place for intermediate riders to step up to the next level. None of the trails consists of any serious length, and if the riding becomes too much, the parking lot is never far away. Nor are easy, descending access roads.

TULIP FESTIVAL

The Skagit Valley's mild climate, evenly distributed rainfall, and fertile farmlands provide an ideal environment for bulb growing, primarily daffodils, tulips, and irises. The total amount of acreage devoted to bulb and flower growing in the Skagit Valley has increased greatly over the years, although it is now threatened by constantly encroaching development. In 1945 just 325 acres were planted, with an approximate value of $300,000. By 1997 approximately 7,000 acres were used for bulb farming, with a value of $42 million. Although the tulip bloom is a major tourist attraction in the Skagit Valley, the tulip industry is concerned primarily with the bulbs themselves. The bulbs are machine graded, and the large bulbs are marketed. The bulbs to be planted usually come from the farm's previous harvests. However, some stock is occasionally purchased from Europe. Planting is done in the fall, mainly in September and October. The flowers are picked beginning in late March. The exact time of the harvest varies due to weather conditions. The festival is usually held in April.

The Skagit Valley Tulip Festival is a community event that actively involves every major city in Skagit County. Officially inaugurated in 1984 by the Mount Vernon Chamber of Commerce, the Tulip Festival has grown into one of Washington State's most popular and colorful happenings. The Mount Vernon Chamber of Commerce, under the direction of director Jerry Diggerness, saw that people were coming by the thousands to view the colors that resembled an explosion in a paint factory and decided to add events and festivities to enhance visitors' trip to the Skagit Valley. In 1994 the Tulip Festival broke off from the Chamber of Commerce and became an entity of its own, headed by a twenty-member board of directors.

From humble beginnings, the Skagit Valley Tulip Festival now boasts an amazing assortment of events. Activities include everything from walks to runs to bike rides. There are several art shows, along with gala celebrations and concerts by the Skagit Symphony and Cheryl Bentyne of Manhattan Transfer. The Downtown Mount Vernon Street Fair has juried arts and crafts, entertainment, and a variety of festival foods. The Kiwanis Salmon Barbecue is a complete salmon dinner held at beautiful Hillcrest Park and hosted by the local Kiwanis Club. Recently added to the Tulip Festival are Woodfest, a celebration of the Sedro-Woolley's logging roots; quilt shows in Anacortes; tours of a third-generation dairy farm in Mount Vernon; a lecture series; a golf tournament; and a black-tie-optional Tulip Ball. For more information, write P.O. Box 1784, Mount Vernon, WA 98273; call (360) 428–5959; or visit www.tulipfestival.org. The Skagit Valley Tulip Festival office is located at 117 North First, in the Carnation Building.

The mileage cues below and the map combine the **Easy Grade Trail,** the **Jam Trail,** the **Walker Valley Trail,** and the **North Trail.** Easy and the Jam Trails gradually climb along the ridge giving mountain bikers a glimpse of the fun to come. The real climbing and thigh-burning challenge comes along when riders hit the Walker Valley Trail (WVT).

The ascent up WVT would be relatively easy except for the deep ruts, eroding trail, and exposed roots and rocks kicked loose by ORVs. There are sections that no mere mortal using pedal power can clean. Most *professionals* would have difficulty riding these sections. However, the trudge through Betty Crocker–like brownie mix is worth the effort once riders reach the top of the North Trail, which begins with a drag-strip straightaway with a few whoop-de-dos thrown in for grins and giggles.

From here the trail begins to descend through banked turns that look as though they were designed with a dual slalom event in mind. However, the turns just keep coming, and the drops get bigger as the ruts grow wider and deeper. The trail is so tough that strong mountain bikers with the ability to finesse their much lighter bikes through the bone-breaking, bike-mangling gauntlet are nearly as fast as less maneuverable motorcycles and four-wheelers. And downhill speed freaks coated in Kevlar and neoprene will blast by all but the best ORV riders. Of course, the motorized crowd will never admit this!

Miles and Directions

0.0 Catch the **Jam Trail** at the back of the parking lot just past the outhouses. Cross the wooden bridge and turn right onto the **Easy Grade Trail.**

0.3 Arrive at a small opening and cross to the Jam Trail. Continue straight past the next three trails.

1.0 The Jam Trail reaches JW-1100. Turn right onto the road and pedal up the hill. Pass a couple of trails, cross the bridge, and pass another couple of trails on the left, all of which join the **Muddled Meanderings Trail.**

1.5 Stay to the left upon reaching the fork of SW-JW-1190. Take the next left on the **Walker Valley Trail,** ahead on the left at Mile 1.53. Begin climbing up a steep ascent over ticktacktoe cinder blocks.

2.0 Climb to the intersection of the **Scratch 'N' Sniff Trail** and the Walker Valley Trail. Continue straight on the Walker Valley Trail.

2.1 Stick to the trail on the left upon reaching the Y.

3.3 Take the trail on the left—the **Old Toad Trail.** Pass through a clearcut, reach another Y, and turn right. (**Note:** It may be confusing here due to the logging. The goal is to bypass the Scratch 'N' Sniff Trail, which descends to the left, and reach the Muddled Meanderings Trail.)

3.6 Reach a T and turn right onto the Muddled Meanderings Trail.

4.3 Reach FS B-1000 and the top of the Muddled Meanderings Trail. Turn left and look for the North Trail on the left. Take the North Trail and let the fun begin! (**FYI:** The first section of the trail is a long straightaway with a shallow descent and several whoop-de-dos. The route is wet but not as muddy as much of the rest of the ride due to the gravel on the trail.)

4.9   The North Trail begins to whip back and forth through a series of S turns complete with big-banked curves. (**Note:** The North Trail is an excellent downhill trail. The trail is littered with large and small jagged rocks, Crisco coated-like slick roots, big drops, super-slimy mud, and ruts that cut deep into the trail surface.)

5.7   The trail straightens out and heads into a clearcut that has been growing back for a number of years. The trail is dry and full of whoop-de-dos as the forest canopy opens up.

6.6   Reach the road (SW-JW-1150) and turn left. Ignore the trail on the right.

6.9   Reach a large turn to the right in the road and the Muddled Meanderings Trail on the left of the apex of the turn.

7.0   Turn left onto SW-JW-1190 and then right onto the Jam Trail.

9.2   Pass three trails.

9.4   Reach the turnaround area and cross to the Easy Grade Trail.

9.7   Reach the beginning of the Jam Trail and turn left.

9.8   Reach the parking lot.

Downhill Directions

For our big-air-speed-freak-neoprene-Kevlar-coated brethren, Walker Valley's North Trail provides more than enough thrills and spine-tingling chills. Burley drops, canyon-sized ruts, deep mud, behemoth banked turns, and steep descents are just a sampling of the challenges that DH riders will find on the North Trail. To access the trail, leave one car at the parking area, then shuttle riders and bikes up JW–1100 all the way to Lake Cavanaugh Road. Turn left and drive to B–1000. Turn left again, and drive to the top of the North Trail. Park on the side of the road and head downhill!

Ride Information

Local Information

Sedro Woolley Chamber of Commerce, (360) 855-1841
Mount Vernon Chamber of Commerce, (360) 428-8457
La Conner Chamber of Commerce, (360) 466-4778

Local Events

Skagit Valley Tulip Festival, late March to early April; Mount Vernon, (360) 428-5959; www.tulipfestival.org
Wildflower Festival, June; Darrington, WA, (360) 436-1794

26 Lake Padden Park

Option 1. Lake Padden Loop

Option 2. Lake Padden Singletrack

Start: Lake Padden Park parking lot
Trail contacts: Bellingham City Parks,
(360) 676–6985
Whatcom County Parks, (360) 733–2900
Fees and permits: None
Schedule: Open year-round
Maps: *Washington Atlas and Gazetteer,* page
109, C5; USGS Bellingham South; Local
Knowledge Trail Map—write to P.O. Box 704,
Bellingham, WA 98227; also available at
Kulshan Cycles

Land status: Bellingham Parks and Recreation
Nearest town: Bellingham
User density: Heavy
Other trail users: Equestrians, hikers, joggers, cross-country skiers
Canine compatibility: Leashed dogs permitted

Finding the Trailhead

From Seattle, head north on I-5. Approximately 9 miles south of Bellingham, take the North Lake Samish Road exit. Turn left at the end of the off-ramp, and continue north for 2.5 miles to the park entrance on the left. For the Lake Padden Loop, stay to the right when the road splits; park in this area. For the Singletrack Loop, stay to the left and park near the rest rooms that sit in front of a large grassy field on the east side of the lake.

The Ride

Located on the outskirts of Bellingham, Lake Padden Park offers trails for all skill levels. The Lake Padden Loop, a short ramble around the lake, is perfect for families and inexperienced riders. The Singletrack Loop—which hosts the annual although somewhat irregular Padden Mountain Pedal—while short, challenges even expert off-road cyclists.

The **Lake Loop** is just under 3 miles of flat, completely nontechnical gravel-covered trails. Still, the park is a fantastic area to spend the day with the family, riding, fishing, swimming, picnicking, and tossing a Frisbee around. Although the trail is completely tame, the route is beautiful and relaxing as it lazily winds around the lake. Lined with alder, vine maple, cedar, and Douglas fir, the trail is rather wide— perfect for riding two, three, or even four across, chatting while riding and even pulling a child carriage.

Located on the south end of the park, the **Singletrack Loop** is short but does contain a couple of steep climbs, a wicked descent full of switchbacks, and technical terrain. Advanced to expert cyclists will want to take the outside loop in order to ride the ascents and downhill sections. They will also want to ride the loop at least

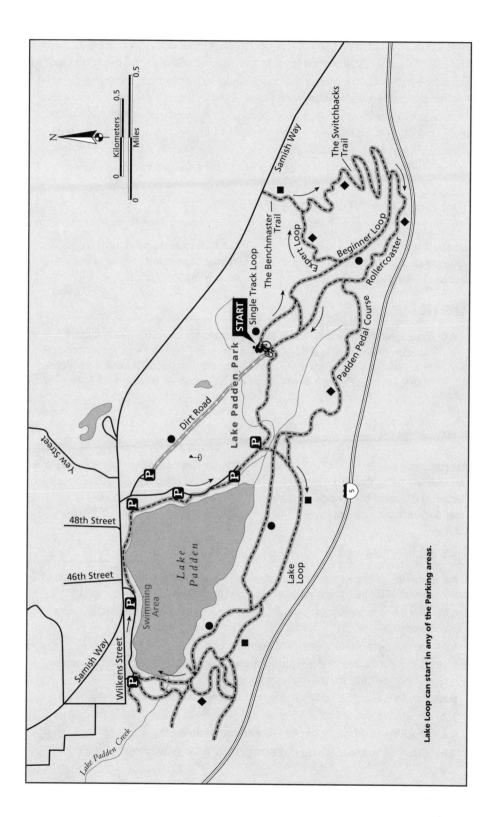

Lake Loop can start in any of the Parking areas.

twice in order to accumulate any mileage at all. Intermediate riders on their way up the skill chain can take the short loop. It does not include the rowdy switchbacks, but there are plenty of banked turns and threatening terrain to keep the ride interesting.

For racers, the Padden Mountain Pedal might be one of the most exciting amateur events in the Northwest. Although there are better courses, the Padden course is short enough for nearly the entire distance to be lined with spectators. Typically they line up at the most difficult sections to cheer racers on. The event has also included a big air event, trials riding, and racing for children.

Option 1: Lake Padden Loop

Length: 2.6 miles
Approximate riding time: 30 to 90 minutes
Technical difficulty: Novice

Trail surface: Wide gravel path
Wheels: Cross-country and hybrids
Hazards: No real hazards

Miles and Directions

0.0 From anywhere in the park, access the wide gravel path around the lake and pick a direction. Begin pedaling and simply stay on the wide gravel path as it wraps around the lake. Pass the showers, rest rooms, picnic areas, and baseball fields either at the beginning or the end of the ride, depending on which direction you chose.

Option 2: Lake Padden Singletrack

Length: 3 miles
Approximate riding time: 1 to 1½ hours
Technical difficulty: Intermediate to advanced
Trail surface: Hard-pack singletrack

Wheels: Cross-country to light full suspension
Hazards: Switchbacks and technical sections; mud and slippery roots and rocks

Miles and Directions

0.0 From the parking lot, ride to the south end of the park and look for the map board. Go to the left of the board and pedal down the wide dirt path.

0.01 Pass the wide gravel trail on the right. This is the return trail. Continue straight into the woods.

0.04 The trail narrows to singletrack and begins to climb.

0.06 Bust out of the trees and ride under the power lines. Pass the trail on the right; stick to the main trail with the golf course on the left.

0.08 Turn left and begin climbing the advanced section of the trail.

1.2 Stick to the right at the Y and continue climbing.

1.4 Reach the top of the ascent. Start downhill and let the fun begin.

1.7 Reach the bottom after navigating through steep, rutted switchbacks.

1.8 Turn left on the trail and drop down the hill. (If you miss it, you'll end up at the Mile 0.08 marker where you turned left and headed up the hill.)

2.0 Reach a T and turn left, crossing under the power lines again.

2.2 Reach a Y and stay to the right. The trail on the left is for horses only.

2.3 Hit the large trail and head back down to the main entrance.

3.0 Reach the map board. Are you up for another lap? Try it in the opposite direction this time.

Ride Information

Local Events

Padden Mountain Pedal, usually held in early May

Restaurants

Oriento Grill & BBQ, (360) 733-3322

Pandapalace, (360) 752-1818

Giuseppe's Italian Restaurant, (360) 714-8412

Luccis Bayshore Pizzeria, (360) 733-7100

El Nopal Family Mexican Restaurant, (360) 988-0305

Note: Above restaurants are all located in Bellingham.

27 Galbraith Mountain

Start: Whatcom Falls Park
Length: Up to 30 miles
Approximate riding time: 2 to 4 hours
Technical difficulty: Difficult to expert due to climbing, tight turns, dense forest, and technical descents
Trail surface: Singletrack and gravel access roads
Trail contacts: Whatcom County Parks, (360) 733-2900; www.co.whatcom.wa.us/parks · Bellingham Parks & Recreation, (360) 676-6985 · Bellingham/Whatcom County Convention & Visitors Bureau, (360) 671-3990; www.bellingham.org
Fees and permits: None
Schedule: Open year-round
Maps: *Washington Atlas and Gazetteer,* page 108, C5; USGS Bellingham South; Local Knowledge Trail Map—write to P.O. Box 704,

Bellingham, WA 98227; also available at Kulshan Cycles
Land status: Public and private property
Nearest town: Bellingham
User density: Heavy
Other trail users: Equestrians, hikers, joggers, cross-country skiers
Canine compatibility: Dogs permitted without a leash, but it's a good idea to keep them on a leash while crossing Electric Avenue and riding up Birch Street. There are a few small ponds that dogs can drink from, but it's best to bring an extra water bottle for your canine companion.
Wheels: Cross-county to light dual suspension recommended due to length and steepness of initial climb and teeth-rattling descents
Hazards: Technical sections of the trail, other trail users

Finding the Trailhead

From Seattle, take I-5 north to exit 253 and turn east onto Lakeway Drive. Pass the cemetery and turn left into Whatcom Falls Park. Park here. *Do not park* on Birch Street. From the parking lot, cross Electric Street and head straight up Birch Street. Follow it south (uphill) to the end, and then follow the gravel road up and to the left. This is the start of the Ridge Trail, which connects to the Galbraith circuit of singletrack.

The Ride

More than thirty individual trails and numerous gravel access roads weave throughout the forest of Bellingham's Galbraith Mountain like a spider's web gone wrong. Navigating the labyrinth of thigh-burning lactic acid–churning climbs, deep ruts, treacherous drops, and tight technical singletrack that winds, twists, turns, crisscrosses, zigs, zags, climbs, and descends is a serious challenge all by itself. Galbraith is as hardcore as it gets without donning downhill gear and hurling your bike down a mountain. None of these trails is for pseudo mountain bikers. If you are not physically fit or do not have strong skills, Galbraith will run over you like a jacked up NFL line backer.

For strong intermediate and advanced riders, the crazy maze of trails and burly terrain is like a siren's call that mountain bikers can't ignore. In fact, Galbraith attracts

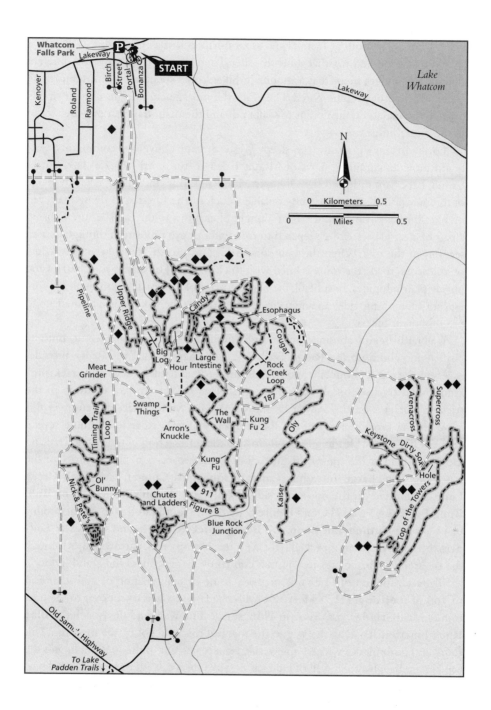

Whatcom Falls Park

START

Kenoyer
Roland
Raymond
Birch Street
Bonanza
Portal

Lakeway

Lake Whatcom

Lakeway

N

Kilometers
0   0.5
Miles
0   0.5

Pipeline

Upper Ridge

Candy

Esophagus

Cougar

Big Log

2 Hour

Large Intestine

Rock Creek Loop

Meat Grinder

187

Swamp Things

The Wall

Kung Fu 2

Oly

Arenacross

Supercross

Keystone

Dirty So...

Timing Trail

Loop

Arron's Knuckle

Kung Fu

Hole

Ol' Bunny

Chutes and Ladders

Figure 8

911

Kaiser

Top of the Towers

Nick & Pete's

Blue Rock Junction

Old Sam... Highway

To Lake Padden Trails ↓

riders from as far south as Tacoma and as far north as British Columbia. Galbraith is simply that good and has that much to offer. There are so many trails and different options to connect them that a mountain biker could spend an entire summer on Galbraith and not become bored. Therefore, the mileage cues in this chapter simply provide the main entrance point to Galbraith and the main trail that provides access to the entire mountain.

Located right up against the sleepy Western State University community, Galbraith provides stunning views of Mount Baker to the north (10,750 feet), Puget Sound, Lake Sammish, and the Olympic Mountains. But riders must take advantage of the viewpoints when they are available. Much of the forest is so dense that even on blue-bird days, only timid rays of sunlight filter down to the trail. Be sure to bring a pair of clear glasses, or be prepared to ride without eye protection through certain sections of the trail. When the trail does break out into the sunlight, mostly while on the access roads, the route is lined with thick walls of Himalayan blackberries and purple prairie lupines. Best of all, the massive maze of trails snaking through the forest on Galbraith provides an adrenalin-charged day in the saddle for intermediate to pro mountain bikers.

Galbraith begins abusing cyclists right from the start with a steep, technically challenging climb up the **Ridge Trail.** The good news is that the Ridge provides access to the entire mountain and its trail surface is all hard-packed singletrack, providing solid traction on all but the dampest days. Be sure to pay attention to the trickier problems on the way up, as most rides end with a sweet descent over this same terrain. From the top of the Ridge Trail (900 feet) riders can choose several different directions. Heading east and crossing the intersection of the Ridge Trail and the gravel road at the top of this first climb provides access to the majority of the trails. **Big Log, Large Intestine, Candy, Esophagus, Cougar,** and **Rock Creek Loop** are located on the northwest side of Galbraith. **Arron's Knuckle, The Wall, Kung Fu, Kung Fu 2, 911,** and **Figure 8** are farther south but higher on the mountain than the **Timing Tail Loop, Ol' Bunny, Nick & Pete's,** and **Chutes & Ladders.** Nearly every trail is packed tight with turns, drops, ruts, narrow gashes through the trees, and roller-coaster terrain that constantly taxes a rider's lungs and limbs.

To reach the top of Galbraith, pick any route or combination of trails that lead to **Top of the Towers** (1,785 feet). Probably the fastest way is to cut over to the bottom of **MeatGrinder,** pass **Swamp Things,** ride **The Wall,** and then catch the **Blue Rock Junction Road** all the way to the top. But this may not be the most fun. This route cuts out miles of wicked singletrack. Ninety percent of the trails leading to the top blaze through a solid wall of Douglas fir, Sitka spruce, western hemlock, and big-leaf and vine maples that practically grow on top of one another. The canopy allows minimal light to reach the forest floor, making the already extremely narrow trails even more challenging. In certain spots the trail is so dark that it is like riding in the twilight just before the sun drops out of the sky.

Fido needs a drink!

The Top of the Towers is roughly 6 to 9 miles from Whatcom Falls Park, depending on your chosen route. Riders usually catch a break here before bombing back down the mountain. The toughest downhill sections start right from the top, as riders cut back into the woods. Before clipping into the pedals, it's a good idea to lower your saddle. You'll need the extra clearance to survive the treacherous terrain about to be served up. The trails begin as a steep descent riddled with wide, deep ruts, several big drops, roots, and sharp rocks. Riders who can clear this section without dabbing (putting a foot down) deserve the respect of all their fat-tire friends. Fortunately this part of the trail is short. While it's a blast and it pushes a rider's abilities, too much time on a trail like this will pound riders and bikes into utter submission.

From here the trail never lets up as mountain bikers are faced with trails like **Super Cross** and **Arena Cross,** both of which cause several crashes every weekend. Super Cross is probably the worse of the two. The trail is not that steep, but throw in a 3- to 4-foot trench that rips its way right down the middle of the trail, and you've got a serious recipe for disaster. Riders can't stay on one side of the trench because the trail is badly eroded and slants toward a gaping gash in the middle. While the front wheel is riding high on the trail, the back wheel is often sliding and seemingly being sucked in. Riders must hold on until the trench comes up out of the trail for a few feet and then cross over to the other side and repeat the process once again in the other direction. Clear Super Cross without any scrapes, bruises, or stitches and you *Da Man!*

Heading west from here deposits riders back to trails Cougar, Rock Creek Loop, Esophagus, Candy, and Large Intestine. All of them, as well as various other unnamed and untamed trails, lead back to the Ridge Trail. From here it is all downhill—and it's all good, baby!

Miles and Directions

(**Note:** The mileage cues simply provide the main entrance point to Galbraith and the main trail that provides access to the entire mountain.)

0.0 From the parking lot cross Electric Avenue and Lakeway Drive. Follow Birch Street (south) to gate.

0.2 Reach the gate and trailhead. Ride to the right of the gate and begin climbing on the Ridge Trail.

0.4 Turn right, then left, and continue climbing.

0.5 Ignore the spur trail on your right.

0.6 Follow either trail; they lead to the same place.

0.9 Cross the trail intersection and continue climbing.

1.0 Reach the road or stay on the trail. If you take the road, pick up the trail just a few feet up the road on the right.

1.5 Reach the road again, and take a soft right or stay on the trail.

1.6 Reach the crest of climb where the Ridge Trail intersects with the gravel road. Across the road and to the east, there are two trails that provide access to all Galbraith Mountain.

Ride Information

Local Events

Bellingham Festival of Music, late July to mid-August; Performing Arts Center, (360) 676-5997. Two weeks of world-class symphony, chamber, and jazz music festival features the music of Beethoven and other great composers and artists; performances nightly. **Mt. Baker Blues Festival,** late July; River's Edge Christmas Tree Farm. Outdoor music festival at its best. Former performers include The Chris Duarte Group, Joanna Connor Band, Jude Bowerman Band, Cafe Blue, Incognito, Badd Dog Blues Society, and Daddy Treetops.

Restaurants

The Archer Ale House, (360) 647-7002
Dirty Dan Harris Restaurant, (360) 676-1011
Elephant & Castle Restaurant & Pub, (360) 671-4545
Dos Padres, (360) 733-9900
Note: Above restaurants are all located in Bellingham.

Accommodations

A Secret Garden B&B, (360) 671-5327
Anderson Creek Lodge B&B, (360) 966-0598
Eagle's Bluff, (360) 733-1963
Fairfield Manor B&B, (360) 756-8470
Note: Above accommodations are all located in Bellingham.

Olympia and the Kitsap Peninsula

I n the mid- to late '90s, the Kitsap Peninsula (Bremerton/Silverdale) was once voted the most livable area in the United States. The ranking was based on density of population, quality of the public schools, the job market, annual income, and the environment, to name a few criteria. Since then, the area has fallen in ranking, but if mountain biking were to become one of the criteria, Kitsap might reach the top honors again. Add in Capitol Forest just south of Olympia, and it's game over. The riding is that good.

Capitol Forest has long been the epicenter of the mountain bike universe in Washington State. Miles of singletrack cover the Black Hills of south Puget Sound, providing stunning views of Mount Rainier, Mount Saint Helens, the Olympics, and the Cascades. Carved by years of ORV use, the trails are buffed; well maintained by the Department of Natural Resources, supersonic fast, and technically challenging. In addition, for years Capitol Forest has hosted some of the biggest amateur races in the state.

On the peninsula the riding is as good or better. Tahuya State Forest is similar to its neighbor to the south but with less climbing and more standing water during the rainy season. Home to the annual Valentines Day Classic, Tahuya has been to known to grind cyclists and bikes up every February. But in summer, Tahuya, as well as Wildcat and Beaver Pond, is a plush playground full of mountain bike thrills and adventures.

28 Capitol State Forest

Option 1. Green Line to Mima Porter Loop

Option 2. Lost Valley Loop

Option 3. Larch Mountain Loop

Option 4. Rock Candy Mountain

Trail contacts: Department of Natural Resources, (360) 748-2383 or (800) 527-3305
Fees and permits: None, unless noted in specific option
Schedule: Open year-round but nearly unridable in the rainy season
Campgrounds: April 1 to October 31
Trails closed to ORVs and horses November 1 to March 31.
Maps: *Washington Atlas and Gazetteer*, page 45, A7-8, page 61, D7-8; USGS Capitol Peak

and Kamiliche Valley; Washington State Department of Natural Resources—Captol Forest
Land status: State forest—Washington Department of Natural Resources
Nearest town: Littlerock, Tumwater, Olympia
Other trail users: Equestrians, hikers, ORVs
Canine compatibility: Dogs permitted on a leash
Wheels: Hard-tail to light dual suspension
Hazards: Deep, thick, sticky Capitol Forest clay; horse dung; slippery wooden footbridges; motocross cycles; ORVs.

Capitol Forest Summary

Conveniently located just 5 miles south of Olympia, Capitol Forest is home to some of the state's most outstanding off-road riding. Mountain bikers will discover miles and miles of joy-inducing singletrack weaving throughout 90,000 square acres of Douglas fir, western red cedar, hemlock, red alder, big-leaf and vine maples, willow, and cascara. Open to the public since 1955, the forest holds adventures for hikers, campers, hunters, equestrians, and motocross riders. And although more than 150,000 outdoor enthusiasts visit Capitol Forest each year, the trails are fairly traffic free. There are simply so many miles of trails that riders won't run into too many other people—unless you're caught in a motocross poker run. Don't worry; below you'll find four trails to choose from. ORVs are permitted on only two.

The forest spreads out over the Black Hills of the south Puget Sound region, which were once completely underwater some fifty million years ago. Ironically, the hills earned their moniker only after the forest burned to the ground. Today the forest contains a massive circuit of trails with hundreds of banked turns, wild descents, whoop-de-dos, and miles of plush singletrack. Managed by the Department of Natural Resources, the trails are well maintained and constantly being improved. In addition, numerous signs provide directions and mileage markers. Even when logging takes place, detour routes and signs are provided. Yes, Capitol Forest is logged

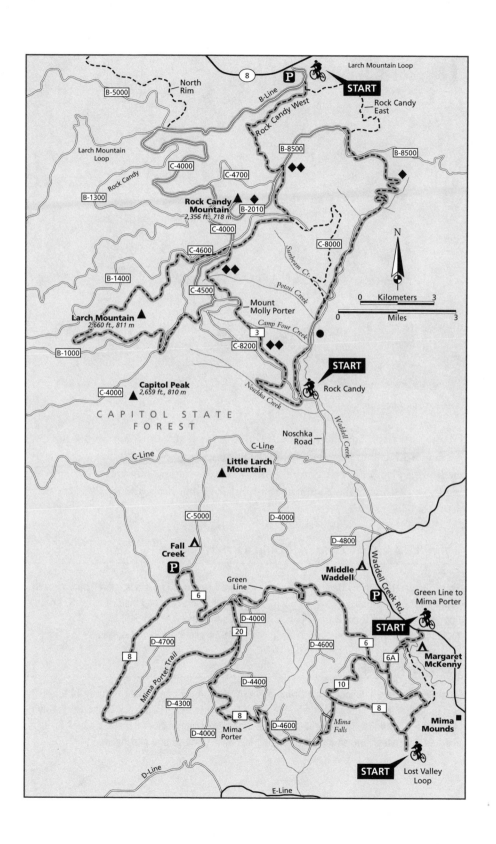

Larch Mountain Loop

⑧

START

Rock Candy East

B-5000

North Rim

Larch Mountain Loop

B-Line

Rock Candy West

B-8500

B-8500

C-4000

C-4700

Rock Candy

B-1300

Rock Candy Mountain
2,356 ft., 718 m

B-2010

C-4000

C-8000

Sunbeam Cr.

C-4600

B-1400

C-4500

Potosi Creek

Mount Molly Porter

Larch Mountain
2,660 ft., 811 m

B-1000

Camp Four Creek

③

C-8200

N

0   Kilometers   3

0   Miles   3

START

Rock Candy

Capitol Peak
2,659 ft., 810 m

C-4000

C A P I T O L   S T A T E
F O R E S T

Noschka Creek

Noschka Road

Waddell Creek

C-Line

C-Line

Little Larch Mountain

C-5000

D-4000

D-4800

Fall Creek

P

D-4000

Middle Waddell

Waddell Creek Rd.

P

Green Line to Mima Porter

⑥

Green Line

START

D-4700

D-4000

⑳

D-4600

⑥

6A

Margaret McKenny

⑧

Mima Porter Trail

D-4400

⑩

D-4300

⑧

Mima Falls

⑧

D-4000

⑧

Mima Porter

D-4600

Mima Mounds

D-Line

START

Lost Valley Loop

E-Line

Another silky turn in Capitol State Forest

on a regular basis, but never more than one-sixtieth at a time. In summer the trails are fast, technical, and rowdy. During the rainy season, however, riding certain lower sections of Capitol Forest can be a nightmare of clinging clay and mind-boggling mud that destroys brake pads, rims, bushings, bearings, seals, and nearly every other part of a bike.

Option 1: Green Line to Mima Porter Loop

Start: Margaret McKenny Campground
Length: 12.6-mile loop
Approximate riding time: 3 to 4 hours
Technical difficulty: Intermediate to advanced

Trail surface: Fire roads, gravel, hard-packed singletrack, clay, and mud
User density: Moderate
Other users: Equestrians, hikers

Finding the Trailhead

From Seattle, take I-5 south past Olympia to exit 95. Turn right onto State Highway 121, which cuts through Maytown toward Littlerock. Reach a T on other side of Littlerock. To the left is Gate Mima Road Southwest. To the right is Waddell Creek Road. Turn right and follow Waddell Creek Road for 2.5 miles. Turn left into the Margaret McKenny Campground parking lot.

The Ride

Among the fat-tire community, **The Green Line to Mima Porter Trail** is the least-well-known ride in the area. Mountain bike traffic is minimal, and motorized vehicles are not allowed on this trail. Noise and air pollution are nonexistent during the entire route. However, the trail is shared with equestrians, so the smooth singletrack tends to take an extra beating, not to mention the lovely deposits of horse manure, which can be rather pungent at times.

The climb to the top of the ride is relatively easy and is made even more pleasant by the trail upgrades performed by the Department of Natural Resources. Various stretches of the climb have been covered with crushed gravel and packed tight to make climbing a breeze—especially in the raining season. Green Line has a lower elevation than the other Capitol Forest trails listed here. The result is a morass of thick, clinging pudding-like clay and mud that eats through bike parts and stops your bike in its tracks. The gravel-covered sections provide a much-needed respite from the treacherous slime and ooze, allowing riders to actually ride for a time. Even certain sections of the descent have been layered with gravel to make the trail more accessible year-round. The downside, however, is that the singletrack is simply not as smooth.

Miles and Directions

0.0 From the parking lot ride back toward Waddell Creek Road, following the park entrance.

0.1 Turn left off the park entrance road onto the singletrack. The sign reads ACCESS TO TRAILS #6 AND #8. The trail immediately drops down a short, steep hill. Ignore the spur trail on the left.

0.3 Reach the bottom of the hill and Waddell Creek. Pass the trail on the left, and ride along the creek to the bridge.

0.4 Cross Waddell Creek; turn right, begin climbing, and take the next right.

0.6 Reach the intersection of Road E9500, the Waddell Loop, Green Line, and #6A. (**Note:** The route is slightly confusing here. Pay close attention to the actual turns, and loosely follow the signs marking the route.) Take a soft right on the road, and make the immediate right on the Waddell Loop Trail; drop down the shallow descent.

0.8 Turn right onto Green Line #6.

1.1 Reach the intersection of Green Line Trails #6 and #10. Follow Green Line to the right. (**FYI:** During the rainy season the trail alternates between hard-packed dirt, maintained gravel singletrack, and slimy, sticky, clinging mud.) The route will eventually return riders to Green Line #6 via #10.

3.4 Begin the first serious climbing of the ride. The trail emerges from the forest into a clearcut area as well.

3.5–3.6 The trail is manicured and maintained with new crushed rock. The climbing continues, but the gravel makes it an easy ride.

3.7 The trail nearly crosses the road but makes a turn just a few feet from the road and then parallels it for 50 feet or so.

3.8 Cross Road D4600. Pass a large mound of gravel on the right, and head back into the forest.

4.0 Shortly after crossing the road again, the gravel gives way to mud and clay. Continue following the trail as it rides the ridge and the edge of the clearcut.

4.5 Reach the road and turn right, following the trail to the yellow gate. Ride around the yellow gate to the intersection of D4000 and D4600. Stay on D4600 and continue down the hill.

4.9 Turn left back onto Green Line #6. Ignore the trail on the right that heads out to the road.

5.2 Reach the junction of Green Line #6 and Trail #20. Turn left and begin descending. (**FYI:** Trail #20 is nearly unridable when wet and muddy.)

5.7 Stay to the left and follow the **Mima Porter Trail,** which climbs back up the ridge through a clearcut. Cross a wooden bridge and head back into the trees at Mile 6.8.

7.2 Reach the top of the T formed by D4000 and D4400. The trail is diagonal across the T.

7.4 Cross D4400 and follow the Mima Porter Trail. Continue descending and cross at least three wooden bridges. (**FYI:** Remember, when it is raining the bridges are very slick. A strong pedal stroke can cause the rear wheel to spin out and slide sideways.)

8.6 Cross D4600 and follow the section of maintained gravel trail.

9.0 Cross D4600 again and another wooden bridge a short distance down the trail.

9.5 Reach Mima Falls and cross the bridge. (**FYI:** This is a great spot for a quick rest before the tail end of the ride. The falls are small, but you can walk to the bottom for a pleasant view.) Continue on and cross the bridge.

9.8 Turn left onto Trail #10, following signs back to McKenny Campground.

11.2 Cross Road E9000 and turn right onto Green Line #6. This is the same intersection you rode through at Mile 2.54.

11.9 Turn left onto #6A and climb to Road E9500.

12.1 Cross the road and follow Green Line #6A.

12.3 Turn right and descend toward the bridge and Waddell Creek. Cross the bridge and turn right.

12.4 Stay to the left, and climb up the hill back to the park entrance.

12.6 Turn right onto the park entrance road and return to the parking lot.

Option 2: Lost Valley Loop

Start: Mima Falls Trailhead
Length: 21.4-mile loop
Approximate riding time: 3 to 5 hours
Technical difficulty: Intermediate to advanced

Trail surface: Fire roads, hard-packed single-track, clay, and mud.
User density: Moderate
Other users: Equestrians, hikers

Finding the Trailhead

From Seattle, take I-5 south past Olympia to exit 95. Turn right onto State Highway 121, which cuts through Maytown toward Littlerock. On the other side of Littlerock, reach the T. To the right is Waddell Creek Road. To the left is Gate Mima Road Southwest. Turn left onto Gate Mima Road Southwest and follow to the Bordeaux Road. Turn right and then right again onto Marksman Road. Continue to Mima Falls Trailhead and Campground.

The Ride

The **Lost Valley Loop** shares sections of trail with the Green Line to Mima Loop. Despite being nearly double in length, the LVL is a good ride for strong intermediates and even beginners who are physically fit. There is relatively little climbing, the trails are not overly technical, and riders can always bail out by taking an easy-to-find and easy-to-navigate shortcut (see below in mileage log).

The trail is shared by equestrians but not by ORVs. This has advantages and drawbacks. Riders won't find big banked turns like on the Rock Candy route (Option 4), but there are no serious ruts either. Contending with the smell of horse manure creates its own challenges, as does the damage that hooves do to soft, moist, dirt trails. In many areas the singletrack is like riding through a rock garden because horses have chewed up the trail while it was wet. Then it dries, leaving behind a jarring technical ride at best. The DRN is doing its best to maintain and upgrade the trail by reinforcing it with pea-sized crushed rock, but there are still miles of trail that remains a pitted mess. In the rainy season the LVL is like any other Capitol Forest ride—wet and disturbingly muddy.

Miles and Directions

0.0 From Mima Falls Campground, follow the Mima Porter Trail (Trail #8).

0.4 The trail turns into doubletrack and crosses Green Line Trail (Trail #6). The sign reads CAPITAL PEAK 14.1 MILES; PORTER CREEK CAMP 23.5 MILES; WEDEKIND 18.2 MILES. Stay to the left on the Mima Porter Trail to Mima Falls.

0.5 Reach the intersection of Trails #8 and #6. Stick to #8, and shortly thereafter cross E9000. (Old DNR maps list it as D6000.)

0.7 Arrive at the intersection for Mima Falls—1.7 miles.

2.1 Reach the intersection of Trails #10 and #8. Stay on Trail #8, which is on the left.

2.4 Reach Mima Falls. Be sure to walk down below the falls for the best view. It will only take a minute; the falls are not that large.

3.0 Cross Road D4600 three times in the next 0.5 mile before heading down to Mima Creek.

4.4 Cross Mima Creek on wooden bridge. (Be careful when the bridge is wet. It can be like riding on a greased cookie sheet.)

4.8   Climb up to D4400.

6.3   Cross the road and continue following Trail #8.

6.8   Cross D4000. It may or may not be here because it was slated to be abandoned. Stick to the trail.

7.1   Reach the intersection of D4300 and D4400. Cross through the intersection and stay on Trail #8.

7.7   Take a left and stay on Trail #8, passing the Lost Valley Trail (Trail #20). **Bail-out:** If you're injured or fatigued, this is a good place to head back to the parking lot. Take Trail #20 to #6. Turn right on Trail #6 and follow directions from Mile Marker 15.5. This cuts 2 miles off the return trip, as well as most of the climbing.

10.2   You may reach an old FSR road, but it has been or will be abandoned. Simply stay on the trail.

13.0   Cross the creek, turn right (east) onto Trail #6 (Green Line), and cross D4700, which is listed as D4300 on the old DRN maps.

15.5   Arrive at the intersection with Trail #20. Stay on Trail #6.

15.8   Reach the intersection of D4600 (used to be listed as D4200) and D4000. Continue east on Trail #6 and pass the sign reading NO MOTORIZED VEHICLES.

16.4   There may be two crossings of forest service roads. They have been or will be abandoned. Stay on the trail. Just keep crossing the roads until you reach the intersection of Trails #6 and #10.

19.3   Reach the junction of Trails #6 and #10. Remain on Trail #6.

19.8   Arrive at the intersection between Trails #6A and #6. (**FYI:** Margaret McKinney Camp is 1 mile up Trail #6A; Trail #8 is ahead 2 miles.) Continue on Trail #6.

20.2   Cross E9000 twice, and follow Trail #6 to Mima Falls Campground, ignoring the Waddell Loop Trail.

20.9   Continue following Trail #6, ignoring the trail that connects from behind.

21.2   Cross the road and the road immediately following.

21.3   Reach the intersection of Trail #6, Trail #8, and the trail back to the parking lot.

21.4   Reach parking lot.

Option 3: Larch Mountain Loop

Start: Rock Candy Mountain entrance to Capitol Forest

Length: 20.5-mile loop

Approximate riding time: 2 to 4 hours

Technical difficulty: Intermediate to advanced

Trail surface: Fire roads, hard-packed singletrack, clay, and mud.

Fees: Northwest Forest Pass $5.00 a day, $30.00 for the year

User density: Moderate

Other users: Equestrians, ORVs

Finding the Trailhead

From Seattle, follow I-5 past Olympia to exit 104. Take the exit and head north on U.S. Highway 101, and then catch State Route 8 west toward Aberdeen. Follow SR 8 for just over 10 miles, and turn left onto Rock Candy Mountain Road. The sign is small, so keep your eyes peeled. Rock Candy Mountain Road turns into a gravel road. Shortly after turning to gravel road, the road turns right at the fork. Follow this to the parking lot.

The Ride

The **Larch Mountain Loop** begins with a hardy climb on a forest service road and winds its way around Rock Candy and Larch Mountains. The remaining two-thirds of the ride are on the typical Capitol Forest singletrack that has made the area a Puget Sound favorite for years. Whoop-de-dos, berms, ruts, switchbacks, rock gardens, big drops, roots, and smooth hard pack are all waiting for riders willing to climb the 7 miles to the actual trail.

The only downside to this route is that it is shared with ORV enthusiasts. Capitol Forest is extremely popular with the ORV crowd. On occasion, mountain bikers find themselves caught in the middle of an ORV "poker run." This could mean as many as a hundred motorcycles to contend with. The best way to avoid this potential nightmare is to start early in the day and stay off the trails where the parking lots are loaded with ORV riders. There are several rides to choose from at Capitol Forest. If you arrive at a campground and it's overrun with the motocross crowd, head over to Rock Candy, Greenline to Mima, or the Lost Valley Loop.

Miles and Directions

0.0 From the Rock Candy parking lot, pedal west on the B-Line Road and pass B9000.

0.07 Stay on B-Line as B8000 forks off to the left.

1.5 Pass the Rock Candy Trail on the left. (**FYI:** Some of the old DNR maps list this as the North Rim Trail #1.)

2.3 Continue on the main road, passing the road on the left.

2.5 Arrive at Porter Pass, which intersects B5000. Continue on the B-Line Road until reaching C4000. Turn left here, and head toward Larch Mountain.

7.0 The Larch Mountain Loop begins at the intersection of C4600 and C4000. Find the Mount Molly Trail on the left just past C4600. The trail heads into the woods and around the east side of Larch Mountain. You'll return to this point, as the trail comes back around the west side of the mountain. Follow the trail for a short distance to the sign reading MOUNT MOLLY PORTER #3 FOR BORDEAUX CAMP AND MOUNT MOLLY CAMP. At the first intersection, follow the Mount Molly Trail (Trail #40). Take the right fork; the left fork is Trail #20, which will lead riders back to Rock Candy. The trails become a little hard to follow through this section because there is Mount Molly #3, Mount Molly #40, Trail #20, and Trail #30. They seem to alternate back and forth while on the same trail. Simply continue

Capitol State Forest after a wind and lightning storm

in a southwest direction, as this route parallels C4000 and uses a short section of C4500 to connect two different sections of Trail #40.

8.9 At the intersection of Trails #40 and #30, turn right onto Trail #30 and head back toward C4000 (west) for a short distance before the trail turns south again and follows C4000.

9.3 Arrive at C4000. Stay on the trail and cross the road.

9.9 Trail #30 parallels B1000 for a short distance and then actually drops riders onto the road. Follow the road to the main intersection. Turn right up the hill until reaching Trail #30—about 100 yards. Follow Trail #30. (**FYI:** On the old DNR maps, B1000 is listed as C4400. The trail follows B1000 and then B1500 as the road splits.)

11.4 Cross a logging road.

11.9 Continue straight on Trail #30 as another trail comes in on the left. The trail parallels B1500 (on the right-hand side of the trail) as it winds around the west side of Larch Mountain (2,660 feet) and then parallels C4600 on the left.

15.0 Reach C4000 and turn left. Follow the road for a short distance, looking for the trail on the right.

15.3 The Larch Mountain Loop returns to the intersection of C4000 and C5000—the same point at Mile 7.0. Cross C4000 and follow the signs to Trail #20 down the east side of Rock Candy Mountain.

15.6 Cross C4600, then turn left onto Trail #20 and head back to the parking lot.

16.3 Cross B8500. (By turning left here, mountain bikers can explore Rock Candy Peak. Simply follow the directions from Mile 7.0 in the Rock Candy route [Option 4].)

19.3 Reach the intersection of Trail #20 and Rock Candy West. Turn right. (**FYI:** Rock Candy West is labeled as North Rim Trail #1 on the old DRN maps.)

19.4 Cross the small stream.

19.8 Cross B8000 and remain on the trail that continues descending.

20.5 Turn left and reach the parking lot.

Option 4: Rock Candy Mountain

Start: Remains of old Bordeaux Campground
Length: 18.7-mile loop
Approximate riding time: 3 to 4 hours
Technical difficulty: Intermediate to advanced

Trail surface: Singletrack
User density: Heavy
Other users: ORVs

Finding the Trailhead

From Seattle, take I–5 south past Olympia to exit 95. Turn right onto State Highway 121, which cuts through Maytown toward Littlerock. Reach the T on other side of Littlerock. To the left is Gate Mima Road Southwest. To the right is Waddell Creek Road. Turn right onto Waddell Creek Road and drive for just over 4 miles to a T in the road. Turn left and head west for just over a mile, and then turn left onto the gravel Noschka Road. Follow Noschka Road for 1 mile, and park at the barricade made of stumps in front of the old gate to the closed-down Camp Bordeaux.

The Ride

Sammy Hagar sang it best in the 1973 Montrose song "Rock Candy": "Baby, you're hard, sweet, and sticky!" For the under-thirty crowd, Montrose was a hard-rock band with one great album. It is some of Sammy's best work, and whether you like him or not, or even like rock and roll for that matter, the chorus is a perfect description of this ride.

Steep climbs blanketed with sharp jagged rocks, descents tattooed with deep ruts and surprising drops, deep sticky mud, and banked turns littered with forest debris and loose gravel make this ride hard on the body and the bike.

Hard-packed smooth sections of singletrack, rolling terrain, the whoop-de-do mile, big, bad and ugly berms, views of Mounts Rainier, Adams, and Saint Helens, The Olympics, and south Puget Sound make the ride extremely sweet.

In the rainy season, mud as thick as molasses clings to bikes and riders like fly-paper to a cartoon character. Once you get it on you, it's nearly impossible to get it off, giving new meaning to the word *sticky*.

Miles and Directions

0.0 From the parking area in front of the closed-down Camp Bordeaux, ride up FSR C8000. (This is the road on the right as you look back up Noschka Road, virtually the same spot as the parking area.) The road immediately begins to climb.

0.2 Turn left onto the singletrack trail and climb a steep grade up to FSR C8200. Alternatively, you can follow C8000. They arrive at roughly the same place.

0.3 Reach the road, turn right, drop down the hill, and turn left onto C8000. Ignore any other roads and spur trails until the next designated turn.

1.4 Cross the bridge and take the next right onto the North Rim Trail #1. (There is no sign here, but the DNR does use this spot to store gravel for trail maintenance. The North Rim Trail is an old railroad grade.)

1.8 Continue past the trail on the right. (**FYI:** Riders will now start to notice North Rim Trail signs with mileage markers. Don't worry about the mileage in the book or on your computer being different from the mileage markers. There will be about 0.5 mile difference, depending on where you accessed the North Rim Trail.)

2.2–2.30 The trail here has been reinforced with ballast gravel—crushed rock the size of hardballs. This section is difficult to ride because of the size of the rocks and the instability of the surface. However, the trail does drain much better, and cyclists don't have to fight motorcycle-induced ruts.

2.5 The trail makes a hard turn to the right, crosses a bridge, and begins to climb.

2.6 Follow the trail around to the left. Do not continue straight and cross the bridge. Enjoy the Whoop-de-do Mile. Can you count the number of whoop-de-dos? Fifty? Sixty? Maybe more?

3.5 Cross two bridges in quick succession.

5.46 Cross FSR B8500.

6.0 Continue straight on the North Rim Trail #1 as the Rock Candy Trail connects on the right-hand side.

6.1 Reach FSR B8500 and turn right. Follow the North Rim #1 tail signs. (Take your time through this section as the signs are hard to spot.)

6.4 Pass the spur road on the right and stay to the left at the Y. Ignore the spur road on the right.

6.7 The main road ends and narrows down to a jeep trail as it climbs up a steep, rocky section.

7.0 The jeep trail ends at a four-way intersection. Climb up the steep, wide trail covered in sharp and nasty looking loose rock. (You can wimp out and turn left, beginning the descent back to Camp Bordeaux, but you'll miss the views of Rainier, Saint Helens, Adams, the Olympics, south Puget Sound, and Olympia. Get up that hill, maggot!)

7.2 Reach FSR B2010 and turn left.

7.6 Pass the trail on the right.

8.5 Turn right onto the FSR.

8.8 Reach the tip-top of Rock Candy Mountain (2,364 feet).

9.0 Turn left and head back down the hill on FSR B2010.

10.2 Turn right and head back down the trail.

10.5 Reach the bottom of the steep rocky section and the four-way intersection. Turn right onto Trail #20. Enjoy the singletrack.

11.2 Cross FSR C4600.

12.6 Arrive at a switchback that turns up the hill and to the right. Go straight on the Mount Molly Porter Trail #3 that starts at the apex of the switchback.

12.7 Stay to the left on Mount Molly Porter #3. (**Note:** The trail signage becomes a bit confusing in this area, as it alternates between Mount Molly Porter #3 and Mima Porter. To make matters worse, the DNR map only reads mount molly porter #3. Following both signs will transport you to the parking lot.)

14.3 Cross FSR C4600 twice.

16.0 Cross FSR C8200 and follow the trail right back out to the road. Look for the trail on the right.

16.5 Cross C8200 again, and follow the trail down between the wooden fences.

17.0 Cross the road again and look to cross a bridge a short distance farther.

17.7 Reach the beginning of North Rim Trail #1 and pass the trail on the right.

18.0 Cross the bridge.

18.4 Reach FSR C8200 and head down the trail. (This spot is used by the DNR to store gravel and dirt. Occasionally the trail is blocked from view.)

18.5 Turn right at the road, and roll down to the parking lot.

Ride Information

Local Information

The Olympia/Thurston Visitors and Convention Bureau, (360) 704-7544, or (877) 704-7500; www.visitolympia.com

Restaurants

The FarmBoy, Maytown, (360) 754-8442 homemade soups, chili fries, multiflavored milkshakes, pizza burgers, and the best bacon cheeseburgers in the south Puget Sound area.

Brewery City Pizza, Olympia, (360) 754-7800

Thai Garden, Olympia, (360) 786-1959

Brotherhood Tavern, Olympia, (360) 352-4153

Budd Bay Café, Olympia, (360) 357-6963

29 Tahuya State Forest

Start: Mission Creek Trailhead
Length: 14.3-mile loop
Approximate riding time: 2 to 3 hours
Technical difficulty: Intermediate to advanced
Trail surface: Singletrack that is scattered with puddles even after mild rains; sand-and-dirt mix in some areas, loose rock in others.
Trail contacts: Department of Natural Resources, (360) 748-2383 or (800) 527-3305
Fees and permits: None
Schedule: Open year-round, but submerged underwater November to May. Puddles can be as deep as the top tube of even large bikes.

Maps: *Washington Atlas and Gazetteer,* page 62, A1; USGS Lake Wooten
Land status: State forest
Nearest town: Belfair
User density: Heavy on weekends
Other trail users: ORVs, ATVs, equestrians
Canine compatibility: Dogs permitted on a leash but not recommended due to high ORV use.
Wheels: Full suspension, but hard tails okay
Hazards: ORVs

Finding the Trailhead

From Tacoma, take I-5 toward State Route 16. Cross the Narrows Bridge and head west to State Route 3. Follow SR 3 south to Belfair and then turn right onto Northeast Clifton Lane. Follow Clifton until it becomes State Route 300 and then go north on Shore Road. Drive 3.5 miles and turn right onto Northeast Belfair-Tahuya Road. Drive 1 mile, and look for the Mission Creek Trail parking lot.
From Seattle, you can take the ferry across the sound. The ride is much more relaxing but takes about the same amount of time. For ferry schedules and pricing, visit www.wsdot.wa.gov/Ferries or call (888) 808-7977 (in Washington).

The Ride

Tahuya is filled with more than 200 miles of singletrack trails. Mission Creek (the main trail) twists and turns over roots, whoop-de-dos, slow, sandy, pebbly sections, and through puddles deep enough to be named as lakes. Managed by the Department of Natural Resources, the trails are open to everyone . . . including ORVs. In fact, the area is extremely popular with them. The best plan is to ride the area during the week or early in the morning to avoid the noise and air pollution the ORVs create.

Located on the southeast tip of the Kitsap Peninsula, Tahuya Forest lacks any serious elevation gain, and topography rolls up and down through new-growth forest and an ever-changing number of clearcuts. While the trails are not pretty, they do provide clear views to the Olympic Mountains, which rise as high as 8,000 feet above sea level. And with more than 200 miles of trails, there are more possible

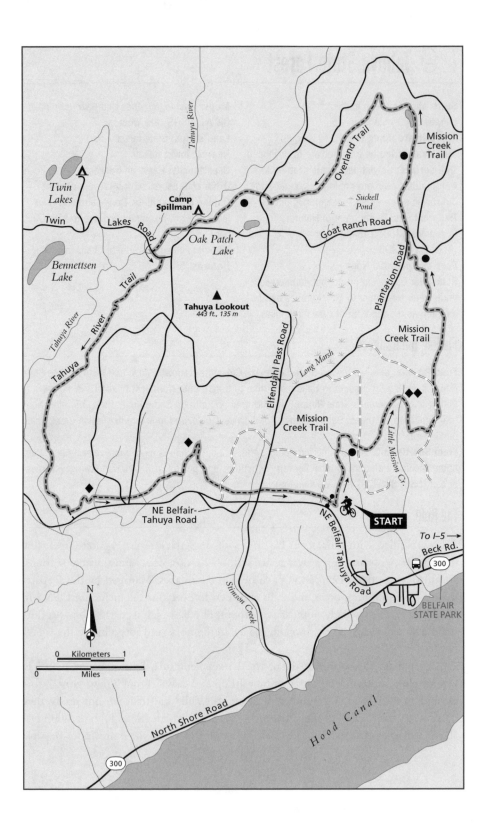

Twin
Lakes

Twin   Lakes   Road

Tahuya River

**Camp
Spillman**

*Oak Patch
Lake*

*Bennettsen
Lake*

Tahuya River

River   Trail

Tahuya

▲
Tahuya Lookout
443 ft., 135 m

*Suckell
Pond*

Goat Ranch Road

**Mission
Creek
Trail**

Plantation Road

**Mission
Creek Trail**

Elfendahl Pass Road

Long Marsh

Overland Trail

**Mission
Creek Trail**

Little Mission Cr.

◆

◆

START

NE Belfair–
Tahuya Road

NE Belfair Tahuya Road

Stimson Creek

To I–5 →

Beck Rd.

300

**BELFAIR
STATE PARK**

N

0   Kilometers   1

0   Miles   1

North Shore Road

300

Hood Canal

routes in the area than Boeing has employees living and working in the Puget Sound area.

Tahuya is open year-round, but from November to May, many of the trails are submerged underwater. The water combined with the fine dirt, sand, and grit takes a serious toll on cyclists and machines alike. Count on spending a few hours cleaning your mount after a day of riding in the rainy season. And if you are one of the insane racers who brave the elements during the Annual Valentine's Day Classic, count on replacing parts on your bike—and perhaps completely rebuilding it. The puddles can be as deep as 4 or 5 feet—nearly deep enough to consume an entire bike! Still, when Tahuya is dry, the trails are fast and fun. Big burly banked turns carved out by the ORVs and mile after mile of hard-packed smooth singletrack make Tahuya worth the trip to the peninsula.

Miles and Directions

0.0 From the Mission Creek Trailhead, follow the trail to the right of the parking area. Look for the blue-and-gray diamonds nailed to the trees.

1.4 Follow the trail as it bears to the right and intersects with a road. Keep on the lookout for a quick right-hand turn back onto the trail.

2.1 Reach the fork, and stick to the trail on the right.

2.2 Cross a bridge and start a short, steep climb.

2.4 Reach the crest of the hill, and follow the trail as it turns to the right.

3.0 Turn left onto the road and pedal for about 150 feet, looking for the trail on the right. Take the trail and head back into the forest.

5.1 Arrive at an intersection and turn left. Stay on the main trail, following the blue-and-gray diamonds and ignoring the numerous spur trails.

7.6 Cross the Goat Ranch Road and connect with the trail on the other side.

8.5 Remain on the Mission Creek Trail.

10.6 Take the hard right at the four-way intersection onto the Tahuya River Trail.

11.9 Ride over the bridge at an unmarked intersection. Continue following the blue-and-gray diamonds.

14.3 Arrive back at the trailhead.

Ride Information

Local Information

North Mason Chamber of Commerce, (360) 275-5548; www.nmcoc.com
Mason County Transit, (360) 426-9434; www.olympicpeninsula.com/travel/gettingabout/busmason.html

Local Events and Attractions

Belfair State Park, (800) 233-0231; www.parks.wa.gov/belfair.html
Kitsap County Fair, late August, (360) 692-3655

30 Wildcat and Beaver Pond Trail

Start: Wildcat Trailhead or Green Mountain Camp and Picnic Area
Length: 12.9-mile loop
Approximate riding time: 2 to 3 hours
Technical difficulty: Novice to advanced
Trail surface: Singletrack and gravel road
Trail contacts: Department of Natural Resources South Puget Sound Region, (360) 825-1631 or (800) 527-3305
Fees and permits: None
Schedule: Trail is open year-round. Access to the campground is limited—9:00 A.M.–6:00 P.M. Saturday and Sunday, June through September.
Maps: *Washington Atlas and Gazetteer,* page 78, C2–D2; USGS Wild Cat Lake

Land status: Department of Natural Resources
Nearest town: Bremerton
User density: High
Other trail users: Hikers, motorcycles, equestrians
Canine compatibility: Dogs permitted on a leash
Hazards: Other trail users, wooden bridge that's extremely slippery when wet, horse manure on the trail
Wheels: Cross-country and light dual suspension

Finding the Trailhead

From Seattle, drive south on I-5 to Tacoma. Take State Route 16 north across the Narrows Bridge toward Bremerton. Just south of Bremerton bear right onto State Route 3 (north), and take it past Bremerton to the Chico Way exit. At the end of the ramp, turn left onto Chico Way. Turn right onto Northlake Way, and then bear right onto Seabeck Highway. Drive 3.2 miles, and then turn left onto Holly Road. Travel 1.9 miles and find Green Mountain's Wildcat Trailhead on the left.

If you ride the ferry from Seattle to Bremerton, take State Route 304 west. Turn right onto SR 3, and go north to the Chico Way exit.

Riders can also take the ferry from Seattle to Bainbridge Island. The ferry ride is shorter (thirty-five minutes compared with sixty), but the drive to the trailhead is longer. Take State Route 305 north from the ferry terminal. Follow to SR 3, and head south to Chico Way exit. Follow directions above.

(Ferry note: Fares range from $6.50 to $8.25 per vehicle and driver. Each additional passenger is $2.50 to $4.00. There is also an additional charge of $8.25 for vehicles over 7' 6". This means most automobiles with bikes and roof racks. Ferries run roughly every forty to seventy minutes. Check www.wsdot.wa.gov/ferries for actual times, or call (888) 808-7977.)

The Ride

Located in the Green Mountain Forest on the Kitsap Peninsula, the **Wildcat** and **Beaver Pond Trails** have been carved out of the forest primarily by motocross riders, making for sweet twisting singletrack full of turns and berms. A few steep climbs

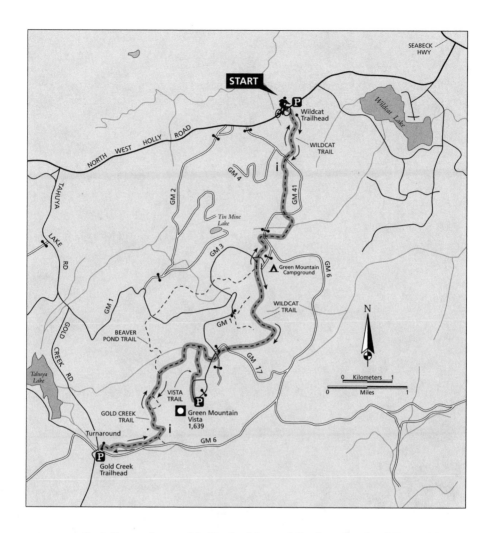

pose a small challenge for aerobically fit riders, while the summit of Green Mountain provides an excellent vantage point for viewing the Olympic Mountains, Hood Canal, Bainbridge Island, and Puget Sound.

The Wildcat and Beaver Pond Trails are favorites with local riders from Bremerton and Silverdale. On weekends the trailhead parking lot is frequently loaded with cars most of the day. To avoid the traffic, hit the trailhead early in the morning.

From the parking lot the singletrack heads through a small clearcut and then shoots into the trees. The dense forest canopy acts as a natural buffer, keeping the trails relatively dry during the rainy season and cool on those sweltering days in late July and August. The route has been buffed out by years of motocross riding, making for smooth, twisting singletrack that is loaded with quick turns and surly berms.

A cold, wet, Puget Sound day

Take them slow or fast, but there is nothing quite like riding high up in a turn, leaning your bike over, and letting the terrain guide the bike out the other side of the curve.

Despite the 1,100 feet of climbing, the ascent is gradual with just a few steep technical sections. This makes Wildcat and Beaver Pond an excellent early-season ride when the legs and lungs are not quite in shape. Plus, the length of each trail is novice friendly as well as being easy on the body still locked in its winter coat.

The trail rolls up and down with the terrain, crossing gravel access roads, small sections of harvested land, and beautiful groves of wild pink rhododendron. Once at the top (1,690 feet) the views of Puget Sound, the Olympic Mountains, and Bainbridge Island are stunning. On a clear bluebird day, riders are rewarded with an almost 360-degree view of the area.

The rest of the ride is nearly all downhill. The twisting ribbon of dirt is velvety smooth. Riders can rocket through the berms or take them at a less aggressive speed. With only a few steep technical sections, strong beginners to advanced riders will find the descent to be a blast. The trail winds back and forth through the trees, up and down over humps and bumps, all the while leading riders down a super route of singletrack. This is definitely a ride worth doing more than once.

Miles and Directions

0.0 Start from the Wildcat Trailhead. A short distance in, the trail winds through a small clearcut.

0.9 Cross the dirt road (GM 41). The trail begins a series of short semisteep climbs. Novice riders and some intermediates may have to walk some of the tougher sections.

1.3 Reach the crest of the hill, viewpoint, and bench constructed of logs. Begin short descent through the small section of clearcut.

1.6 Turn left at the gravel road (GM 41) and make an immediate right back onto the trail marked WILDCAT TRAIL and into the forest.

1.9 Cross dirt road (GM 41) and continue up trail. Terrain morphs from smooth, twisting singletrack to rocky, littered, short steep climbs.

2.7 Cross gravel road (GM 3) at the three-way intersection. Green Mountain Camp and Picnic Area is just a short distance to your left. Cross the road and turn right up the steep trail to the Trail Vista.

2.8 Pass the river wash on the right, and stay on the trail to the left. Cross the road again (GM 17), turn right, and continue on the Wildcat Trail to the left.

3.4 Reach gravel road (GM1) and the Y intersection; follow the trail around the gate.

3.9 Cross GM 41 and head back into the woods.

4.3 Reach the Gold Creek, Beaver Pond, and Vista Trails junction.

To reach the vista: Take a hard left up the Vista Trail, and ride to the Green Mountain Vista parking lot. Riders will find a picnic area and sanicans. Follow the trail around the gate and up to the viewpoint (0.2 mile). To continue the ride, backtrack to the Vista Trail. Vista excursion is now included in the mileage log.

4.5 Upon reaching the bottom of the Vista Trail, turn left and follow the sign toward the Gold Creek–Beaver Pond Trail.

6.1 Arrive at the intersection of Gold Creek and Beaver Pond Trails. Stay to the left and follow the Gold Creek Trail.

6.4 Ignore both trails on the right. Sounds from Gold Creek Trail are now audible if you listen closely.

7.1 Reach the Gold Creek Trailhead and the parking lot. Turn around and pedal back up the trail.

8.1 Arrive at the Gold Creek–Beaver Pond junction and turn right. Riders can also turn left on the Beaver Pond Trail, which leads back to the Green Mountain Campground.

8.3 Stay on the Beaver Pond Trail passing the Vista Trail to the viewpoint.

9.7 Reach the Wildcat Trail (Mile Marker 4.3).

10.1 Cross GM 41 and head downhill back into the woods.

10.6 Cross GM 1 and ride around the gate.

11.2 Cross GM 17 and continue following the trail.

11.3 Cross gravel road (GM 3) at the three-way intersection. Green Mountain Camp and Picnic Area is just a short distance to your right. Cross the road and turn right up the steep trail to the Trail Vista.

11.6 Reach the crest of hill, viewpoint, and bench constructed out of logs. Continue back toward the parking lot away from the clearcut.

12.0 Cross GM 41 for the last time.

12.9 Arrive back at the trailhead.

Ride Information

Local Information
Bremerton/Kitsap Peninsula Visitor and Convention Bureau, (360) 297-8200

Local Events
Blackberry Festival, Bremerton, WA; August, (360) 377-3041

Restaurants
19th Hole Tavern, (360) 479-9077
Ammirato's Airshow Pub & Grill, (360) 377-0837
Azteca Mexican Restaurant, (360) 373-9315
Big Apple Diner, (360) 373-8242
Boat Shed Restaurant, (360) 377-2600.
Note: Above restaurants are all located in Bremerton.

Highway 410

Mile for mile, the region surrounding Highway 410 may be home to the best mountain biking in the state of Washington. Located in the southwest corner of the Mount Baker Snoqualmie National Forest and just northeast of Mount Rainier National Park, the area is stacked with miles of suede leather–smooth singletrack, technical root and rock gardens, savage descents, lung-bursting climbs, icy-cold rivers and streams, crystal-clear alpine lakes, mountain meadows filled with wildflowers, and amazing views of Washington's most famous landmark: Mount Rainier.

From the top of nearly every ride but one, Mount Rainier looms big, bold, and beautiful. The snow-covered slopes, ice-blue glaciers, and angry, rocky crags seem so close you can almost reach out and touch them. Granted, Washington's most famous peak is visible from almost anywhere west of the Cascades. But from the peak of Crystal Mountain, Sun Top, Ranger Creek, Corral Pass, and Dalles Ridge, the views are simply spiritual. The only location with a better view of the mountain is standing atop a 14,411-foot peak.

Rainier also acts as an umbrella, keeping this area slightly drier than the rest of the Puget Sound region. The mountain is so large that cloud formations moving west to east must unload the majority of their precipitation in order to climb up and over the peak. However, thunderstorms and even snowstorms in mid-July are not uncommon. In fact, for thirty years prior to 1999, Rainier held the official world record for most snowfall in a single season—1,122 inches—until Mount Baker unofficially broke the record with 1,124 inches in 1999. Be sure to prepare accordingly.

If there is a complaint about riding in this area, it is the distance from the Puget Sound cities. For most, reaching Highway 410 requires at least a one-hour drive. Not bad really, until you consider that in such areas as Moab and Sun Valley, the trails are accessible right from town and in many cases your backdoor. One to two hours behind the wheel both ways isn't all that attractive, which is why riding in this area has not attracted much national attention. Even on the weekends most mountain bikers end up sharing the trails with just a few locals. Then, again, maybe that drive is not such a bad thing after all.

31 Ranger Creek

Start: From the bottom of Forest Service Road 72
Length: 24-mile loop
Approximate riding time: 3 to 4 hours
Technical difficulty: Advanced due to length of climb and precariously slim singletrack on the side of steep fall lines
Trail surface: Gravel forest service roads, smooth hard-packed singletrack, and a short paved section at the end of the ride
Trail contacts: USDA Forest Service, White River Ranger District, Enumclaw, (360) 825-6585 · Department of Natural Resources, (360) 835-1631 or (800) 527-3305
Fees and permits: Parking lots require a Northwest Forest Pass. Passes are available at all REI locations, all ranger stations, and online at www.naturenw.org; $5.00 per day, $30.00 for annual pass good for a year from day of purchase.
Schedule: Open year-round, weather/snow permitting; usually unridable November through mid-June
Maps: *Washington Atlas and Gazetteer,* page 64, D4; USGS Sun Top, Noble Knob
Land status: National forest
Nearest town: Greenwater
User density: Light
Other trail users: Hikers, equestrians
Canine compatibility: Dogs permitted on a leash but not recommended due to speed of descents.
Wheels: Front to light dual suspension
Hazards: Superman impersonations off the side of steep fall lines, dangerous switchbacks, horseflies, a climb that will make your lungs feel as though they are filled with acid.

Finding the Trailhead

From Seattle, take I-5 south to State Route 18 east to Auburn. Take the Enumclaw exit and follow SR 164 to Enumclaw. Follow the main road (Highway 410) through Enumclaw and Green Water to FSR 72 (5.7 miles past the Greenwater General Store). Turn left and drive for 25 to 50 yards; park at the fork in the road.
From Tacoma, take I-5 north to SR 18. Then follow directions above.
From the East Side area, take I-405 south to Renton. Then take the Maple Valley Highway/SR 169 south to Enumclaw. Turn left onto Highway 410 toward Greenwater, and follow the above directions. Or you can bypass Enumclaw by taking a left onto Southeast 416th Street (there is a Shop and Stop convenience store on the corner). Then turn right onto 284th Avenue Southeast after about a mile. Follow 284th to Highway 410, and turn left. Follow the above directions.

The Ride

Ranger Creek is simply *da-bomb.* A relentless no-rest-for-the-weary ascent; porcelain-smooth, supermodel-slim singletrack cut into savagely steep fall lines; intimate views of Mount Rainier; vicious switchbacks that strike fear into the hearts of mere mortals; glacier-fed creeks; a 30-plus mile per hour shot through an old-growth forest of fir, pine, hemlock and cedar; banked turns; and drops and dips make Ranger Creek one of the most explosive rides in Washington—never mind the entire Puget Sound area.

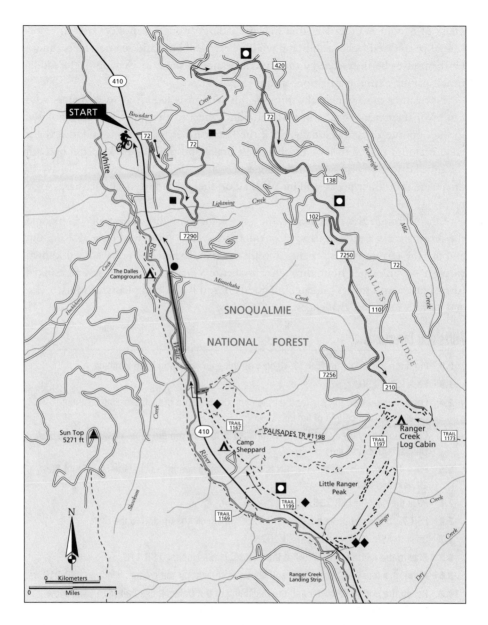

START

410

420

72

72

72

138

102

72

7290

7250

110

DALLES RIDGE

Boundary

Creek

Lightning   Creek

White   River

The Dalles
Campground

Minnehaha   Creek

SNOQUALMIE

NATIONAL   FOREST

7256

210

Huckleberry   Creek

Sun Top
5271 ft

N

0   Kilometers   1

0   Miles   1

Skookum   Creek

410

White   River

TRAIL
1167

PALISADES TR #1198

Camp
Sheppard

TRAIL
1197

Ranger
Creek
Log Cabin

TRAIL
1173

Little Ranger
Peak

TRAIL
1199

TRAIL
1169

Ranger   Creek

Creek

Dry   Creek

Ranger Creek
Landing Strip

Taxenpehlt   Creek

Mile   Creek

Ranger Creek is for serious riders only. If the 10-plus-mile climb isn't enough to dissuade most weekend warriors, the technically challenging descent ought to be. Most of the trail itself is as smooth as Samuel L. Jackson and just as dangerous as his character in the movie *Pulp Fiction*. Make one wrong move and you'll be headed to the hospital with broken bones, red-ribbon gouges, and purple-and-yellow bruises. For the first half of the downhill, the singletrack is no more than 20 inches wide. No big deal, except that it is cut into a fall line that is darn near a sheer wall. While the views of Mount Rainier are stunning, and riding through slopes covered in a collage of purple, red, yellow, and blue wildflowers is sublime and serene, riders cannot let themselves be distracted by the natural beauty of the area. Staying in the saddle means paying extreme attention on this ride.

Navigating the switchbacks through this section is hellish as well. Riders who can pivot their rear wheel around their front wheel so that their bikes are pointed in the opposite direction usually clock the fastest times to the bottom. However, it takes titanium nerves to lock up that front brake and pull the back of the bike off the ground while balancing on the edge of a huge drop. Many riders will have to disengage from their pedals and lift the bike off the ground to make the sharp-angle turns.

Once through the switchbacks, the ride mellows slightly. The trail widens, and the drops are not nearly as ugly. Most riders are secure enough to let it all hang out and use the terrain to help them navigate the trail. Expert riders have been known to push 40 miles per hour through this section. Finally, there are several banked turns, bumps, and rollers for catching good air. You'll also find plenty of roots, rocks, and various technical challenges.

Miles and Directions

0.0 From the car, pedal up FSR 72. (Ignore all the spur rides and keep climbing!)

1.5 Pass FSR 7290.

2.4 Pass an unmarked logging road on the right. Continue up the hill, crossing Lightning Creek at least a couple of times.

3.5 Cross Boundary Creek. (**FYI:** After climbing 1,500 feet, you are at an elevation of 3,750. Only 1,700 feet to go!)

5.5 Pass the viewpoint on the left. This is a great spot to see the Enchantments, Mount Stewart, and Mount Rainier.

7.1 Pass the sign for FSR 138.

7.4 FSR 72 begins to descend. Take FSR 7250, which climbs up and to the right.

7.7 Stick to FSR 7250 and pass FSR 102.

8.6 Stay to the right on FSR 7250 at the Y intersection, ignoring FSR 110.

9.6 Arrive at a four-way intersection and continue straight up the gradual climb on FSR 210.

10.2 Reach the end of FSR 210 and the beginning of the Dalles Ridge Trail (#1173). Follow the Dalles Ridge Trail, and climb away from the road.

10.7 Find the sharp right-hand turn onto the Ranger Creek Trail (#1197). The Dalles Ridge Trail continues straight ahead. (**Note:** For CTC riders, this is the junction between the Dalles Ridge Trail and Ranger Creek. You'll be riding from Corral Pass toward Ranger Creek via Dalles Ridge Trail and the Noble Knob Trail.)

11.9 Arrive at the Ranger Creek log cabin/shelter. Follow the trail around the left of the shelter. (Cyclists can choose either the Palisades Trail (#1198) or the Ranger Creek Trail. Palisades is in front of the shelter and Ranger Creek is to the left. The Palisades Trail adds more climbing and more technical challenges.)

14.3 Pass the junction for the Ranger Peak Viewpoint.

16.9 Drop down almost on top of Highway 410, passing the trail on the left. Take a hard right onto the White River Trail (#1199) toward Camp Sheppard (2 miles). Follow the new spur trail as it parallels Highway 410 and crosses a wooden bridge.

18.2 Reach the intersection between the Buck Creek Trail (#1169) and the Snoquera Falls Trail (#1167). Continue straight on Trail #1199.

18.5 Arrive at the Snoquera Falls Loop (for hikers only) and continue straight through the four-way intersection. Cross a bridge and another four-way intersection (go straight).

18.9 Reach Camp Shepherd and make a soft right, keeping the camp on your left. (If the climbing becomes steep, double back and stay closer to the edge of the camp.) **Side trip:** If you're tired, you can always follow the camp entrance to the highway and cut out the last portion of singletrack.

19.4 After crossing through three small clearings, continue straight through a four-way intersection.

19.8 Pass the Dalles Creek Trail (#1169) connecting in on the right. Head straight, following the side of the drainage. Turn right onto Powerline Way and then right again onto Highway 410.

23.0 Turn right onto FSR 72 and reach the car.

Ride Information

Local Information

Campground reservations, (800) 280-2267; radio AM 530 in Enumclaw provides the latest weather, road conditions, and mountain-area information.

Local Events

King County Fair, Enumclaw; July, (360) 825-7666

Pacific Highland Games, Enumclaw; July, (360) 825-7666

Restaurants

The Naches Tavern, (360) 663-2267
Buzzey's Greenwater Cafe, (360) 663-2421
Note: Both establishments are located in Greenwater.

32 Sun Top

Start: Trailhead off Buck Creek Road
Length: 21.8 miles
Approximate riding time: 3 to 4 hours
Technical difficulty: Advanced due to length of climb and supersteep descent off the crest of Sun Top.
Trail surface: Gravel forest service roads, smooth hard-packed singletrack, and a short paved section at the end of the ride
Trail contacts: USDA Forest Service, White River Ranger District, Enumclaw, (360) 825-6585 · Department of Natural Resources, (360) 835-1631 or (800) 527-3305
Fees and permits: Parking lots require a Northwest Forest Pass. Passes are available at all REI locations, all ranger stations, and online at www.naturenw.org; $5.00 per day, $30.00 for annual pass good for a year from day of purchase.

Schedule: Open year-round, weather/snow permitting; usually unridable November through mid-June due to snow and weather conditions
Maps: *Washington Atlas and Gazetteer,* page 64, D3-4; USGS Sun Top
Land status: National forest
Nearest town: Greenwater
User density: Heavy on the access roads but light on the trail
Other trail users: Equestrians, hikers, ORVs
Canine compatibility: Dogs permitted on a leash but not recommended due to speed of descent.
Wheels: Front to light dual suspension
Hazards: Logging trucks and automobiles on the access road, steep drop-off at the top.

Finding the Trailhead

From Seattle, take I-5 south to State Route 18; follow SR 18 east to Auburn. Take the Enumclaw exit and follow State Route 164 to Enumclaw. Follow the main road (Highway 410) through Enumclaw and Green Water to Forest Service Road 73 (6.4 miles past the Greenwater General Store). Turn right (east) and follow for 0.3 mile. Cross the White River and park just over the bridge across from the Skookum Flats Trailhead.
From Tacoma, take I-5 north to SR 18, then follow directions above.
From the East Side area, take I-405 south to Renton, then take Maple Valley Highway/State Route 169 south to Enumclaw. Turn left onto Highway 410 toward Greenwater and follow the above directions.

The Ride

A classic Puget Sound ride, **Sun Top** combines all that is right, good, and decent about mountain biking into one epic adventure. Miles of thigh-burning climbing, spectacular views of Mount Rainier and surrounding peaks, steep descents, technical trials of skill and stamina, and creamy peanut butter–smooth singletrack make Sun Top another must-ride. It is also the last and most difficult leg of the daunting Cascade Triple Crown. (See Ride 35.)

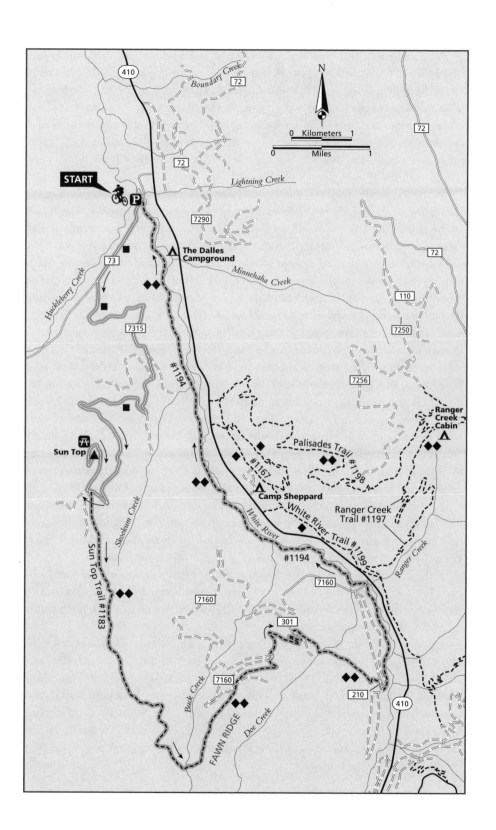

Another serious ride, Sun Top begins with a 7-mile climb and an elevation gain of 3,340 feet. Compared with the Ranger Creek ascent (11 miles and 3,290 feet in climbing), which is located just across Highway 410, Sun Top does not seem nearly as intimidating. However, Sun Top gains more elevation in 4 fewer miles. The climb is much steeper and more taxing on the mind and body. Upon reaching the saddle, cyclists often believe they have reached the tip-top. Alas, there are still at least 2 more miles of climbing. And this does not include the **Skookum Flats Trail,** which presents its own set of challenges. Stay tuned . . .

While the DNR spent the summer of 2001 widening the trail and rerouting the last section to the top (it now takes a more gradual approach around the west side of the ridge), the fall line is still punishing. Unfortunately, the change in the trail detracts from the magnificent views of the surrounding area. You can still reach the top by climbing up the old descent as it connects into the new trail. The best plan is to leave the bikes on the lower trail and walk the 50 to 75 feet to the top. The reward for the extra effort is spectacular views of Mount Rainier, Crystal Mountain, Green Mountain, Huckleberry Ridge, Huckleberry Mountain, and Noble Knob.

Cyclists are relieved to reach the first descent, but, again, they may be disheartened to learn there is still more climbing to be done. The trail follows the spine of the ridge, with frightening fall lines on either side; and once the trail begins to drop, it drops at warp speed. But then it climbs back up the ridge—again and again and again for roughly 2 to 3 miles. Each descent and return trip up the ridge tests a cyclist's stamina, determination, bike-handling skills, and reflexes. The first few hundred feet are about as steep as it can get without stepping off the edge of a cliff and simply dropping to the valley below. Worst of all, the climb usually saps precious energy needed for quick reactions to the challenging terrain. Obstacles seem to appear out of nowhere. Hit one and you'll be unceremoniously bounced out of the saddle.

Aerobically fit dirt mongers, however, will enjoy Sun Top immensely. Although the ride is hardcore, sections of the singletrack do allow for opening up on the throttle. The banked turns and switchbacks will check your speed. A good thing, considering the trail is used by hikers and horses as well as mountain bikes.

If there is a problem with Sun Top, it is the fact that this area sees frequent logging. The trail through the clearcut is well maintained, and the switchbacks are much more negotiable than those of Ranger Creek. However, no matter how intoxicating the trail is, clearcuts are just plain ugly.

Upon reaching the bottom, cyclists are faced with a choice. Head out to Highway 410 and ride the smooth forgiving pavement back to the car, or catch the punishing Skookum Flats Trail (see Ride 33) and ride back to the car. The only thing "flat" about Skookum Flats is the trail's lack of elevation gain. Skookum Flats can be a severe lesson in humility. The elevation gain is slight, but Skookum is simply one of the most technically taxing rides in Washington State. From start to finish, cyclists are faced with a seething mass of slimy, twisting roots bubbling up out of the pine needles, dirt, rocks, and mud.

The only flat spot on Sun Top

Miles and Directions

0.0 Ride up FSR 73. Be aware of logging trucks and other traffic.

1.1 Turn left onto FSR 7315 and continue climbing. Pass all the spur roads, staying on the main trail.

5.9 Pass the Sun Top Trail on the left, and continue pedaling up the road to the saddle and the intersection between FSR 7315 and Sun Top Trail #1183. Stick to the right on FSR 7315.

6.8 The road ends at the Sun Top Lookout (5,270 feet). (**FYI:** Mount Rainier is so close you can almost reach out and touch it. Noble Knob, Huckleberry Ridge, Green Mountain, Crystal Mountain, and Huckleberry Mountain are also visible from the viewpoint.) Turn around and descend to the saddle.

7.7 Reach the intersection and head left for about 50 feet. Then take Trail #1183 to the right and climb up the ridge for about a mile. The first section is supersteep, requiring most riders to dismount and walk.

8.9 Bust out of the trees onto the ridge (5,440 feet). (**Note:** The drop from the ridge is super-steep. It is a good idea to check to make sure your brakes are functioning properly before descending.) Drop down for about 0.5 mile, and then ride the roller-coaster ridge as the ridgeline mellows but still continues to descend.

11.4 Cross Buck Creek and keep descending.

12.5 Cross FSR 7160 and continue downhill.

12.8 Stick to the left as the trail splits. The right fork is for hikers only.

13.2 Hit FSR 7160 again. Turn right onto the road and follow for about 80 feet to the trail on the right. Make the turn and continue downhill. If the trail splits again, stay to the right one more time. (**Note:** The area is logged on a regular basis, so the trail may change a bit. However, finding the trail is usually fairly easy.)

13.4 The trail ends at a logging spur. Follow the road to the left, and then look for the trail on the right.

14.4 Cross Spur Road 310. Follow the trail as it parallels Doe Creek.

15.0 Stay to the right as the trail splits again.

15.4 Cross the overgrown road and continue following the trail.

15.5 Go to the left at the Y, descend a steep hill, and cross the usually dry creekbed. Just on the other side of the creekbed, arrive at a multi-intersection. Turn right, and then make the immediate left and follow the trail out to Spur Road 210.

15.7 Take a right onto Spur Road 210 and pedal south to a sharp curve in the road. Leave the trail here, and head to the left through a gravel-covered parking area and the Ranger Creek airstrip to Skookum Flats Trail #1194. Follow this trail to Highway 410.

15.9 Turn left onto Highway 410.

21.5 Turn left on FSR 73.

21.8 Cross the White River and reach the car.

Ride Information

Restaurants
The Naches Tavern, (360) 663–2267
Buzzey's Greenwater Cafe, (360) 663–2421
Note: Both establishments are located in Greenwater.

33 Skookum Flats

Start: Skookum Flats Trailhead parking lot
Length: 16.6 miles or 11.5 miles
Approximate riding time: 2 to 4 hours
Technical difficulty: Strong intermediate to advanced due to technical riding over and through a tangled mass of roots and rocks.
Trail surface: Singletrack, gravel access roads, and blacktop.
Trail contacts: USDA Forest Service, White River Ranger District, Enumclaw, (360) 825-6585 · Department of Natural Resources, (360) 835-1631 or (800) 527-3305
Fees and permits: Parking lots require a Northwest Forest Pass. Passes are available at all REI locations, all ranger stations, and online at www.naturenw.org; $5.00 per day,

$30.00 for annual pass good for a year from day of purchase.
Schedule: Open year-round, weather and snow permitting
Maps: *Washington Atlas and Gazetteer,* page 64, D4; USGS Sun Top
Land status: Mount Baker-Snoqualmie National Forest
Nearest town: Greenwater
User density: Light
Other trail users: Hikers, equestrians
Canine compatibility: Dogs permitted on a leash
Wheels: Light full suspension
Hazards: Slippery roots and rocks

Finding the Trailhead

Route One—The North End

From Seattle, take I-5 south to State Route 18 east to Auburn. Take the Enumclaw exit and follow State Route 164 to Enumclaw. Follow main road through Enumclaw and continue east on Highway 410 through Greenwater. Turn right onto Forest Service Road 73, 6.4 miles past the Greenwater General Store. Cross the bridge and travel 0.04 mile to parking lot on the right. Skookum Flats Trail (#1194) is on the left side of the road.

From Tacoma, take I-5 north to SR 18, then follow directions above.

From the East Side area, take I-405 south to Renton. Then take Maple Valley Highway/State Route 169 south to Enumclaw. Go left on Highway 410, and follow directions above.

Route Two—The South End

From Seattle, take I-5 south to SR 18 and follow it east to Auburn. Take the Enumclaw exit and follow SR 164 to Enumclaw. Follow main road through Enumclaw and continue east on Highway 410 through small town of Greenwater. Drive for 11.3 miles past the Greenwater General Store, and turn right onto Forest Service Road 7160. Parking area is on the right-hand side of the road.

From Tacoma, take I-5 north to SR 18, then follow directions above.

From the East Side area, take I-405 south to Renton. Then take Maple Valley Highway/SR 169 south to Enumclaw. Follow signs through Enumclaw to Highway 410, and follow above directions.

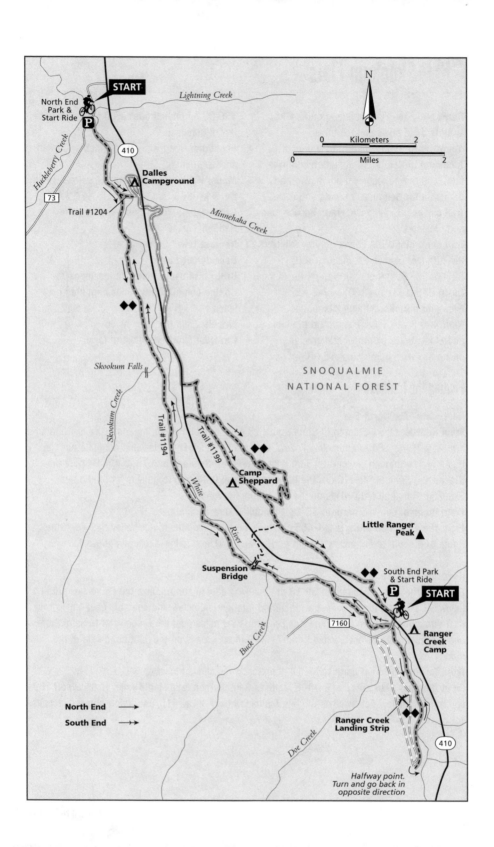

START

North End
Park &
Start Ride

P

410

Dalles
Campground

Trail #1204

Lightning Creek

N

0   Kilometers   2

0 ————— Miles ————— 2

Huckleberry Creek

73

Minnehaha Creek

Skookum Falls

Skookum Creek

Trail #1194

Trail #1199

White

River

Camp
Sheppard

Suspension
Bridge

S N O Q U A L M I E

N A T I O N A L   F O R E S T

Little Ranger
Peak ▲

South End Park
& Start Ride

P   START

Ranger
Creek
Camp

7160

Buck Creek

North End   ⟶
South End   ⟶⟶

Ranger Creek
Landing Strip

410

Doe Creek

*Halfway point.
Turn and go back in
opposite direction*

The Ride

Listening to the river and looking up into the forest canopy above **Skookum Flats** gives the impression that the ride will be a tranquil roll through the woods. But just a few pedal strokes into the forest, and fat-tire fanatics realize Skookum Flats is anything but tranquil. In fact, the only thing "flat" about Skookum Flats is the trail's lack of elevation gain. Skookum Flats can be a severe lesson in humility. The rise in elevation is minimal, but the trail is simply one of the most punishing rides in the Pacific Northwest. Imagine riding over a seething mass of greasy tentacles bubbling up out of the pine needles, dirt rocks, and mud. Mountain bikers who lose focus—and even those who don't—are routinely and sometimes viciously catapulted out of their saddles. Even strong and experienced riders are sometimes seriously challenged by the constant barrage of natural obstacles. Add in the usual sogginess that goes with riding along the bank of the White River, and Skookum Flats will either improve your technical skills or simply beat you to a pulp. No matter who you are, it will probably do a little of both.

The word "Skookum" is derived from Chinook Indian language. Based on trade, the language was developed by various tribes to talk business among one another. Translations of the word include "strong," "strength," "demon," and "evil spirit." The latter two translations may be most appropriate when it comes to mountain biking here. Riding Skookum Flats requires strong riding skills and serious physical strength. Without both, riders will feel as though evil spirits and demons haunt the trail each time an innocent-looking root throws them out of the saddle.

Located just north of Mount Rainier, Skookum Flats follows the White River as it gradually ascends 500 feet—not much of a climb until you realize the trail climbs over tricky technical problems again and again and again. The trail climbs up and away from the river and then drops back down—again and again and again. The river is aptly named for its distinctive pale hue, a result of the glacier flow coming off Mount Rainier's Emmons Glacier. The pulverized rock looks like plaster dust and turns the river milky white. Eighty percent of the ride is singletrack riddled with roots that more often than not are slippery and slimy. The forest canopy is thick, so even in summer the forest floor may not dry out completely.

▶ Puget Sound-area Native Americans call Mount Rainier "Tahoma," for "large white peak," or "Tacobet," for "nourishing breast," for the mountain's life-giving rivers and streams. The White River and its tributaries support coho, sockeye, and chinook salmon, as well as elk, deer, and other wildlife.

Route One creates a loop that includes part of the **Buck Creek Trail** and 3 miles of Highway 410 as well as the Skookum Flats Trail. This route heads south to north toward the tiny community of Greenwater. **Route Two,** the shorter of the two routes, begins on the north end of the trail and remains entirely on the Skookum

Yet another awesome adventure

Flats Trail. Mountain bikers ride south in one direction and then north back to the trailhead. First time Skookum riders are amazed by how different the same trail is when ridden in the opposite direction.

Both routes twist and turn along the river over fallen trees, gnarly roots, rocks, water-eroded sections of trail, and a suspension bridge across the river. No matter which trail you choose, expect you and your bike to be punished. The good news is that riding Skookum on a regular basis improves your technical skills dramatically.

Miles and Directions

Route One—Starting from the North End of Skookum Flats

0.0 From the Skookum Flats Trailhead (#1194), head south, or upriver.

1.1 Pass a small trail on the right, and continue following the river.

1.2 Begin crossing a series of wooden bridges for the next 0.2 mile.

2.2 Cross the stream.

3.7 Cross the wooden bridge with handrails.

4.1 Arrive at a trail intersection with a sign that reads ROAD 73—4.1 MILES; SKOOKUM FALLS—2 MILES. On the left, riders will find a suspension bridge that crosses the White River. Enjoy the thrill of walking out on the bridge, then continue heading up the stream on Trail

#1149. **Bailout:** If riders need to return to the parking lot, the quickest way is to cross the bridge and head west on Highway 410.

5.5 Turn left and follow the river.

5.6 Turn left at the Y intersection.

5.9 Pass the spur trail on the right that leads to the Ranger Creek Airport.

6.5 Pass Ranger Creek Camp off to the right. Arrive at a T intersection and turn left heading toward the White River. (Turning right deposits riders at Ranger Creek Camp.)

7.1 Pass an equestrian camp, turn right, and follow the trail to a concrete bridge. The trail parallels the airstrip and Forest Service Road 210.

8.3 Reach the top of the airstrip (the halfway point), turn around, and follow the trail in the opposite direction.

9.5 Cross the concrete bridge, turn left, and pass the equestrian camp.

10.1 Pass Ranger Creek Camp off to the left and turn right at the T intersection, heading toward the White River.

10.7 Pass the spur trail on the left that leads to Ranger Creek Airport.

11.0 Stay to the right at the Y intersection.

11.1 Turn right and follow the river downstream.

12.5 Arrive back at trail intersection with sign that reads ROAD 73—4.1 MILES; SKOOKUM FALLS—2 MILES. The suspension bridge is now on the right.

12.9 Recross the wooden bridge with handrails.

14.4 Recross the stream.

15.5 Pass the small spur trail on the left.

16.6 Reach the parking lot.

Route Two—Starting from the South End of Skookum Flats

0.0 From the trailhead, follow the trail north (downstream) along the river.

0.1 Turn right to remain on Trail #1194.

0.2 Turn right again at an unmarked intersection.

1.2 Reach the suspension bridge that crosses White River and heads to Highway 410. Bear to the left before the bridge to remain on the trail.

1.6 Turn right at the next intersection.

4.6 Reach the campsite. Stay on the right fork that follows the river.

5.0 The trail forks again. Stay to the right, following the jeep trail.

5.2 The trail turns back into singletrack.

5.8 Hit the gravel road and turn right. Cross the concrete bridge.

5.9 Turn right onto Trail #1204. Cross three short bridges and pedal toward the Dalles Campground.

6.4 Enter the Dalles Campground. Turn left and follow the paved road through the campsite.

6.9 Reach the camp entrance and cross Forest Service Road 7150.

7.1 The road levels out as it turns to the right. Stay on the main road, ignoring the spur roads to private cabins.

Steady, Steeaady

8.0 Turn left onto Highway 410.

8.6 Slow down and look for a super-small and difficult-to-spot trail on the left-hand side of the road. The trail looks like a small traffic pullout. Turn left and make the short, steep climb. Riders will quickly reach a set of power lines, where the trail bears to the right.

8.75 The trail divides. Turn left and pedal away from the power lines onto White River Trail #1199.

8.9 Reach another intersection, but stay on Trail #1199.

9.2 Continue through the intersection, and remain on Trail #1199.

9.64 Enter Camp Sheppard, where the route becomes a jeep trail.

9.75 Across from the buildings on the right, find the sign on the left that reads TRAIL. (Riders may have to look closely for this trail, as it is hard to spot.) Take the trail, and then bear right, riding above the Camp Sheppard buildings.

10.0 Continue straight on Trail #1199.

10.3 Continue straight on Trail #1199.

11.3 Turn right and leave the White River Trail. Ride a short distance down to Highway 410. Cross the highway and turn left.

11.4 Turn right onto Doe Creek Road.

11.5 Cross the river and reach parking lot.

Ride Information

Local Information

Campground reservations, (800) 280-2267; radio AM 530 in Enumclaw provides the latest weather, road conditions, and mountain-area information.

Restaurants

The Naches Tavern, (360) 663-2267
Buzzey's Greenwater Cafe, (360) 663-2421
Note: Both establishments are located in Greenwater.

34 Crystal Mountain

Option 1. Sport Loop

Option 2. Northway Trail

Start: Crystal Mountain Ski Resort parking lot

Trail maintenance hot lines: Crystal Mountain Ski Resort, (360) 663-2265 or (888) 754-6199; www.crystalmt.com · USDA Forest Service, (360) 825-6585 · U.S. Department of Natural Resources, (360) 825-1631 or (800) 527-3305

Fees and permits: Lift tickets are $14.00 for adults (age 11 and older) and $9.00 for children ages 5 to 10; free for children ages 5 and younger.

Schedule: Late June to September 4 for the chairlift, 10:00 A.M.–5:00 P.M.—last ride at 4:00 P.M. · For riders willing to do all of the climbing, trails are open from sun up to sundown and weather/snow permitting.

Maps: *Washington Atlas and Gazetteer,* pages 48, A4, and 49, A5; USGS White River Peak, Norse Peak

Land status: National forest

Nearest town: Greenwater

Other trail users: Hikers, equestrians

Canine compatibility: Dogs permitted on a leash but not on chairlift

Wheels: Cross-country, light dual suspension, and downhill bikes

Hazards: Horseflies, falling off trails that ride the edges of steep ridges, summer snowstorms, lung-bursting climb

Finding the Trailhead

From Seattle, take I-5 south to State Route 18 and follow east to Auburn. Take the Enumclaw exit and follow State Route 164 to Enumclaw. Follow main road through Enumclaw and continue on to Crystal Mountain Access Road on State Route 410—14.4 miles past the Greenwater General Store. Turn left and drive up access road to parking lot.

From Tacoma, take I-5 north to SR 18, then follow directions above.

From the East Side area, take I-405 south to Renton, then take Maple Valley Highway/State Route 169 south to Enumclaw. Turn left onto Highway 410 to Crystal Mountain Access Road.

Option 1: Sport Loop

Length: 7.2-mile loop

Approximate riding time: 1½ to 3 hours

Technical difficulty: Difficult to expert due to the climbing and potentially treacherous descents

Trail surface: Singletrack, gravel access roads, and blacktop

User density: Light

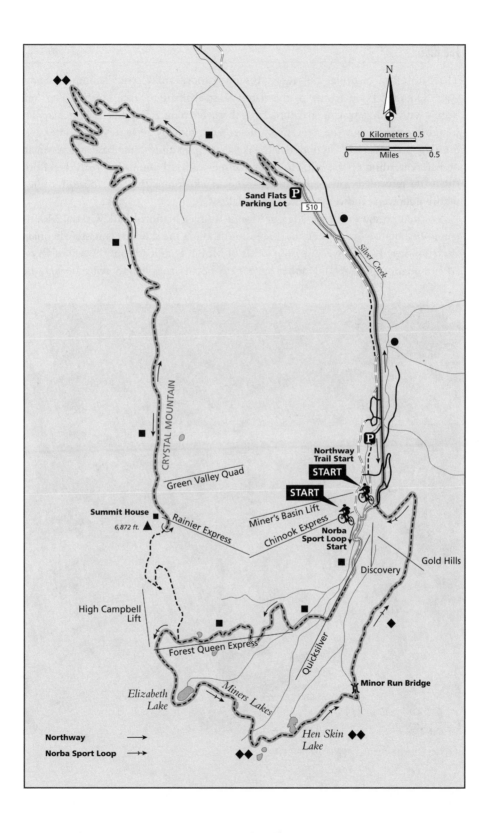

N

0 Kilometers 0.5

0 Miles 0.5

Sand Flats
Parking Lot P

510

Silver Creek

P

Northway
Trail Start

START

START

Miner's Basin Lift

Summit House

6,872 ft.

Green Valley Quad

CRYSTAL MOUNTAIN

Rainier Express

Chinook Express

Norba
Sport Loop
Start

Discovery

Gold Hills

High Campbell
Lift

Forest Queen Express

Quicksilver

Minor Run Bridge

Elizabeth
Lake

Miners Lakes

Hen Skin
Lake

Northway →

Norba Sport Loop →→

The Ride

The NORBA (National Off Road Biking Association) Crystal Mountain Sport Cross Country Loop is one of the state's most challenging race courses. The trail begins with a lung-tearing, backbreaking, thigh-burning 2.5-mile climb. It may not sound like much, but the excessively steep pitch quickly separates the contenders from the pretenders. It's a good idea to take a few spins around the base area to warm up before heading up the hill. However, the self-inflicted trauma is worth the effort; riders are rewarded with satin-smooth singletrack, romps through meadows filled with wildflowers, and crystal-clear alpine lakes.

Located on the northeast edge of Mount Rainier National Park, Crystal Mountain is Washington State's premier ski resort. Although the skiing is fantastic, the main attraction may be the awe-inspiring views of Mount Rainier. From the top of Crystal Mountain (6,872 feet), Rainier appears to be an arm's length away. In fact, the

World Cup racing at Crystal Mountain

only vantage point that may be better than the view from Crystal Mountain—barring a helicopter flight—is the one that mountain climbers find upon reaching the top of the 14,410-foot peak.

During summer, instead of being covered in a white downy blanket of snow, the slopes of Crystal Mountain are covered with bright green meadows that are heavily speckled with colorful wildflowers. Add in sharp, angry crags, icy-blue alpine lakes, peaceful silence, and ultrasmooth singletrack, and the Sport Loop simply provides some of the best riding in the country—if you can stomach the initial climb. Two and a half miles does not sound like a terribly long distance to some, but the climb begins at the base and does not relent until riders have pedaled or pushed their bikes up 1,600 feet of access roads littered with loose dirt, gravel, and rocks. Plan on lactic acid burning through the entire body! Ah, but the reward is more than worth the effort. Once the singletrack begins, it is all downhill and nearly all crushed-velvet smooth. The trail travels around three alpine lakes, underneath King Peak, through creek beds, and along the ridge high above the base of the area.

Riders reach Elizabeth Lake, which lies in Avalanche Basin at the bottom of Silver King Peak (7,012 feet), shortly after the crest of the climb. This is a good place to rest, cool off in the lake (the water is chilly!), and take in the scenery. The water is clearer than glass, and Silver King Peak looks menacing. From here the trail rides the edge of the lake and begins to descend over a few steep technical sections with large, burly roots and drop-offs. Riders pass Jake's Lake and Henskin Lake, located in

An intimate view from the top of Crystal Mountain

Silver Basin at the bottom of Three Way Peak (6,796 feet), and the heart-stopping natural beauty is quickly forgotten as riders enter into the adrenaline-factory singletrack descent.

The waiflike slender trail rides the ridge on a precariously steep pitch. Now would not be a good time to fall. Crash up the fall line, and lunch is a dirt salad with granite-chunk croutons. The alternative is worse—although the drop is not completely vertical, the speeds riders are traveling will launch them out into thin air, guaranteeing a hard landing and a trip to the hospital in Enumclaw. Focus on the trail out in front of the bike, and don't hug the upside of the trail. It tends to kick riders in the opposite direction. In the midst of this steep, narrow line, cyclists also must navigate a couple of jagged, rocky drops.

Nearing the bottom the trail, cyclists break out of the forest up above the lodge for a short distance before the trail cuts back into the trees for the last section of the ride. The singletrack is steep and technical, but after surviving the nasty downhill on the ridge, riders should have no problem working their way to the bottom.

Miles and Directions

0.0 Standing on the slope side of the lodge looking up the mountain, follow the access road between Chinook Express Quad on the right and the Quick Silver chairlift on the left. The access road cuts beneath Quick Silver a couple of times but generally heads straight up the steep ski slope.

0.62 Turn right as the access road turns back under Quick Silver.

0.88 Turn right at the bottom of the Forest Queen sextuple chairlift.

1.06 Turn left up the access road. Follow the route under the Forest Queen, down the dip in the road, and begin climbing again.

1.4 Continue straight, while the access road turns to the right. Make the next right for a short trip through the trees, and then turn left onto the road.

1.9 Cross under the chairlift and stay to the left, then head to the singletrack off the main access road.

2.2 Turn right on the dirt access road directly in front of the creek. Follow this road for a short distance, ignoring trails to the left; continue up the access road.

2.4 Take a left onto a wide singletrack and climb up the rutted trail.

2.6 Turn right, or go straight for a little extra climb and singletrack. Both routes connect into the same location. (There is a small alpine lake/pond on the left.) Stay to the left, reach the top, and head downhill, crossing underneath the Forest Queen.

3.0 Hit the road and turn right; make a quick turn on the left, and then go left again.

3.1 Reach Elizabeth Lake, located in Silver Basin at the bottom of Silver King Peak. Follow the trail around the southwest side of lake, cross the wooden bridge, and climb up above the southeast side of the lake.

3.5 Turn right and continue straight past Jake's Lake on the right. Descend down a steep technical section full of 1- to 3-foot drops in the trails. Cross the creek and continue through another steep technical section with large drops.

4.4 Reach and pass the Minor Lakes, then turn right and continue across the creek, ignoring any spur trails for 0.25 mile.

4.7 Turn left onto narrow singletrack. (Do not hug the uphill side of the fall line. It will kick your bike toward the other side of the trail. The edge is not a cliff, but with momentum you will fly like a bird . . . at least for a little while.)

4.90 Turn right, reach Hen Skin Lake, make another right, stick to the left, cross the creek, and stay left again. Prepare yourself for another steep, rocky, technical section. Do not fall here!

6.3 Cross Major Creek and a bridge called Minor Run. Break out of the woods above the Quick Silver chairlift. The lodge will be down the hill on the left.

6.5 Descend straight down dual track that turns into a gravel road.

6.8 Turn left back onto the singletrack. The trail is steep with big drops and roots. Make the next right, and then turn left above the lodge.

7.2 Reach the bottom.

Option 2: Northway Trail

Length: 16.1-mile loop
Approximate riding time: 3 to 5 hours
Technical difficulty: Difficult to expert due to the climbing and the potentially treacherous descents.

Trail surface: Singletrack, gravel access roads, and blacktop.
User density: Moderate

The Ride

Crystal's Northway Trail contains nearly every aspect of mountain biking that causes otherwise sane individuals to quit their jobs, sell everything they own, and spend their lives in the saddle of a two-wheeled mechanical steed. Porcelain-smooth singletrack, sweeping banked turns, serpentine switchbacks, cruising through fields of wildflowers, trips around alpine lakes, supersonic descents, blood-pumping climbs, and inspiring views of Washington's most recognized landmark, Mount Rainier, make this ride one of the best in North America.

Seemingly created by knobular gods who love velvety singletrack, Northway might be the most popular of the three rides located at Crystal Mountain. From the parking lot the route heads back down the Crystal Mountain Access Road. The actual trailhead begins at the Sand Flats Camps, which is also the base of CM Trail #1163. Skiers and boarders who have ventured out into the North Backcountry will recognize this small gravel parking lot as the pickup spot for the shuttle bus. From here the trail begins to climb and doesn't let up for the next 6 miles. Take it slow and steady; the climb can be grueling; especially on a hot summer day.

Sections of the ascent are steep, but probably the most difficult part of the climb is ignoring the precariously steep pitch down the fall line of the mountain. Be sure not to hug the up hillside of the trail—it tends to kick riders out toward the edge. Although not a cliff, the pitch is steep enough to cause serious bodily harm to riders who go over the edge. And on the way down, the danger increases as the speed ratchets up.

Just past the 5-mile mark, bikers are rewarded with the first of many stunning views of Mount Rainier. A short spur trail delivers riders to the edge of the other side of the ridge and provides an uninterrupted line of sight to the giant beauty. Be sure to get your views of the mountain in while climbing or at the summit. On the way down, you'll be having too much fun ripping down the trail to think about stopping to take in the view.

The forest has also opened up as the trail continues to climb along the ridge and through mountain meadows covered with wildflowers of nearly every color of the rainbow. Even the most macho gearheads can't help but appreciate the brilliance of the landscape.

The last section of the ascent to the summit is over a pox ridden rock field that is tough on both bike and body. Fortunately, it's only a short distance, and the welcome sight of the lodge motivates riders to push hard for the top. Cyclists can refuel in Washington's highest restaurant, use the rest rooms, and refill water bottles or hydration packs. Just be sure not to overdo it on food and drink, because the descent requires a clear head and a comfortable stomach.

The first part of the descent is over the rock field. Think light thoughts, and avoid the sharper rocks to avoid flatting. Once through the rock field, the trail opens up to an unruly ride through the meadows; the singletrack is smooth and fast. Be careful. Once the trail becomes steeper; the switchbacks are difficult to see and come up fast—not to mention, they are tight and covered in loose rock and dirt. (Betcha can't navigate every one of them without dabbing a foot.) Many riders are intimidated by the steepness of the pitch of the fall line. Their natural instincts are to shy away from the edge of the trail. However, because the trail is so narrow and the up hillside so steep, hugging the inside of the trail kicks bikes back toward the edge. Fight those instincts; ride down the middle of the trail, looking forward and not down the fall line.

Once the trail cuts back under the thick forest canopy, the fall line becomes less steep, allowing cyclists to increase their speeds. The trail continues to drop while rolling up and down the ridge. Have fun, but note that horses and other bikers are least visible on this section of the route. At the bottom, head out to the road and back to the lodge and parking lot.

Miles and Directions

0.0 From the parking lot, head back down the Crystal Mountain access road.

1.6 Turn left onto gravel/dirt road on Forest Service Road 510.

2.0 Enter singletrack at back of the Sand Flats parking lot and to the right of the power pole. Begin climbing; forest is dense this low on the trail.

5.1 Turn right onto spur trail for 20 feet for a viewpoint of Mount Rainier.

6.8 Riders can go left or straight. Both deliver them to the same location, although the trail on the left is less steep.

8.1 Reach the Summit House (6,872 feet); rest, eat lunch, refill water bottles, and head back down the way you came.

8.3 Stay to the left of the top of the chairlift and behind the mountain.

14.1 Reach Sand Flats parking lot, and pedal out to Crystal Mountain access road.

14.6 Turn right onto the road.

16.1 Reach the lodge.

Ride Information

Local Information

Campground reservations, (800) 280-2267

Alta Crystal Resort, (800) 277-6475; chalet-style condominiums in old-growth forest, 5 miles from base of Crystal Mountain

Crystal Mountain Lodging Suites, (888) ON-THE-MT; condominiums with completely equipped kitchens

Radio AM 530 in Enumclaw provides the latest weather, road conditions, and mountain-area information.

Restaurants

The Summit House; enjoy an on-mountain lunch with breathtaking views of Mount Rainier—tasty burgers, chili, sandwiches, brew and other beverages

The Snorting Elk Deli and Cellar; ride in for delicious homemade soups, sandwiches, pizza, and pastries. Grab an espresso or a microbrew and cool off in the European wine cellar

Note: Above establishments are all located on Crystal Mountain.

The view of Mount Rainier from the back side of Crystal Mountain

CRYSTAL MOUNTAIN WILDFLOWERS

In addition to the breathtaking beauty of Mount Rainier and the surrounding Cascade peaks, Crystal Mountain is blanketed in green mountain meadows from late June to early October. The green fields are dotted with freckles of blue, white, pink, red, orange, yellow, and purple. The source of all that color is the several species of wildflowers that grow on the slopes of Crystal every summer. Here's a sampling of what you might find:

Marsh marigold. White flowers with yellow centers, 1 to 2 inches across; heart-shaped leaves with round-toothed edges; up to 12 inches tall. Found below melting snowbanks and streams—early to mid-July.

Phlox. Flowers white, pink, or violet; approximately ½-inch clusters, blooming low; short-needle leaves forming thick mats across the ground. Found in dry, rocky places—early to mid-July.

Shootingstar. Purplish-pink flowers about 1 inch long; narrow, rounded leaves are clusters at base of stem; 6 to 8 inches tall. Found in subalpine meadows still wet from snowmelt—early to mid-July.

Lupine. Flowers blue-violet, about ½-inch long, clustered along top of stem; leaves seven to ten radiating leaflets, 1 to 3 inches long; up to 4 feet tall. Found in moist sites in open and shady places—midsummer.

Stonecrop. Flowers yellow, star shaped; leaves oval and fleshy; 3 to 8 inches tall. Found in dry, rocky subalpine meadows—midsummer.

Bluebells. Flowers blue, ½-inch long, funnel shaped; leaves 1 to 4 inches long; 1 to 3 feet tall. Found in clusters in very wet areas and along stream banks—midsummer.

Dwarf aster. Flowers purple, centers yellow, 1 to 2 inches across; narrow leaves; up to 7 inches tall. Found in wet subalpine meadows to dry alpine ridges—late summer.

Indian paintbrush. Red-orange to purplish-pink flowering heads of leaves; leaves alternate, up to 1 ½ inches long; up to 12 inches tall. Found in dry-to-moist subalpine meadows—late summer.

35 Cascade Triple Crown

Seattle's Mountain Bike Iron Man

Start: Crystal Mountain parking Lot
Length: 50.3-mile point-to-point with shuttle back to the start location
Approximate riding time: 8 to 10 hours
Technical difficulty: Extreme due to length of the ride, the amount of climbing, and technical downhills
Trail surface: Singletrack, gravel access roads, and a small amount of pavement
Trail contacts: USDA Forest Service, White River Ranger District, Enumclaw, (360) 825-6585 · Department of Natural Resources, (360) 835-1631 or (800) 527-3305
Fees and permits: None
Schedule: Open year-round, snow permitting, but best July through September

Maps: *Washington Atlas and Gazetteer,* page 64, D3-4 (shuttles 1 and 2), pages 48, A4, and 49, A5 (shuttle 3); USGS Sun Top, Norse Peak, and White River Peak
Land status: National forest
Nearest town: Greenwater
User density: Light
Other trail users: Equestrians, hikers
Canine compatibility: Dogs not recommended due to length of ride and speed of descents.
Wheels: Cross-country and light full suspension
Hazards: Horseflies, falling off trails that ride the edges of steep ridges, summer snowstorms, lung-busting climbs

Finding the Trailhead

From Seattle, take I-5 south to State Route 18 and follow east to Auburn. Take the Enumclaw exit and follow State Route 164 to Enumclaw.

Shuttle 1: From Enumclaw, follow the main road (Highway 410) through Enumclaw and Greenwater to Forest Service Road 73 (6.4 miles past the Greenwater General Store). Turn right (east) and follow for 0.3 mile. Cross the White River and park just over the bridge across from the Skookum Flats Trailhead. Park the first vehicle here.

Shuttle 2: From Enumclaw, follow the main road (Highway 410) through Enumclaw and continue east on Highway 410 through the small town of Greenwater. Drive for 11.3 miles past the Greenwater General Store, and turn right onto Forest Service Road 7160. Parking area is on the right-hand side of the road. Leave the second vehicle here.

Shuttle 3: Continue with bikes to the Crystal Mountain Access Road on Highway 410, 14.4 miles past the Greenwater General Store. Turn left and drive up access road to parking lot. The ride begins here.

The Ride

Looking for a serious challenge? Try the Cascade Triple Crown (CTC), Puget Sound's mountain bike version of the Iron Man. The CTC links six separate trails, climbs three separate peaks (11,000 feet), and covers 50 miles of terrain—all in a single day.

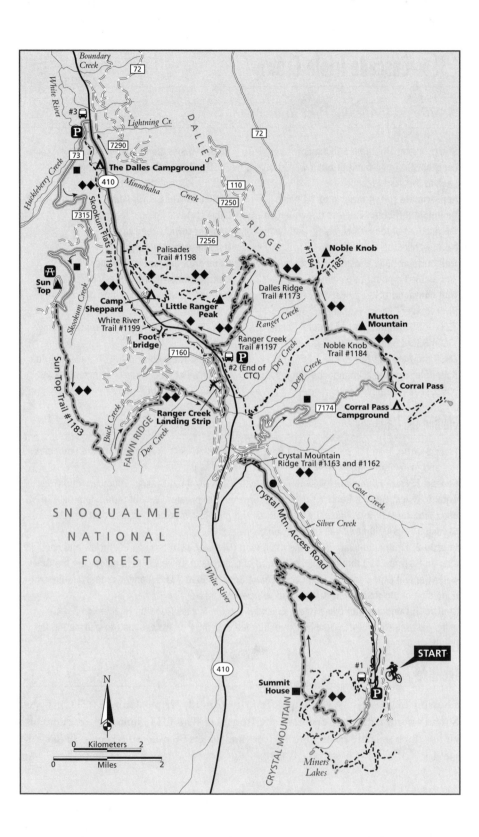

Boundary Creek

72

White River

#3

Lightning Cr.

D A L L E S

72

7290

73

The Dalles Campground

110

410

Minnehaha Creek

7250

Huckleberry Creek

Skookum Creek

7315

Skookum Flats #1194

R I D G E

7256

Palisades Trail #1198

#1184

#1185

Noble Knob

Sun Top

Dalles Ridge Trail #1173

Camp Sheppard

Little Ranger Peak

Ranger Creek

Mutton Mountain

White River Trail #1199

Ranger Creek Trail #1197

Dry Creek

Noble Knob Trail #1184

Deep Creek

Foot-bridge

7160

P

#2 (End of CTC)

Corral Pass

Sun Top Trail #1183

Buck Creek

FAWN RIDGE

Ranger Creek Landing Strip

7174

Corral Pass Campground

Doe Creek

Crystal Mountain Ridge Trail #1163 and #1162

Goat Creek

SNOQUALMIE

NATIONAL

FOREST

Silver Creek

Crystal Mtn. Access Road

White River

410

Summit House

#1

P

START

CRYSTAL MOUNTAIN

Miners Lakes

N

0   Kilometers   2

0   Miles   2

Mile 13 . . . only 37 more to go!

Located near Mount Rainier, the CTC is a combination of Crystal Mountain's Northway Loop, the Crystal Mountain Ridge Trail, Noble Knob, Ranger Creek, Sun Top, Skookum Flats, and small stretches of Highway 410. Four of the six trails are packed full of slim singletrack, rock gardens, relentless thigh-burning climbs, a giant Crayola crayon box of colorful wildflowers, alpine lakes, and abundant wildlife.

The first CTC was completed in 1997 by Keith "Goat Boy" Rollins, Wayne "Crazy Legs" Grevey, and Reltney Watkins—all Seattle area cross-country racers. The ride was inspired by their friendly competition and has become an annual event that acts as a truth serum when it comes to determining riding ability, strength, and cycling prowess. Mountain bikers who can complete the CTC in one piece in less than eight hours have proven their ability, skills, and stamina beyond a shadow of a doubt. Either that, or they are plain goofy in the head!

For many, the CTC requires at least three vehicles to complete the ride: one to transport riders to the base of the Crystal Mountain Ski Area, a second to take riders back to Crystal Mountain once the CTC is finished, and a third to leave at Forest Service Road 73 just off Highway 410. Use this spot as a pit stop before the last and most difficult climb of the day—Sun Top. Consider stocking the vehicle with a fresh change of clothes, food, and water. Park the second car at Buck Creek/Forest Service Road 7160. This is the end of the CTC, and you'll use this vehicle to shuttle back to the base of Crystal Mountain.

The best time to ride the CTC is late July/early August, when days are longer. Riders will need the extra daylight to navigate the treacherous descent off Sun Top—especially after climbing 11,000 feet and riding roughly 40 miles already. Attempting the CTC this time of year also provides riders with plenty of time to train and prepare for the physical demands of the ride. Start training early; the CTC requires solid skills and more stamina than any other ride in Washington state.

Miles and Directions

0.0 Standing on the slope side of the lodge looking up the mountain, follow the access road between Chinook Express Quad on the right and the Quick Silver chairlift on the left. The access road cuts beneath Quick Silver a couple of times but generally heads straight up a steep, rocky, gravel road.

0.6 Turn right as the access road turns back under Quick Silver. The road traverses across the mountain for a short distance before turning left and heading up the mountain. Follow main access road as it heads northwest and up the steep switchbacks. If you are looking at a Crystal Mountain ski map, the road heads in the direction of the Sunny Side ski run before cutting up the ridge to the Summit House.

3.0 Reach the Summit House (6,872 feet). (This is a good spot to rest, eat lunch, and refill water bottles.) Head north along the ridge.

3.3 Stay to the left of the top of the chairlift and behind the mountain. (**FYI:** Enjoy the single-track, but be careful of the steep switchbacks—they are difficult to see when you're moving at high speeds. Parts of the trail are narrow as they follow the edge of the ridge. Falling off means you are going to do your best Superman impression.)

9.2 Reach Sand Flats parking lot. Follow the gravel road and look for a trail on the left just after leaving the cul-de-sac parking area. Take the trail on the left, immediately cross the wooden bridge, and pedal through the equestrian parking lot. On the other side of the lot, continue along the trail up to the road.

9.6 The first leg of the CTC is complete. Now turn left onto the Crystal Mountain access road. (Be careful, and watch for cars.)

13.2 Descend down the road and look for the large gravel turnout on the right. Take the Crystal Mountain Ridge Trail (#1163—it reads #1162 at the bottom of the trail in the cabin area) as it drops off the road. Follow the switchbacks for 0.5 mile.

13.7 Reach a four-way intersection and continue straight out to the gravel road. Turn left on the road and drop down the hill.

13.8 Turn left again at the bottom of the hill and quickly cross Silver Creek. Follow this gravel road to FSR 7174. Turn right onto FSR 7174, and let the climbing begin.

18.8 Reach the top of Corral Pass and turn left onto Spur Road 210. Look for the trail at the back of the parking area at the end of Spur Road 210. Follow this trail, which is the Noble Knob Trail, or #1184.

19.5 The trail widens to the size of a road. Stick to the left and follow the wide trail. Over the next 1.5 miles pass two trails on the left and four on the right.

20.3 Stay to the left as the trail splits and climb the steep hill. If you can ride this, you are huge!

20.7 Pass Trail # 1196 on the left. Stick to the Noble Knob Trail (#1184).

21.6 Reach the crest of the ridge and drop down the other side. The trail drops below and to the right of a large, angry crag.

21.8 Reach the junction between the Noble Knob Trail and Dalles Ridge Trail #1173. Take the hard left/switchback onto Trail #1173.

22.9 Turn left onto Ranger Creek Trail #1197. Enjoy the switchbacks!

23.1 Reach the junction between the Palisades and Ranger Creek Trails and the Ranger Creek log cabin/shelter. Follow the trail around the shelter and to the left. Continue to descend as the switchbacks become even more ferocious.

26.3 Continue straight.

28.8 Pass the sign reading LITTLE RANGER CREEK, DALLES RIDGE, AND PALISADES TRAILS.

29.0 The trail drops down almost onto Highway 410. Pass the trail on the left and follow White River Trail #1199 to Camp Shepherd.

30.2 Stay left at the Y. (There is a sign that reads BUCK CREEK TRAIL #1169, HIGHWAY 410, AND SKOOKUM FLATS #1194.)

30.4 Turn right onto the grass-covered trail as it breaks out into the open for a short distance. Make the next left back onto dirt singletrack and back into the trees. Reach Highway 410, but turn right and continue on the trail. Cross the clearing and continue on the trail as it parallels the highway.

30.7 Reach the Camp Shepherd entrance and turn left. Reach Highway 410 and turn right. Be careful of moving vehicles! (The second leg of the CTC is now complete.)

34.0 Reach FSR 73 and turn left. Cross the bridge and reach the shuttle vehicle. (**FYI:** This is a good spot to rest and refuel.) Head up FSR 73.

35.5 Turn left onto FSR 7315 and continue climbing. Pass all the spur roads, staying on the main road.

40.3 Pass the Sun Top Trail on the left and continue pedaling up the road to the saddle and the intersection of FSR 7315 and Sun Top Trail #1183. Stick to the right on FSR 7315.

41.2 The road ends at the Sun Top Lookout (5,270 feet). (Mount Rainier is so close you can almost reach out and touch it. Noble Knob, Huckleberry Ridge, Green Mountain, Crystal Mountain, and Huckleberry Mountain are also visible from the viewpoint.) Turn around and descend to the saddle.

42.1 Reach the intersection and head left for about 50 feet. Then take Trail #1183 to the right and climb up the ridge for about a mile. (The first section is super-steep, requiring most riders to dismount and walk.)

43.3 Bust out of the trees onto the ridge (5,440 feet). (The drop from the ridge is super-steep. Make sure your brakes are functioning properly before descending.) Drop down for about 0.5 mile, and then ride the roller-coaster ridge as the ridgeline mellows but still continues to descend.

45.8 Cross Buck Creek and keep descending.

46.9 Cross FSR 7160 and continue downhill.

47.2 Stick to the left as the trail splits. The right fork is for hikers only.

47.6 Hit FSR 7160 again. Turn right onto the road and follow for about 80 feet to the trail on the right. Make the turn and continue downhill. If the trail splits again, stay to the right one more time. (**Note:** The area is logged on a regular basis, so the trail may change a bit. However, finding the trail is usually fairly easy.)

47.8 The trail ends at a logging spur. Follow the road to the left and then look for the trail on the right. Continue to and cross Spur Road 310. From here the trail parallels Doe Creek.

49.4 Stay to the right as the trail splits again. Cross the overgrown road a short distance later and continue following the trail.

49.9 Go to the left at the Y, descend a steep hill, and cross the usually dry creekbed. Just on the other side, arrive at a multi-intersection. Turn right and then make the immediate left, following the trail out to Spur Road 210.

50.1 Turn left onto Spur Road 210 and parallel the Ranger Creek Airport landing strip on either the road or the wide gravel trail between the road and the airstrip.

50.3 Turn right on FSR 7160 and reach the shuttle car.

Ride Information

Local Information

Campground reservations, (800) 280–2267
Alta Crystal Resort, (800) 277–6475; chalet-style condominiums in old-growth forest, 5 miles from base of Crystal Mountain
Crystal Mountain Lodging Suites, (888) ON-THE-MT; condominiums with completely equipped kitchens

Radio AM 530 in Enumclaw provides the latest weather, road conditions, and mountain-area information.

Restaurants

The Naches Tavern, (360) 663–2267
Buzzey's Greenwater Cafe, (360) 663–2421
Note: Both establishments are located in Greenwater.

The Outer Limits

—Or just because they are so good we couldn't leave them out

The Outer Limits is the only section in this guide that includes rides outside the ninety-minute drive time radius from the boundaries of the Puget Sound area—the boundaries running from Olympia to Bellingham and Kitsap to the East Side. The Outer Limits is not really a region at all but simply a collection of my favorite trails just a few steps beyond the Puget Sound area.

It's not as easy as he makes it look!

Each of the six rides in this section has been included for either its scenic beauty, awesome trails, or both. For instance, **Devils Gulch** ought to be called Heaven's Gate, because if God decided to go on a freaky fat-tire adventure, He'd ride here. The views of the North Cascades, Mount Stewart, and Mission Creek are nothing short of heavenly, not to mention the ride's more than 12 miles of velodrome-smooth single track. Then there is **Mission Ridge,** which some cyclists claim is even more epic than the Gulch.

Mad Lake is also accessible from State Route 2. Complete with romper-room terrain, the savage beauty of its massive rockslides, silky-smooth singletrack, and the icy-cold emerald-clear waters of Mad Lake, this ride is totally amazing.

To the south and easily accessible from I–5, riders will find **Kachess Ridge** and **Taneum Creek.** More smooth singletrack, spectacular views of Mount Rainier, angry crags, and long-sustained descents make both rides the subject of many fat-tire fantasies.

36 Devils Gulch and Mission Ridge

Start: From Devils Gulch–Mission Ridge parking lot along Forest Service Road 7100
Length: 24.4 and 26.4 miles
Approximate riding time: 4 to 5 hours
Technical difficulty: Advanced to expert due to the long climbs and the dangerous descents
Trail surface: Singletrack, dirt and gravel roads
Trail contacts: Leavenworth Ranger District, (509) 548-6977 · Lake Wenatchee Ranger District, (509) 763-3103 or (800) 452-5687
Fees and permits: $5.00 per car per day, $30.00 for an annual pass
Schedule: June to late October, depending on the snow level. Call the ranger district before heading out.

Maps: *Washington Atlas and Gazetteer,* page 67, B5; USGS Mission Peak
Land status: National forest
County: Chelan County
Nearest town: Cashmere
User density: Heavy
Other trail users: Hikers, equestrians
Canine compatibility: Not recommended; descents are too fast for most dogs to keep up.
Wheels: Cross-country, dual suspension, and downhill
Hazards: Rapid descents, big-air drops over steep slopes

Finding the Trailhead

From Seattle, take I-90 east just past Cle Elum. Turn left on State Route 970 and follow to U.S. Highway 97. Follow over Blewett Pass and then turn right onto U.S. Highway 2. Head east on U.S. 2 until reaching Cashmere. Turn right onto Division Street and follow around Vale School, where Division turns into Pioneer Street. Take the immediate left onto Mission Creek Road and follow to Binder Road. Turn right and then make a quick left back onto Mission Creek Road. Follow for 10.4 miles to the fork in the road. Turn left onto FSR 7100 for 2.6 miles to the Mission Ridge and Devils Gulch Trailhead.

The Ride

Despite the long drive to Devils Gulch and Mission Ridge, these trails are simply two of the best in Washington State. Porcelain-smooth singletrack, views of the North Cascades and Mount Stewart, Mission Creek, mountain meadows filled with wildflowers, more downhill than uphill, burly banked turns, sneaky switchbacks, roller-coaster terrain, and insanely steep descents make both trails a must-ride for any fat-tire enthusiast.

Devils Gulch

Located just outside Cashmere on the east side of the Cascades and roughly two hours from Seattle, the Gulch and the Ridge attract all types of riders searching for a day of blazing saddles. Skinny-legged climbers routinely pedal to the top of the

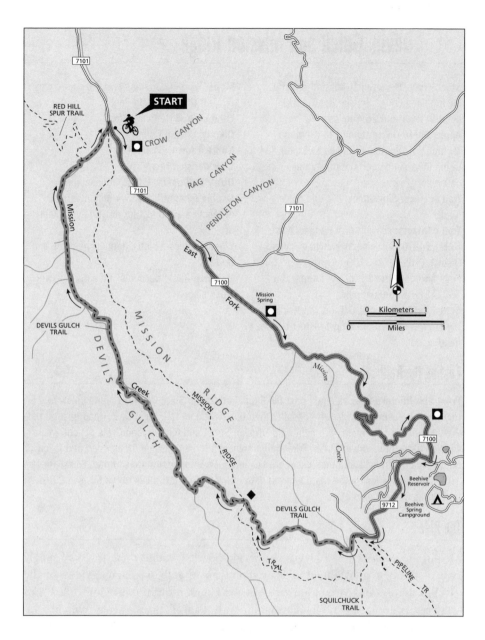

trails in about ninety minutes—sometimes less. They rest for a few minutes, chow down an energy bar, and gloat in their superior athletics while their neoprene-Kevlar-clothed downhillers routinely load up one vehicle with several bikes and simply drive to the top. These cross-country climbers then shoot down the trail at reasonably safe speeds.

Devils Gulch is a heavenly ride.

The gravity-defying speed freaks, on the other hand, don their protective gear and bomb down the trail at speeds most would find terrifying—only after scratching their heads and wondering why anyone in his or her right mind would want to make the 11-mile climb in the saddle when they could simply drive to the top in a matter of twenty minutes. No matter how a rider reaches the top or the bottom, everyone agrees that Devils Gulch is a heavenly adventure.

For an 11-mile climb, Devils Gulch is relatively easy on the thighs and lungs. The elevation gain is slow, and after a couple of miles of riding on gravel, the road turns into smooth hard-packed dirt. The ascent is fairly easy from here on up to the top.

Just past the halfway point in the climb, the fire road crosses into the Mount Baker Wenatchee National Forest. Views of Wenatchee, the Columbia River, Mission Ridge's chairlifts, Bomber Bowl, and Glacier Peak open up. Mount Stewart is also visible to the north.

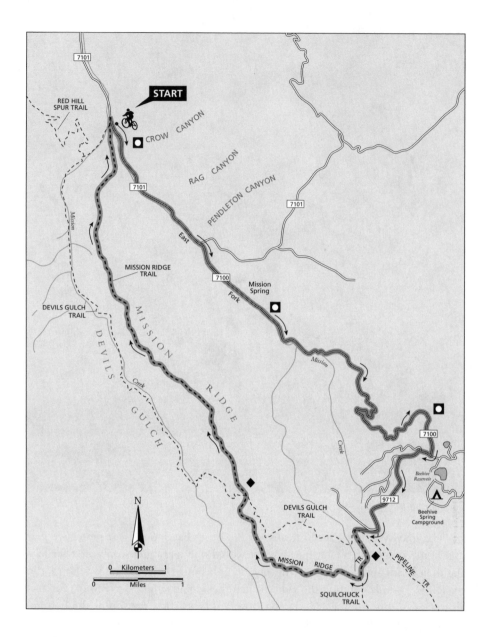

The top section of the route covers velvety-smooth singletrack, perfect for railing down the trail. The descent is not steep at all, and the forest of ponderosa pine and subalpine firs is open enough so that riders can see several yards down the trail. Enjoy this nonthreatening terrain while you can. Once the trail reaches the edge of the Gulch and begins to descend, it becomes extremely clear where the "Devil" in Devils Gulch came from.

Riding the edge of the Gulch, the trail is slim and laced with conniving switchbacks. Go over the edge and it's a long, long way to the bottom—it's doubtful you'd be riding out aboard anything other than a helicopter. The switchbacks are equally dangerous. Difficult to see and navigate, they surprise even riders who have ridden the Gulch more than once.

After the steepest and nastiest part of the descent, the trail widens and begins to cross back and forth across Mission Creek. With each crossing, the trail climbs a short distance up each side of the Gulch but continues to drop in elevation as it heads back to the parking area.

Mission Ridge

If you like climbing, then Mission Ridge will be even more fun than Devils Gulch. After reaching the Devils Gulch trailhead, continue for another 3 miles of steep climbing. This is the steepest part of the entire ride, and your lungs and thighs will be tested. However, the rewards are sweet. The trail, all singletrack, opens up along the ridge and rolls up and down with the terrain. Riders will encounter tight switchbacks, but they are not nearly as unforgiving as the switchbacks of Devils Gulch.

The Mission Trail intersects with Devils Gulch after about 4 miles, signaling the beginning of the coolest part of the ride. The route follows the ridge, providing stunning views of the North Cascades, Wenatchee, and the Columbia River. Best of all, the downhill is pure adrenaline. Steep is a bit of an understatement. Your glutes will be out behind your saddle, which will be pressed up against your belly. Be alert for more switchbacks and dangerous drops in the terrain, either on or off the trail.

Miles and Directions

Devils Gulch

- **0.0** Start from the small parking lot and ride up FSR 7101.
- **2.5** Stay to the right on FSR 7100, following the east fork of Mission Creek. The road begins to climb and doesn't stop for the next 9 miles.
- **5.5** The gravel road turns to hard-packed dirt, making the climb a little easier.
- **6.0** Enter national forest boundary.
- **9.2** Turn right onto FSR 9712.
- **9.5** Look for the sign that reads BEEHIVE SOIL AND MANAGEMENT AREA.
- **9.7** Pass the spur road and stay on FSR 9712.
- **10.4** Pass the road on the right.
- **11.5** Turn right into the parking lot of Devils Gulch Trailhead. Devils Gulch Trail is at the back of the lot.
- **14.0** The trail levels off and the trees open up, providing excellent visibility. The smooth terrain here allows for maximum speed!

15.8 Look out for the treacherous switchbacks. They are difficult to see and sneak up on riders, especially when you're moving at high speed. Miss the turn and it is a long, long way down. The trail navigates back and forth across Mission Creek and other fingers several times, climbing up each side of the Gulch in the process.

18.0 The trail continues to roll up and down each side of the Gulch and across Mission Creek. (**Note:** The ride is less demanding in that going over the edge at this point means fewer consequences.)

24.4 Return to the Devils Gulch–Mission Creek Trailheads.

Mission Ridge

0.0 Start from the small parking lot and ride up FSR 7101.

2.5 Stay right onto FSR 7101.

9.2 Turn right onto FSR 9712.

9.5 Look for the sign that reads BEEHIVE SOIL AND MANAGEMENT AREA.

9.7 Pass the spur road and stay on FSR 9712.

10.4 Pass the spur road on the right.

11.5 Pass the Devils Gulch Trailhead on the right. Instead, take the **Pipeline Trail** on the left, which delivers riders to the Mission Ridge Ski Area via the **Squilchuck Trail.**

13.8 Pass the Squilchuck Trail, which takes riders to the Mission Ridge Ski Area. The Mission Ridge Trailhead is on the right. Let the singletrack begin!

17.7 Cross the Devils Gulch Trail by going straight through the four-way intersection; begin to climb.

26.2 At the T intersection, turn right onto Devils Gulch Trail.

26.4 Reach the Devils Gulch–Mission Ridge Trailhead.

Ride Information

Accommodations
Cashmere's Village Inn, Cashmere, (509) 782-3522
Icicle River RV & Campground, Leavenworth, (509) 548-5420
Pine Village KOA, Leavenworth, (800) 562-5709

Restaurants
Casa Sanchez, Cashmere, (509) 782-1364
Best of the Wurst, Leavenworth, (509) 548-7580
Big Y Cafe, Peshastin, (509) 548-5012
Cafe Mozart Restaurant, Leavenworth, (509) 548-0600

37 Mad Lake

Start: Chikamin Creek Trail parking area
Length: 20.1 miles
Approximate riding time: 4 to 6 hours
Technical difficulty: Advanced to expert due to the amount of climbing, technically challenging rock gardens, and loose, fine silt/dust/dirt that causes bikes to drift while moving at high speeds
Trail surface: Singletrack
Trail contact: Wenatchee National Forest, Lake Wenatchee Ranger District, (509) 763-3103 or (800) 452-5687
Fees and permits: $5.00 day pass, $30.00 annual pass
Schedule: Open mid-July to late October, depending on snow levels; call the ranger station for exact dates.

Maps: *Washington Atlas and Gazetteer,* page 82, A3; USGS Chickamin Creek
Land status: Wenatchee National Forest
Nearest town: Cole's Corner, Leavenworth
User density: Light
Other trail users: Hikers, equestrians, ORVs
Canine compatibility: Dogs permitted on a leash but not recommended due to speed of descents and ORV's.
Wheels: Free ride, cross-country, and light full suspension
Hazards: Rapid descents, rockslides, bears, bobcats, mosquitoes, horseflies, dust, near clifflike drops, ORV riders

Finding the Trailhead

From the East Side, take State Route 2 east over Steven's Pass to Cole's Corner. Turn left (north) onto Highway 207 toward Lake Wenatchee. At 4.5 miles, the road crosses the Wenatchee River and splits in two. Stick to the right, and follow the Chiwawa Loop Road for 1.3 miles (pass Midway General Store at 0.8 mile). Turn left onto Meadow Creek Road, the start of FSR 62 (Chiwawa Valley Road). Follow for 9.2 miles, cross bridge (Chikamin Creek), and then turn right onto FSR 6210 (0.35 mile). Pass the Chikamin Creek Loop Trailhead and drive uphill for 8.1 miles; park just past where the trail crosses the road. (**FYI:** On Sundays, be sure to cross SR 2 back to Seattle by 4:00 P.M. The highway travels through three or four small towns with only one lane in each direction. After 4:00 P.M. you'll be stuck in bumper-to-bumper traffic for nearly 20 miles.)

The Ride

A crystal-clear emerald lake, panoramic views of the Entiat Mountains, massive rock gardens, a mountain meadow filled with wildflowers, and Velodrome-smooth singletrack make the Mad Lake Trail an off-road cyclist's dream. This route is not for average mountain bikers, however, due to its large amount of climbing and the toll it exacts on a rider's mind. The route climbs and then descends . . . then climbs and descends . . . then climbs and descends three more times for a total of roughly 3,500 feet. Even worse, the climbs include steep, sharp switchbacks and desert-dry, dusty, deep silt.

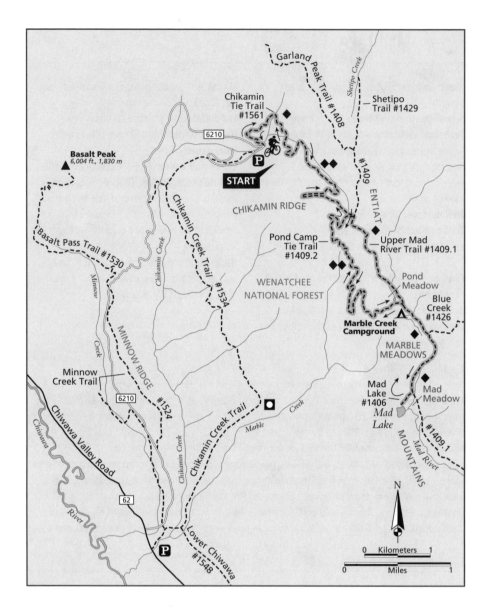

Mad Lake is the best trail in the Lake Wenatchee area—first due to its spectacular beauty and second due to the fact that all the lower level trails are usually desert-dry all summer long. Despite the parched nature of the trail, be absolutely sure to bring extra clothing in late season. This area rests at a high elevation and can grow cold and dangerous quickly. And don't forget the mosquito repellant—something strong that deters horseflies, bees, June bugs, and every other kind of insect. The buggers will drive you mad throughout the entire summer without strong protection.

Serenity on the edge of Mad Lake

A tough, no warm-up singletrack climb through the trees starts the journey. The grade generally eases up, with the exception of the steep switchbacks. Not only are they steep in relation to the fall line of the mountain, but they also are constructed with crisscross cinder blocks and form steep banked turns. The combination causes riders to fall to the inside of the turns, which can be dangerous due to the cinder blocks and the steepness of the fall line. Strong pedal strokes on the outside pedal help keep the bike upright and away from the center of the turn.

Climbing over the section of trail that cuts through the rock gardens is challenging as well. In fact, few cyclists can clean this section. Most will have to walk this portion of the trail. If any of your riding partners snicker at you, simply tell them that you dismounted so that you could enjoy the view. The giant rockslides are amazing in their power and size.

The route reaches a plateau at just over 6,400 feet. Don't be fooled by the short burst of sweet downhill. There are still miles of climbing to be done as the trail rolls up and down the ridge two more times before completely dropping into Marble Meadow. And remember, all of these short downhill sections will be uphill sections on the return trip.

Upon reaching Mad Lake, mountain bikers may be amazed by the clearness of the water and the complete lack of sound other than the wind. Despite the name, the area is an oasis of serenity—provided your bug juice is still working. Perspiration

An angry rockslide

tends to decrease repellant's effectiveness. It might be a good idea to pack a small can with you, but be sure to carry it where it can't be punctured! And be sure to pack along plenty of water; the dust can make your throat feel like sandpaper. Mad Lake is located at the edge of Mad Meadow and is a peaceful and serene location to relax and down some grub. When it is extremely hot, walk out to the end of the log, dip your feet in the lake, and use your jersey to give yourself a sponge bath. You'll cool off immediately, and the moist jersey will keep you cool as you climb back up the ridge.

One more set of climbs back to the top of the ridge, and then the real fun begins. Banked turns and trails slimmer than marathon runners with steep drops are common, as are creek crossing, dips, and drops. And remember those steep switchbacks you had to climb. They look even steeper from the top. Proceed with caution. As you near the bottom of the trail, be aware that the silt/dirt/dust causes bikes to drift over the trail. Your bike may be difficult to control, and no amount of tread or breaking seems to make much of a difference.

If you haven't had enough by the time you reach the bottom, cross the road and ride down the Chikamin Creek Trail. (See "Extended Ride" for more info.)

Miles and Directions

0.0 From the parking area, find and then follow the **Chikamin Tie Trail** (#1561). The Ride begins with a steep climb but levels out once the trail is away from the road.

0.07 Cross the first of several small creeks that have been fortified with gravel or ticktacktoe cinder blocks.

3.3 Break out of the trees and navigate the large field of boulders, the result of a gigantic rockslide. It's best not to dally through this section.

4.1 The Chikamin Tie Trail ends (finally) at 6,200 feet and a four-way intersection. To the left is the **Shetipo Trail** (#1429). Straight ahead is the **Upper Mad River Trail.** Turn right onto the **Pond Camp Tie Trail** (#1409.2) and continue to climb the ridge.

7.8 Reach the junction of the Pond Camp Tie Trail and the Mad River Trail (#1409.1). **Option:** Turning left will deposit riders at the Shetipo Trail after 3 miles of riding. The Shetipo Trail leads back to the Chikamin Tie Trail, so you can use this as an alternate route. To continue on to the lake, turn right on the Mad River Trail (closed to ORVs) and continue past Pond Meadow. The route also follows the edge of Marble Meadow, which is the larger of the two meadows.

8.4 Arrive at the intersection of Blue Creek Trail (#1426) and the Mad River Trail.

9.5 Turn right onto the Mad Lake Trail—only 0.25 mile to the lake.

9.8 The trail ends near a few campsites. Now turn around and head back in the opposite direction.

10.02 Turn left onto the Mad River Trail.

11.1 Return to the intersection of Blue Creek and Mad River Trails. Continue straight on the Mad River Trail.

11.8 Return to the junction of the Pond Camp Tie Trail and the Mad River Trail. Turn left on Pond Camp Tie Trail.

15.5 Return to Chikamin Tie Trail intersection and turn left. Cut back through the boulder field.

20.1 Reach the base of the Chikamin Tie Trail and the car.

Extended ride: For a monster ride and 8.4 additional miles of singletrack, turn left onto FSR 6210 and find the Chikamin Creek Trail just a short distance away. Extending The Ride requires parking one vehicle at the base of the Chikamin Creek Trail and shuttling your bicycles up to the base of the Chikamin Tie Trail—unless you want to ride back up the road for yet another 8 miles! (For details and directions to Chikamin Creek Trail see Ride 38.)

20.1 From your car and the base of the Chikamin Tie Trail, turn left onto FSR 6210 and find the Chikamin Creek Trail just a short distance away.

21.8 Turn left onto Chikamin Creek Trail and climb for roughly a mile. You'll cross three to five fingers of Chikamin Creek. The trail traverses its way across the ridge while heading south. Be cautious; the trail is narrow, and the fall line is dangerously steep.

25.8 Look for the viewpoint to the left and slightly above the trail.

28.0 Arrive at the intersection of the Chikamin Creek Trail and the Lower Chiwawa River ORV Trail.

28.5 Reach the parking area. Now jump in your car and drive to the base of the Chikamin Tie Trail to get the first car.

Ride Information

Local Information

Leavenworth Chamber of Commerce & Visitor Center, (509) 662-2116

Lodging

Camping at Lake Wenatchee
Lake Wenatchee State Park is a 489-acre camping park located 18 miles northwest of Leavenworth, Washington, with 12,623 feet of waterfront on glacier-fed Lake Wenatchee and the Wenatchee River. The park is bisected by the Wenatchee River, creating two distinct areas: South Park, with areas for camping, swimming, and horseback riding; and North Park, in a less developed, forested section, a 0.25 mile walk from the lake. The park is a natural wildlife area, and visitors should be aware of the presence of bears and other potential natural dangers. The park is open year-round. Campground is open mid-April to mid-October; mid-October to March, camping is available in designated day-use area. To make a reservation, call Reservations Northwest at (800) 452-5687.

Restaurants

Visconti's at the Brewery, (509) 548-1213
Dragonfire Pizza & Subs, (509) 548-5519
Northern Lights Pizza & Subs, (509) 548-5585
Gustavs, (509) 548-4509
Happy Clown Restaurant, (509) 763-3266.
Note: All restaurants are located in Leavenworth.

38 Chikamin Creek Loop

Start: Chikamin Creek Trailhead
Length: 16.5-mile circuit
Approximate riding time: 3 to 5 hours
Technical difficulty: Advanced to expert due to amount of climbing, technically challenging rock gardens, and loose fine silt/dust/dirt that causes bikes to drift while moving at high speeds
Trail surface: Singletrack and gravel access road
Trail contact: Wenatchee National Forest, Lake Wenatchee Ranger District, (509) 763–3103 or (800) 452–5687
Fees and permits: $5.00 day pass, $30.00 annual pass
Schedule: Open mid-July to late October, depending on snow levels; call the ranger station for exact dates.

Maps: *Washington Atlas and Gazetteer,* page 82, A3; USGS Chikamin Creek
Land status: Wenatchee National Forest
Nearest town: Cole's Corner, Leavenworth
User density: Light
Other trail users: Bikers, hikers, equestrians, ORVs
Canine compatibility: Dogs permitted on a leash; be sure to bring water for your canine friend as well.
Wheels: Free ride, cross-country, light full suspension
Hazards: Rapid descents, steep side cuts, bears, dust, mosquitoes, ORVs

Finding the Trailhead

From the East Side, take State Route 2 east over Steven's Pass to Cole's Corner. Turn left (north) onto Highway 207 toward Lake Wenatchee. At 4.5 miles, the road crosses the Wenatchee Rivers and splits in two. Stick to the right and follow the Chiwawa Loop Road for 1.3 miles (pass Midway General Store at 0.8 mile). Turn left onto Meadow Creek Road, the start of FSR 62 (Chiwawa Valley Road). Follow for 9.2 miles, cross the bridge over Chikamin Creek, and then turn right on FSR 6210 (0.35 mile). Drive to Chikamin Creek Trailhead parking area on the right. (**FYI:** On Sunday, be sure to cross SR 2 back to Seattle by 4:00 P.M. The highway travels through three or four small towns with only one lane in each direction. After 4:00 P.M., you'll be stuck in bumper-to-bumper traffic for nearly 20 miles.)

The Ride

Chikamin Creek is one of the few rides in Washington with as many or more miles to the downhill as there are to the climb. In fact, Chikamin's steep descent is nearly a mile longer than the climb up the forest service road. Mountain bikers won't find spectacular views in the area, as the trail descends through the basin/gully of the creek. All the better, because cyclists will be able to stay focused on navigating the gnarly downhill over hundreds of yards of ticktacktoe cinder blocks, sharp-angle switchbacks, and narrow trails cut into the fall line of the surrounding terrain. Add in ultrafine dust that hangs in the air longer than a young Michael Jordan after a

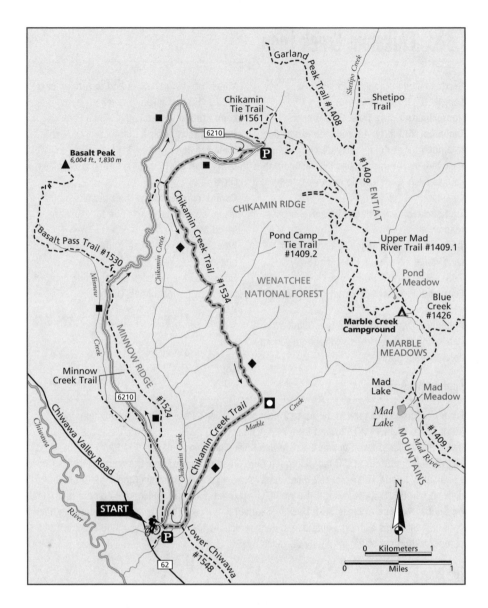

rider passes through, decreasing visibility, and Chikamin Creek is one of the tougher rides listed in this guide.

Early fur traders are responsible for naming Chikamin Creek. "Chikamin" is the Chinook word for money. Traders would ask the local natives, "How much Chikamin for that fur?" Apparently, so much business was conducted in the area that the creek quickly became known as Chikamin Creek. Today, although fur trading is a thing of the past, the wildlife in the area is quite strong. It is not uncommon to see

A couple that rides together stays together.

bears, bobcats, coyotes, deer or elk, foxes, marmots, minks, mountain goats, rabbits, raccoons, skunks, and weasels.

As for the riding, Chikamin Creek is one of the toughest in the area. Although the climb is relatively easy, the downhill is simply punishing. Thank goodness for full suspension! The route crosses Chikamin Creek five times, necessitating the reinforcement of the trail with ticktacktoe cinder blocks. Riding over them is like driving down railroad tracks in an automobile—thud, thud, thud, thud . . .

Riders will find one vantage point a few miles into the downhill with partial views of the Entiat Mountains. More than anything, this is a good place to rest your hands, wrists, elbows, and shoulders. From here the remaining downhill section is steep and continues to punish riders. As lower elevations are reached, the ride becomes more difficult because of the amount of dust that is kicked up. It is as fine as baby powder, and any slight disturbance sends it into the air, decreasing visibility and making it difficult to breathe. Better get out in front and stay out there, or hang back for a few minutes to let the dust settle.

Miles and Directions

0.0 From the parking area, pedal out to FSR 6210 and pedal up the road. Ignore spur roads on the way up.

2.8 Pass the Minnow Ridge Trail access point on the right.

3.0 Pass the Minnow Creek Trail (#1539) on the left.

5.3 Pass the Basalt Pass Trail (#1530) on the left.

7.8 Reach the intersection of FSR 6210 and Chikamin Tie Trail (#1561). Turn right and head downhill.

9.8 Turn left onto Chikamin Creek Trail and climb for roughly a mile. You'll cross three to five fingers of Chikamin Creek.

13.8 Look for the viewpoint to the left and slightly above the trail.

16.0 Turn right at the junction of the Chikamin Creek and Lower Chiwawa Trails.

16.5 Reach the parking area.

Ride Information

Local Information

Leavenworth Chamber of Commerce & Visitor Center, (509) 662–2116

Restaurants

Visconti's at the Brewery, (509) 548–1213
Dragonfire Pizza & Subs, (509) 548–5519

Northern Lights Pizza & Subs, (509) 548–5585

Gustavs, (509) 548–4509

Happy Clown Restaurant, (509) 763–3266
Note: All restaurants are located in Leavenworth.

39 Kachess Ridge Loop

Start: The Kachess Lake area
Length: 19.7 miles
Approximate riding time: 4 to 5 hours
Technical difficulty: Advanced due to length of ride and steep technical terrain
Trail surface: Forest roads, singletrack, creek crossings, and meadows
Trail contacts: Cle Elum Ranger Station, Cle Elum, (509) 674-4411
Fees and permits: None
Schedule: Open June through October, depending on snow levels
Maps: *Washington Atlas and Gazetteer*, page 65, B7; USGS Kachess Lake
Land status: National forest and the Department of Natural Resources

Nearest town: Easton
User density: Moderate
Other trail users: Hikers, equestrians
Canine compatibility: Dogs permitted on a leash but not recommended due to speed of descents.
Wheels: Cross-country to full suspension
Hazards: Walking across the scree-covered slope to access the trail (best to carry the bike) and steep sections and nasty switchbacks that virtually disappear as the trail erodes in various spots. Mosquitoes! Bring the bug repellant.

Finding the Trailhead

From Seattle, take I-90 east over Snoqualmie Pass. Take exit 70 (Easton/Sparks Road). At the stop sign, turn left and cross over I-90 to Sparks Road. Turn left and then take a right onto FSR 4818. Drive toward the power lines, and park beneath them on either side at FSR 201 or 203.

The Ride

A long, steep climb, stunning views of Mount Rainier and Kachess Lake, a hike-a-bike scramble over a scree-covered slope, a rapid-fire shot through mountain meadows, and dangerously eroded switchbacks all combine to make Kachess Ridge an excellent adventure in mountain biking. Located only a few miles on the east side of Snoqualmie Pass and above the tiny town of Easton, Washington, and above Kachess Lake, the Kachess Ridge Loop is a fantastic ride for advanced mountain bikers.

The Kachess Ridge Loop starts off with an easy 4.5-mile warm-up as the access road follows the east side of the lake. But don't let the leisurely ramble fool you. About a third of the way in, the route begins a long, steep climb to the top. Cyclists will climb nearly 3,000 feet in just 4 miles, making this a ride for mid- to late-season conditioning. Early in the season, it is a punishing workout.

The pain is worth the effort. Near the top of the ridge, riders are rewarded with awesome views of Mount Rainier to the south and the lake below. From this high up, the water is a dark Aquavelva green with occasional white slashes formed by the motorboats racing across the lake. The word "Kachess" (many fish or more fish) is derived from the native language of the Yakima Indian tribe.

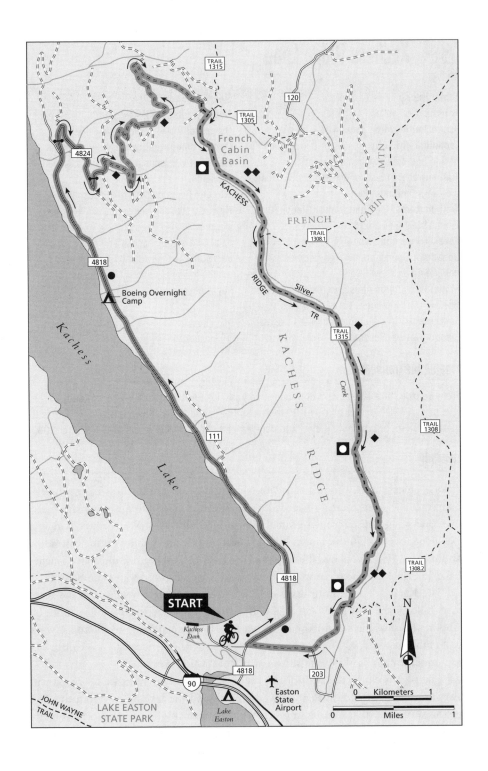

Another spectacular view of Mount Rainier

After dropping off the road and down the first stretch of singletrack, cyclists must carry their bikes across a loose scree-covered slope. This might be the most dangerous part of the ride. If you slip and fall, you're going to tumble for a while before stopping. But once at the top of the hike-a-bike, the real fun begins. From here it is nearly all downhill on fast and furious singletrack.

The trail drops down a short steep section littered with chunky rocks, ruts, drops, and roots before charging through mountain meadows that are often filled with wildflowers. And then the trail gets tricky. The trail dives into the forest, cuts through Silver Creek a number of times, and drops over sections that most riders will want to walk down. Wait—it gets even better. (Note sarcasm here!) Mountain bikers must navigate four to six nasty switchbacks that are badly eroded—so much so that the trail nearly disappears, making it a good plan to dismount and walk through these tight turns. If your riding partners mock you for not riding, simply tell them you believe in proper trail etiquette and preserving the great outdoors. The grade of the descent mellows out from this point on, allowing riders to hammer in the big ring. Be careful however; some mountain bikers prefer to ride up the singletrack instead of the road. Don't forget to find the spur trail that heads up and to the right for awesome views of Quartz Mountain, Easton, and Manastash Ridge.

The only flat section of Kachess Ridge

Miles and Directions

0.0 Ride north (away from I–90) on gravel-covered FSR 4818. (**FYI:** The road is superdry by late May; expect to be inhaling dust whenever an automobile passes by. FSR 4818 follows the east side of Kachess Lake as it heads north.)

2.2 Pass FSR 111.

4.1 Pass Boeing Overnight Camp.

5.9 Turn right onto FSR 4824 and let the climbing begin. Can you say "granny gear"?

7.0 Stay to the main road, ignoring the spur road on the right.

7.4 Stick to the right as the road turns back to the right and intersects with a road coming in on the left at the apex of the turn.

7.7 Follow the main road to the left at the big switchback, and ride through the logging gate at Mile 7.8.

8.8 Stay to the left as the road splits into a Y. Cross three streams in the next one-third mile.

9.9 Turn right at the Y onto FSR 115.

10.6 Turn right at Trail Marker 115. You should be looking at a saddle between a large angry crag on the right and a smaller one on the left.

10.7 After riding a short distance, look for the Kachess Ridge Trail (Trail #1315) on the left. It can be hard to spot, but you will find it at the back of a small cul-de-sac–like area that typically contains the remains of a campfire. The trail drops over the ridge to the north (away from the saddle) before cutting back in the opposite direction.

10.8 Take the right at the bottom of the descent.

STANDARD WASHINGTON STATE CAMPING FEES

$11.00 standard site

$16.00 utility site

$6.00 primitive site

$8.00 primitive site with motorized access

$8.00 daily dock moorage under 26 feet

$11.00 daily dock moorage 26 feet and over

$5.00 daily buoy moorage

$1.00 surcharge April 1 through September 30 at designated popular high-use parks

$2.00 per adult for more than four adults per campsite

$6.00 for second vehicle, unless towed by an RV

$3.00 trailer dump

$3.00–$4.00 boat launch (if camping, this fee included in campground fee)

11.4 Due to erosion, you'll most likely have to carry your bike across this section. Don't worry, the descent is worth it! A short ascent will take you to the top of the saddle to look down on the beautiful meadow below. There is a short, steep descent before the trail levels off as it cuts through the middle of the meadow.

14.7 Cross Silver Creek several times over the next 3 miles.

17.8 Follow the switchback to the left. (Do not cross the blocked trail intersection unless you want to see the viewpoint above I–90.)

18.4 Navigate through several more switchbacks.

19.2 Reach the end of Trail #1315. Stick to the main dirt road, and ride back to the power lines.

19.7 Turn right and reach the parking area.

Ride Information

Local Events and Attractions

Snoqualmie Winery Snoqualmie Pass, (509) 888–4000

Camping and Lodging

Lake Easton State Park, located 1 mile west of Easton on I–90. The park hosts more than ninety tent sites and more than forty utility sites with water, electricity, and sewer hookups. Campers can swim, fish, boat, or bike in summer and cross-country ski or snowshoe in the winter. For reservations call (800) 452–5687

Lake Easton Resort, (509) 656–2255. Open year-round, the resort offers A-frame cabins for $35 a night. Guests can swim, fish, boat, or bike in summer and cross-country ski or snowshoe in winter.

Restaurants

Bob's Barbecue, Friday through Sundays and holidays, 10:00 A.M.–6:00 P.M.

Family Pancake House, open twenty-four hours.

Note: Restaurants are located at the mountain bike center.

40 Fishhook Flats and Taneum Ridge Loop

Start: Taneum Junction Campground
Length: 14.4-mile loop
Approximate riding time: 3 to 4 hours
Technical difficulty: Moderate to advanced due to climb and creek crossings
Trail surface: Hard-pack singletrack, gravel roads
Trail contact: Cle Elum Ranger Station, (509) 674-4411
Fees and permits: $5.00 per car per day, $30.00 annual pass
Schedule: Open year-round, but only ridable early June to October due to the snow level

Maps: *Washington Atlas and Gazetteer,* page 61, D1; USGS Frost Mountain, Quartz Mountain, Ronald, Cle Elum
Land status: National forest
Nearest town: Thorpe
User density: Heavy
Other trail users: Motorcycles, hikers, equestrians
Canine compatibility: Dogs permitted on a leash
Wheels: Cross-country and dual suspension.
Hazards: Water crossings

Finding the Trailhead

From Seattle, head east on I-90 past Cle Elum. Take exit 93 (Elk Heights Road). Turn left and cross over the freeway, and then follow the road to the right. Look for the signs to Taneum Creek. At 0.03 mile, reach the T intersection and turn right, paralleling I-90 for roughly 3.5 miles. Cross back over the freeway and turn right onto West Taneum Creek Road, which turns into FSR 33. Follow for 10.5 miles to FSR 3300 and turn left. Cross the creek and park at the Taneum Junction Forest Camp.

The Ride

Located outside the ninety-minute driving zone from Puget Sound (this ride is simply too good to ignore), the combination of Fishhook Flats and the North Fork Taneum Trail is an interval-style training session of challenging ascents and wicked downhill spurts. Add the Hotwheel track–like trails, banked turns, amazing surroundings, and a soothing symphony of natural sound emanating from Taneum Creek, and this trail is a must ride for any mountain biker.

Despite the name, there is nothing really flat about **Fishhook Flats.** The route immediately begins to climb up the forest service road and then quickly descends to the south fork of Taneum Creek. Riders are allowed to warm up as the terrain rolls up and down along the creek and past a run-down log cabin. There isn't much left to it but it will provide shelter if a sudden mountain storm stirs up. Be prepared for anything—you are riding through the backcountry. The climbing reconvenes shortly after the cabin and doesn't let up until it reaches the high point of the ride (4,200 feet) and the top of the Fishhook Flats Trail.

Here is where the fun begins! The next 2 miles shoot downhill over motorcycle-induced whoop-de-dos, around banked turns, and over drops of various sizes formed

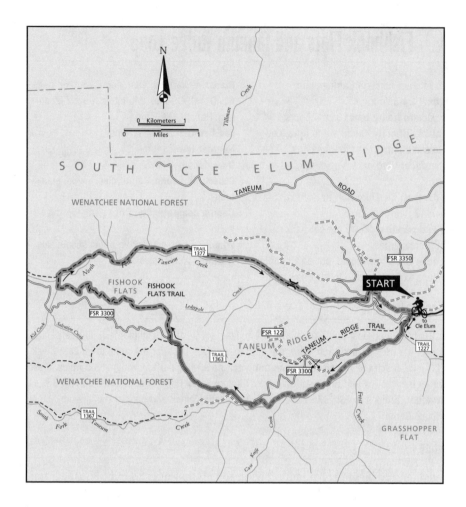

by roots and rocks. Full-suspension bikes will provide riders with a definite advantage. The trail is rough enough to bounce riders out of the saddle on a regular basis.

Due to the area's location on the east side of the Cascades, the trail is usually dry and dusty. In many areas the dirt and dust are so fine that simply riding through causes a cloud to fill the air, making it difficult to breath and to see the trail. It's best to be out in front of the pack or hang back to let the dust settle. Also be aware that it is common for the front wheel to wash out while blasting through those banked turns.

Now get ready for interval training. The route continually loses elevation, but not before riding up and down the ridge to and away from the creek. Both the ascents and the descents are steep, with abrupt transitions. Keep your speed consistent and perhaps even a little slower than normal. It will allow you to time your shifts accurately so that you can pedal up the climbs instead of having to dismount. Every single one of them is ridable, but not if a rider blows the transitions/shifts and tries to climb in the big rings.

One of ten new bridges across Taneum Creek

It used to be that getting wet on this ride couldn't be avoided. The trail crosses Taneum Creek more than ten times, and there used to be no alternative but to ride/wade across. Today, however, the Forest Service has built a bridge at every fording location. Be sure to repay the favor by paying the $5.00-per-day permit fee at the beginning of your ride.

Riders hit the road and the last section of the ride at just over 13 miles. By now most riders are tired, sore, and thirsty. But there is no rest for the weary, as there is one more major climb. The last climb is not the steepest, but after negotiating nearly 90 percent of the route, it will feel like it. The alternative is to hang a right at the road and head downhill. But don't wimp out! Suck it up, climb to the top, and then hang on as the trail heads downhill to the road and Taneum Junction.

Miles and Directions

0.0   From Taneum Junction, ride up FSR 3300.

0.5   Turn left on Spur Road 135. It immediately drops down a small hill and follows the South Fork of Taneum Creek.

0.9   Stay to the right when the road splits, and climb up above the creek. The route alternates between singletrack and dual track.

1.5   Pass a spur road on the right and the remains of a foundation.

1.6   Pass an old log cabin on the right. The trail turns into a dirt road.

3.0   After two or three short but steep climbs, turn left onto FSR 3300.

3.1   Pass trails on the right as well as FSR 3322, and continue the gradual ascent up FSR 3300.

3.8 Cross Spur Road 130.

4.1 Pass unmarked road and yellow gate on the right.

4.5 Pass the Taneum Ridge Trail (Trail #1363) on the right and left. Also pass a gravel road and yellow gate on the right just after Taneum Ridge Trail.

4.7 Pass the dual track on the left and the yellow gate on the right, and then turn right on Fishhook Flats Trail (Trail #1378) at Mile 4.73. (The trail begins to descend toward the north fork of Taneum Creek. This descent rocks! But keep an ear open for motorcycles, and pay attention to the large divots they dig when climbing up this trail. Navigating them can be tricky, and more than one mountain biker has been bounced out of the saddle by them.)

6.1 Reach the bottom of the first major descent and cross a small meadow before climbing up the ridge.

6.9 Take a breather and get ready for the second major downhill section. Be prepared for several short, steep climbs as the trail rolls up and down with the terrain. The transitions are wickedly abrupt.

7.9 Cross the bridge and turn right onto the North Fork Taneum Trail (Trail #1377). Although the route drops in elevation, the trail follows the ridgeline up and down and back and forth away from the creek. (This section takes its toll on riders. Take a quick break and suck some Power Gel or Gu. You're going to need it!)

9.3 Turn left and cross the bridge.

12.5–13.2 Cross the road and begin climbing up the steep section of singletrack. Or turn right and head down the road back to the car.

13.6 The climbing is over! Turn right onto the old dirt road/South Cle Elum Ridge Trail, and head downhill. (The trail is heavily sprinkled with jagged rocks the size of melons, not to mention bunches of whoop-de-dos! Hang on and stay focused!)

14.0 Find the sign to Taneum Junction and make a hard right, continuing downhill.

14.4 Reach the road, cross the bridge, and pedal back to the parking area. Arrive back at Taneum Junction.

Ride Information

Local Information
Cle Elum Chamber of Commerce,
(509) 674-5958

Local Events
Ellensburg Rodeo and Fair, late August—early September; P.O. Box 777, Ellensburg, WA 98926; www.ellensburgrodeo.com

Restaurants
El Caporal Mexican Restaurant,
(509) 674-4284
Little River Soup & Sandwich,
(509) 674-6917

Sunset Cafe & Quetzal Room,
(509) 674-9965
Note: Above establishments are all in Cle Elum.

Camping
Taneum Road #33, 18 miles south of Cle Elum. There are thirteen campsites, twelve picnic sites, vault toilets, tables, stoves, a community kitchen, potable water, and Taneum Guard Station rental. Rates: $10.00 single, $20.00 double, $8.00 per extra vehicle per night.

The Art of Mountain Biking

Within these pages you will find everything you need to know about off-road bicycling in the Puget Sound region. This section begins by exploring the fascinating history of the mountain bike itself, then goes on to discuss everything from the health benefits of off-road cycling to tips and techniques for bicycling over logs and up and down hills. Also included are the types of clothing to keep you comfortable and in style, essential equipment ideas to keep your rides smooth and trouble-free, and descriptions of off-road terrain to prepare you for the kinds of bumps and bounces you can expect to encounter.

The mountain bike, with its knobby tread and reinforced frame, takes cyclists to places once unheard of—down rugged mountain trails, through streams of rushing water, across the frozen Alaskan tundra, and even to work in the city. There seem to be few limits on what this fat-tired beast can do and where it can take us. Few obstacles stand in its way, few boundaries slow its progress, except for one—its own success. If trail closure means little to you now, read on and discover how a trail can be here today and gone tomorrow. With so many new off-road cyclists taking to the trails each year, it's no wonder that trail access hangs precariously between universal acceptance and complete termination. But a little work on your part can go a long way toward preserving trail access for future riders. Nothing is more crucial to the survival of mountain biking than reading the examples set forth in the following pages and practicing their message.

Without open trails, the maps in this book are virtually useless. Cyclists must learn to be responsible for the trails they use—and to share these trails with others. This guidebook addresses such issues as why trail use has become so controversial, what can be done to improve the image of mountain biking, how to have fun and ride responsibly, on-the-spot trail repair techniques, trail maintenance hot lines for each trail, and the worldwide-standard Rules of the Trail.

Mountain Bike Beginnings

It seems the mountain bike—originally designed for lunatic adventurists bored with straight lines, clean clothes, and smooth tires—has become globally popular in as short a time as it would take to race down a mountain trail.

How big is that fork?

Like many other things of a revolutionary nature, the mountain bike was born on the West Coast. But unlike Rollerblades, purple hair, and the peace sign, the concept of the off-road bike cannot be credited solely to the imaginative Californians—they were just the first to make waves.

The design of the first off-road-specific bike was based on the geometry of the old Schwinn Excelsior, a one-speed, camelback cruiser with balloon tires. Joe Breeze was the creator behind it, and in 1977 he built ten of these "Breezers" for himself and his Marin County, California, friends at $750 apiece—a bargain compared with the cost of bikes today.

Breeze was a serious competitor in bicycle racing, placing thirteenth in the 1977 U.S. Road Racing National Championships. After races, he and friends would scour local bike shops, hoping to find old bikes they could then restore.

The 1941 Schwinn Excelsior that Breeze paid just $5.00 for began to shape and change bicycling history forever. After taking the bike home, removing the fenders, oiling the chain, and pumping up the tires, Breeze hit the dirt. He loved it.

His inspiration was not altogether unique, however. Nearly 2,500 miles from Marin County, East Coast bike bums were also growing restless. More and more old beat-up clunkers were being restored and modified. These behemoths often weighed as much as eighty pounds and were so reinforced they seemed virtually indestructible. But rides that take just forty minutes on today's twenty-five-pound featherweights took the steel-toe-booted, blue-jean-clad bikers of the late 1970s and early 1980s nearly four hours to complete.

Not until 1981 was it possible to purchase a production mountain bike, but local retailers found these ungainly bicycles difficult to sell and rarely kept them in stock. By 1983, however, mountain bikes were no longer a fringe item, and large bike manufacturers quickly jumped into the action, producing their own versions of the off-road bike. By the 1990s the mountain bike had firmly established its place with bicyclists of nearly all ages and abilities and now commands nearly 90 percent of the U.S. bike market. Mountain biking is even an official Olympic event.

There are many reasons for the mountain bike's success. Mountain bikes are much friendlier to the cyclist than traditional road bikes because of their comfortable upright position and shock-absorbing fat tires. And because of the health-conscious, environmentalist movement of the late 1980s and 1990s, people are more activity minded and seek nature on a closer front than paved roads can allow. The mountain bike gives you these things and takes you far away from the daily grind—even if you're only minutes from the city.

Mountain Biking into Shape

If your objective is to get in shape and lose weight, then you're on the right track, because mountain biking is one of the best ways to get started.

One way many of us have lost weight in this sport is the crash-and-burn-it-off method. Picture this: You're speeding uncontrollably down a vertical drop that you realize you shouldn't be on—only after it is too late. Your front wheel lodges into a rut and launches you through endless weeds, trees, and pointy rocks before coming to an abrupt halt in a puddle of thick mud. Surveying the damage you discover that, with the layers of skin, body parts, and lost confidence littering the trail above, those unwanted pounds have been shed—instant weight loss!

There is, of course, a more conventional (and quite a bit less painful) approach to losing weight and gaining fitness on a mountain bike. It's called the workout, and bicycles provide an ideal way to get physical.

Cycling helps you shed pounds without gimmicky diet fads or weight-loss programs. You can explore the countryside and burn nearly 10 to 16 calories per minute, or close to 600 to 1,000 calories per hour. Moreover, it's a great way to spend an afternoon.

No less significant than the external and cosmetic changes of your body from riding are the internal changes. Over time, cycling regularly will strengthen your heart as your body grows vast networks of new capillaries to carry blood to all those working muscles. This will, in turn, give your skin a healthier glow. The capacity of your lungs may increase up to 20 percent, and your resting heart rate will drop significantly. The Stanford University School of Medicine reports to the American Heart Association that people can reduce their risk of heart attack by nearly 64 percent if they can burn up to 2,000 calories per week. This is only two to three hours of bike riding!

Recommended for insomnia, hypertension, indigestion, anxiety, and even for recuperation from major heart attacks, bicycling can be an excellent cure-all as well as a great preventive. Cycling just a few hours per week can improve your figure and sleeping habits, give you greater resistance to illness, increase your energy levels, and provide feelings of accomplishment and heightened self-esteem.

Be Safe—Know the Law

Occasionally, even hardcore off-road cyclists will find they have no choice but to ride the pavement. When you are forced to hit the road, it's important to know and understand the rules.

Outlined below are a few of Washington's rules of the road:

- Follow the same driving rules as motorists. Obey all road signs and traffic lights.
- Wear a helmet and bright clothing so that you are more visible to motorists. Bright colors such as orange and lime green are also more visible at night.

- Equip your bike with lights, and wear reflective clothing if you plan to ride at night. Night riders or their bikes must be equipped with a white light visible at least 500 feet to the front and a red light or reflector visible at least 600 feet to the rear.
- Pass motorists on the left, not on the right. Motorists are not expecting you to pass on the right, and they may not see you.
- Ride single file on busy roads so that motorists can pass you safely.
- Stop off the roadway.
- Use hand signals to alert motorists of what you plan to do next.
- Ride with the traffic, not against it.
- Follow painted lane markings.
- Make eye contact with drivers. Assume they they don't see you until you are sure they do.
- Ride in the middle of the lane at busy intersections and whenever you are moving at the same speed as traffic.
- Slow down and announce your presence when passing pedestrians, cyclists, and horses.
- Don't ride out to the curb between parked cars unless they are far apart. Motorists may not see you when you try to move back into traffic
- Turn left by looking back, signaling, getting into the left lane, and then turning. In urban situations, continue straight to the crosswalk and walk your bike across the crosswalk when the pedestrian walk sign is illuminated.
- Never ride while under the influence of alcohol or drugs. DUI laws apply when you're riding a bicycle.
- Avoid riding in extreme foggy, rainy, or windy conditions.
- Watch out for road hazards, such as parallel-slat sewer grates, slippery manhole covers, oily pavement, gravel, wet leaves, and ice.
- Cross railroad tracks as perpendicular as possible. Be especially careful when it's wet out. For better control as you move across bumps and other hazards, stand up on your pedals.
- Don't ride too close to parked cars—a person opening a car door may hit you.
- Avoid riding on sidewalks. Walk your bike. Pedestrians have the right-of-way on walkways. By law, you must give pedestrians audible warning when you pass. Use a bike bell or announce clearly, "On your left/right."
- Slow down at street crossings and driveways.

The Mountain Bike Controversy

Are Off-Road Bicyclists Environmental Outlaws? Do We Have the Right to Use Public Trails?

Mountain bikers have long endured the animosity of folks in the backcountry who complain about the consequences of off-road bicycling. Many people believe that the fat tires and knobby tread do unacceptable environmental damage and that our uncontrollable riding habits are a danger to animals and to other trail users. To the contrary, mountain bikes have no more environmental impact than hiking boots or horseshoes. This does not mean, however, that mountain bikes leave no imprint at all. Wherever humans tread, there is an impact. By riding responsibly, though, it is possible to make that impact minimal—something we all must take care to achieve.

Unfortunately, it is often people of great influence who view the mountain bike as the environment's worst enemy. Consequently, we, as mountain bike riders and environmentally concerned citizens, must be educators, impressing upon others that we also deserve the right to use these trails. Our responsibilities as bicyclists are no more and no less than any other trail user. We must all take the soft-cycling approach and show that mountain bicyclists are not environmental outlaws. For more information on trail preservation and advocacy, call the Back Country Bicycle Trails Club at (206) 283–2995, send an e-mail to bbtc@cycling.org, or visit www.bbtc.org. You can also call the King County Parks Department at (206) 296–2966.

Mountain Bike Etiquette

When discussing mountain bike etiquette, we are in essence discussing the soft-cycling approach. This term describes the art of minimum-impact bicycling and should apply to both the physical and social dimensions of the sport. But make no mistake—it is possible to ride fast and furiously while maintaining the balance of soft-cycling. Here, first, are a few ways to minimize the environmental impact of mountain bike riding.

- **Stay on the trail.** Don't ride around fallen trees or mud holes that block your path. Stop and cross over them. When you come to a vista overlooking a deep valley, don't ride off the trail for a better vantage point. Instead, leave the bike and walk to see the view. Riding off the trail may seem inconsequential when done only once, but soon someone else will follow, then others, and the cumulative results can be catastrophic. Each time you wander from the trail, you begin creating a new path, adding one more scar to the earth's surface.
- **Do not disturb the soil.** Follow a line within the trail that will not disturb or damage the soil.

- **Do not ride over soft or wet trails.** After a rain shower or during the thawing season, trails will often resemble muddy, oozing swampland. The best thing to do is stay off the trails altogether. Realistically, however, we're all going to come across some muddy trails we cannot anticipate. Instead of blasting through each section of mud, which may seem both easier and more fun, lift the bike and walk past. Each time a cyclist rides through a soft or muddy section of trail, that part of the trail is permanently damaged. Regardless of the trail's conditions, remember always to go *over* obstacles across the path, not around them. Stay on the trail.
- **Avoid trails that, for all but God, are considered impassable and impossible.** Don't take a leap of faith down a kamikaze descent on which you will be forced to lock your brakes and skid to the bottom, ripping the ground apart as you go.

Soft-cycling should also apply to the social dimensions of the sport, since mountain bikers are not the only folks who use the trails. Hikers, equestrians, cross-country skiers, and other outdoors people use many of the same trails and can be easily spooked by a marauding mountain biker tearing through the trees. Be friendly in the forest, and give ample warning of your approach.

- **Take out what you bring in.** Don't leave broken bike pieces and banana peels scattered along the trail.
- **Be aware of your surroundings.** Don't use popular hiking trails for race training.
- **Slow down!** Rocketing around blind corners is a sure way to ruin an unsuspecting hiker's day. Consider this: If you fly down a quick singletrack descent at 20 mph, then hit the brakes and slow down to 6 mph to pass someone, you're still moving twice as fast as he or she is!

Like the trails we ride on, the social dimension of mountain biking is very fragile and must be cared for responsibly. By riding in the backcountry with caution, control, and responsibility, our presence should be felt positively by other trail users. By adhering to these rules, trail riding—a privilege that can quickly be taken away—will continue to be ours to share.

Trail Maintenance

Unfortunately, despite all the preventive measures taken to avoid trail damage, we're still going to run into many trails requiring attention. Simply put, a lot of hikers, equestrians, and cyclists alike use the same trails—some wear and tear is unavoidable. But like your bike, if you want to use these trails for a long time to come, you must also maintain them.

Trail maintenance and restoration can be accomplished in a variety of ways. One way is for mountain bike clubs to combine efforts with other trail users (i.e., hikers and equestrians) and work closely with land managers to cut new trails or repair existing ones. This not only reinforces to others the commitment cyclists have in caring for and maintaining the land but also breaks down the barriers that often separate cyclists from their fellow trailmates. Another good way to help out is to show up on a Saturday morning with a few riding buddies at your favorite off-road domain ready to work. With a good attitude, thick gloves, and the local land manager's supervision, trail repair is fun and very rewarding. It's important, of course, that you arrange a trail-repair outing with the local land manager before you start pounding shovels into the dirt. Managers can lead you to the most needy sections of trail and instruct you on what repairs should be done and how best to accomplish the task. Perhaps the most effective means of trail maintenance, though, can be done by yourself—while you're riding. Read on.

On-the-Spot Quick Fix

When riding, most of us have at one time or another come upon muddy trails or fallen trees blocking our path. Over time the mud gets deeper and the trail gets wider as people go through or around the obstacles. We worry that the problem will become so severe and repairs so difficult that the trail's access may be threatened. We also know that our ambition to do anything about it is greatest at that moment, not after a hot shower and a plate of spaghetti. Here are a few on-the-spot quick fixes that will hopefully correct a problem before it gets out of hand—and get you back on your bike within minutes.

Muddy Trails: What do you do when trails develop huge mud holes destined for EPA Superfund status? The repair technique is called corduroying, and it works much like building a pontoon over the mud to support bikes, horses, or hikers as they cross. "Corduroy" (not the pants) is the term for roads made of logs laid down crosswise. Use small- and medium-sized sticks and lay them side by side across the trail until they cover the length of the muddy section (break the sticks to fit the width of the trail). Press them into the mud with your feet, then lay more on top if needed. Keep adding sticks until the trail is firm. Not only will you stay clean as you cross, but the sticks may soak up some of the water and help the puddle dry. This quick fix may last as long as one month before needing to be redone. And as time goes on, with new layers added to the trail, the soil will grow stronger, thicker, and more resistant to erosion. This whole process may take fewer than five minutes, and you can be on your way, knowing the trail behind you is in good repair.

Leaving the Trail: What do you do to keep other cyclists from cutting corners and leaving the designated trail? The solution is much simpler than you may think. (No, don't hire an off-road police force.) Notice where people are leaving the trail, and throw a pile of thick branches or brush along the path, or place logs across the opening to block the way through. There are probably dozens of subtle tricks like these that will manipulate people into staying on the designated trail. If executed well, no one will even notice that the thick branches scattered along the ground in the woods weren't always there. And most folks would probably rather take a moment to hop a log in the trail than get tangled in a web of branches.

Obstacle in the Way: If there are large obstacles blocking the trail, try and remove them or push them aside. If you cannot do this by yourself, call the trail maintenance hot line to speak with the land manager of that particular trail and see what can be done.

We must be willing to sweat for our trails in order to sweat on them. Police yourself and point out to others the significance of trail maintenance. "Sweat Equity," the rewards of continued land use won with a fair share of sweat, pays off when the trail is "up for review" by the land manager and he or she remembers the efforts made by trail-conscious mountain bikers.

Rules of the Trail

The International Mountain Bicycling Association (IMBA) has developed these guidelines to trail riding. These "Rules of the Trail" are accepted worldwide and will go a long way in keeping trails open. Please respect and follow these rules for everyone's sake.

1. Ride only on open trails. Respect trail and road closures (if you're not sure, ask a park or state official first), do not trespass on private property, and obtain permits or authorization if required. Federal and state wilderness areas are off-limits to cycling. Parks and state forests may also have certain trails closed to cycling.

2. Zero impact. Be sensitive to the dirt beneath you. Even on open trails, don't ride under conditions that will cause you to leave evidence of your passing, such as on certain soils or shortly after a rainfall. Be sure to observe the different types of soils and trails you're riding on, practicing minimal-impact cycling. Never ride off the trail, don't skid your tires, and be sure to bring out at least as much as you bring in.

3. Control your bicycle! Inattention for even one second can cause disaster for you or for others. Excessive speed frightens and can injure other trail users, gives mountain biking a bad name, and can result in trail closures.

4. Always yield. Let others know you're coming well in advance (a friendly greeting is always good and often appreciated). Show your respect when passing others by slowing to walking speed or stopping altogether, especially in the presence of horses. Horses can be unpredictable, so be very careful. Anticipate that other trail users may be around corners or in blind spots.

5. Never spook animals. Sudden movements, unannounced approaches, or loud noises spook all animals. Give animals extra room and time so that they can adjust to you. Move slowly or dismount around animals. Running cattle and disturbing wild animals are serious offenses. Leave gates as you find them, or as marked.

6. Plan ahead. Know your equipment, your ability, and the area in which you are riding, and plan your trip accordingly. Be self-sufficient at all times; keep your bike in good repair, and carry necessary supplies for changes in weather or other conditions. You can help keep trails open by setting an example of responsible, courteous, and controlled mountain bike riding.

7. Always wear a helmet when you ride. For your own safety and protection, wear a helmet whenever you are riding your bike. You never know when a tree root or small rock will send you flying.

Thousands of miles of dirt trails have been closed to mountain bicycling because of the irresponsible riding habits of just a few riders. Don't follow the example of these offending riders. Don't take away trail privileges from thousands of others who work hard each year to keep the backcountry avenues open to us all.

Food and Water

It's essential to keep yourself hydrated and energized when you're on the trail.

- **Water.** Without it, cyclists may face dehydration, which may result in dizziness and fatigue. On a warm day, cyclists should drink at least one full bottle of water during every hour of riding. Remember, drink *before* you feel thirsty.
- **Food.** This essential item will keep you rolling. Cycling burns up a lot of calories and is among the few sports in which no one is safe from the "Bonk." Bonking feels like it sounds. Without food in your system, your blood sugar and energy level collapse, resulting in fatigue and light-headedness. So when you're filling your water bottle, remember to bring along some food. Fruit, energy bars, or other forms of high-energy food are highly recommended. Candy bars are not, however; they will deliver a sudden burst of high energy, only to let you down soon after, causing you to feel worse than before. Energy bars are available at most bike stores and are similar to candy bars, but they provide complex carbohydrate energy and high nutrition rather than fast-burning simple sugars.

Be like a Boy Scout

Essential Equipment

Do you remember the Boy Scout motto? Like them, you should always be prepared. The following is a list of essential equipment that will keep you from having to walk out a long trail, being stranded in the woods, or even losing your life.

- Spare tube
- Tire irons: See "Repair and Maintenance" for instructions on fixing flat tires.
- Patch kit
- Pump

- Money (Spare change for emergency calls.)
- Spoke wrench
- Spare spokes to fit your wheel. Tape these to the chain stay.
- Chain tool
- Allen keys: Bring appropriate sizes to fit your bike.
- Compass
- First-aid kit: See sidebar.
- Rain gear: For quick changes in the weather.
- Matches
- Guidebook: If all else fails and you must start a fire to survive, this guidebook will serve as excellent fire starter!

To carry these items, you'll need some type of bike bag or pack. A bag mounted in front of the handlebars provides quick access to your belongings but changes the steering ability of the bike. A saddle bag fitted underneath the saddle keeps things out of your way but carries very little. Panniers, which mount on each side of the rear or front wheels, carry a tremendous amount of cargo. But they change the weight and feel of the bike considerably. You won't need them to do any of the rides in this book, and unless you are riding and camping, panniers will only decrease the fun you can have on a bike.

A backpack will be sufficient to carry the items on the list. There are currently many streamlined backpacks with hydration systems on the market to choose from. Many cyclists, though, prefer not to use a pack. They just slip all they need into their jersey pockets, and off they go.

Be Safe–Wear Protection

While on the subject of jerseys, it's crucial to discuss the clothing you must wear to be safe, practical—even stylish. The following is a list of items that will help save you from disaster, outfit you comfortably, and, most important, keep you looking cool.

- **Helmet:** A helmet is an absolute necessity—it protects your head from complete annihilation. It is the only thing that will not disintegrate into a million pieces after a wicked crash on a descent you shouldn't have been on in the first place. A helmet with a solid exterior shell will also protect your head from sharp or protruding objects. Of course, with a hard-shelled helmet, you can paste several stickers of your favorite bicycle manufacturers all over the outer shell, giving companies even more free advertising for your dollar.
- **Shorts:** Padded cycle shorts provide cushioning between your body and the bicycle seat. Cycle shorts also wick moisture away from your body and prevent chafing. Form-fitting shorts are made from synthetic material and have smooth

seams to avoid chafing. If you don't feel comfortable wearing form-fitting shorts, baggy-style padded shorts with pockets are also available.

- **Gloves:** You may find well-padded cycling gloves invaluable when traveling over rocky trails and gravelly roads for hours on end. When you fall off your bike and land on your palms, gloves are your best friend. Long-fingered gloves may also be useful when branches, trees, assorted hard objects, and, occasionally, small animals reach out and whack your knuckles. Insulated gloves are essential for winter riding.

- **Sunglasses.** Not only do sunglasses give you an imposing presence and make you look cool (both are extremely important), they also protect your eyes from harmful ultraviolet rays, invisible branches, creepy bugs, and dirt—and may prevent you from being caught sneaking glances at riders of the opposite sex also wearing skintight, revealing Lycra™.

- **Shoes:** Mountain bike shoes are constructed with stiff soles in order to transfer more of the power from a pedal stroke to the drive train and to provide a solid platform to stand on, decreasing fatigue in your feet. You can use virtually any good light outdoor hiking footwear, but specific mountain bike shoes (especially those with inset cleats) are best. They are lighter, breathe better, and are constructed to work with your pedal strokes instead of the natural walking cadence.

- **The layered look:** To prepare for Washington's weather, dress in layers that can be added or removed as weather conditions change. In cold weather, wear a wicking layer made of a modern synthetic fiber next to your skin. Avoid wearing cotton of any type, which dries slowly and does not wick moisture away from your skin, thus chilling you directly as it evaporates. The next layer should be a wool or synthetic insulating layer that helps keep you warm but also is breathable. A fleece jacket or vest works well as an insulating layer. The outer layer should be a jacket and pants that are waterproof, windproof, and breathable. Your ears will also welcome a fleece headband when it's cold out.

First-Aid Kit

- Band-Aids
- mole skin
- various sterile gauze and dressings
- white surgical tape
- an Ace bandage
- an antihistamine
- aspirin
- Betadine solution
- a first-aid book
- Tums
- tweezers
- scissors
- antibacterial wipes
- triple-antibiotic ointment
- plastic gloves
- sterile cotton-tip applicators
- syrup of ipecac (to induce vomiting)
- thermometer
- wire splint

Oh, Those Cold, Wet, Puget Sound Days

If the weather chooses not to cooperate on the day you've set aside for a bike ride, the following can help you stay comfortable:

- **Tights or leg warmers.** These are best in temperatures below 55°Fahrenheit. Knees are sensitive and can develop all kinds of problems if they get cold, including tendonitis, bursitis, and arthritis.

- **Plenty of layers on your upper body.** When the air has a nip to it, layers of clothing will keep the chill away from your chest. If the air is cool, wear a polypropylene or Capilene™ long-sleeved shirt against the skin beneath other layers of clothing. Polypropylene or Capilene, like wool, wicks moisture away from your skin to keep your body dry. Avoid wearing cotton or baggy clothing when the temperature falls. Cotton, as mentioned before, holds moisture like a sponge, and baggy clothing catches cold air and swirls it around your body. Good cold-weather clothing should fit snugly against your body but not be restrictive.

- **Wool socks.** Don't pack too many layers under those shoes, though. If you restrict circulation, your feet will get real cold, real fast.

- **Thinsulate™ or Gortex™ gloves.** There is nothing worse than frozen feet—unless it's frozen hands. A good pair of Thinsulate™ or Gortex™ gloves should keep your hands toasty warm.

- **Hat or helmet on cold days.** When the weather gets really cold and you still want to hit the trails, it's sometimes tough to stay warm. A large percent of the body's heat escapes through the head (overactive brains, I imagine), so it's important to keep the cranium warm. Ventilated helmets are designed to keep heads cool in the summer heat, but they do little to help keep heads warm in subzero temperatures. Capilene™ skullcaps are great head and ear warmers that fit snugly over your head beneath the helmet so that head protection is not lost. Another option is a helmet cover that covers those ventilating gaps and helps keep the body heat in. These do not, however, keep your ears warm. Some cyclists will opt for a simple knit cycling cap sans the helmet, but these have never been shown to be very good cranium protectors.

All of this clothing can be found at your local bike store, where the staff should be happy to match your garb to the seasons of the year.

To Have or Not to Have . . . Other Very Useful Items

There is no shortage of items for you and your bike to make riding better, safer, and easier. We have rummaged through the unending lists and separated the gadgets from the good stuff, coming up with what we believe are items certain to enhance your mountain bike riding experience:

- **Tires.** Buying a good pair of knobby tires is the quickest way to enhance the off-road handling capabilities of a bike. There are many types of mountain bike tires on the market. Some are made exclusively for very rugged off-road terrain. These big-knobbed, soft-rubber tires virtually stick to the ground with magnetlike traction but tend to deteriorate quickly on pavement. Other tires are made exclusively for the road. These are called "slicks" and have no tread at all. For the average cyclist, though, a good tire somewhere in the middle of these two extremes should do the trick. Realize, however, that you get what you pay for. Do not skimp! As your primary point of contact with the trail, tires may be the most important piece of equipment on a bike. With inexpensive rubber, the tire's beads may unravel or chunks of tread actually rip off the tire. If you're lucky, all you'll suffer is a long walk back to the car. If you're unlucky, your tire could blow out in the middle of a rowdy downhill, causing a wicked crash.

- **Clipless pedals.** Clipless pedals, like ski bindings, attach your shoe directly to the pedal. They allow you to exert pressure on the pedals during both the down and up strokes. They also help you maneuver the bike while in the air or climbing various obstacles. Toe clips may be less expensive, but they are also heavier and harder to use. Clipless pedals and toe clips take a little getting used to, but they're definitely worth the trouble.

- **Bar ends.** These clamp-on additions to your original straight bar will provide more leverage, an excellent grip for climbing, and a more natural position for your hands. Be aware, however, of the bar end's propensity for hooking trees on fast descents, sending you airborne. Opinions are divided on the general usefulness of bar ends these days, and over the past few years bar ends have fallen out of favor with manufacturers and riders alike.

- **Backpack.** These bags are ideal for carrying keys, extra food and water, guidebooks, foul-weather clothing, tools, spare tubes, and a cellular phone—in case you need to call for help.

- **Suspension forks.** For off-roaders who want nothing to impede their speed on the trails, investing in a pair of suspension forks is a good idea. Like tires, there are plenty of brands to choose from, and they all do the same thing—absorb the brutal beatings of a rough trail. The cost of these forks, however, is sometimes more brutal than the trail itself.

- **Bike computers.** These are fun gadgets to own and are much less expensive than in years past. They have such features as trip distance, speedometer, odometer, time of day, altitude, alarm, average speed, maximum speed, heart rate, and global satellite positioning. Bike computers will come in handy when following the maps in this book—or to help you determine just how far you've ridden in the wrong direction.

- **Hydration pack.** This is quickly becoming an essential item for cyclists pedaling for more than a few hours, especially in hot, dry conditions. The most popular brand is the Camelback™, and these water packs can carry as much as one hundred ounces of water in their bladder bags. These packs strap on your back, with a handy hose running over your shoulder so that you can be drinking water while still holding onto the bars with both hands on a rocky descent. These packs are a great way to carry a lot of extra liquid on hot rides in the middle of nowhere, plus keys, a camera, extra food, guidebooks, tools, spare tubes—and that cellular phone.

Trail Types and Obstacles

Lay of the Land

- **Rails-to-Trails.** Abandoned rail lines are converted into public resources for exercising, commuting, or just enjoying nature. Old rails and ties are torn up and a trail, paved or unpaved, is laid along the existing corridor. This completes the cycle from ancient Indian trading routes to railroad corridors and back again to hiking and cycling trails.

- **Forest Roads.** These dirt and gravel roads are used primarily as access to forestland and are generally kept in good condition. They are almost always open to public use. Although a gravel road may sound tame and inviting, it can be even more dangerous than a singletrack trail. Riders must contend with logging trucks, automobiles, dust, and unstable trail surfaces.

- **Singletrack.** This is the reason we live to ride and ride to live. No other trail is as fun as a silky-smooth ribbon of narrow, fast, roller coaster–like, kinky, challenging singletrack.

- **Open land.** Unless there is a marked trail through a field or open space, you should not plan to ride here. Once one person cuts his or her wheels through a field or meadow, many more are sure to follow, causing irreparable damage to the landscape—and the ire of the landowner or manager.

Back-Road Obstacles

- **Logs.** When you want to hop a log, throw your body back, yank up on the handlebars, and pedal forward in one swift motion. This clears the front end of the bike. Then quickly scoot forward and pedal the rear wheel up and over. Keep the forward momentum until you've cleared the log; by all means, don't hit the brakes, or you may do some interesting acrobatic maneuvers!

- **Rocks and roots.** Worse than highway potholes! Stay relaxed, let your elbows and knees absorb the shock, and always continue applying power to your pedals. Staying seated will keep the rear wheel weighted to prevent slipping, and a light front end will help you to respond quickly to each new obstacle. The slower you go, the more time your tires will have to get caught between the grooves.

- **Water.** Before crossing a stream or a puddle, first check the depth and bottom surface. An unseen hole or large rock hidden under the water could wash you up if you're not careful. After you're sure all is safe, hit the water at a good speed, pedal steadily, and allow the bike to steer you through. Once you're across, tap the breaks to squeegee the water off the rims.
- **Leaves.** Be careful of wet leaves. These may look pretty, but a trail covered with leaves may cause your wheels to slip out from under you. Leaves are not nearly as unpredictable and dangerous as ice, but they do warrant your attention on a rainy day.
- **Mud.** If you must ride through mud, hit it head on and keep pedaling. You want to part the ooze with your front wheel and get across before it swallows you up. Above all, don't leave the trail to go around the mud. This just widens the path and leads to increased trail erosion.

Urban Obstacles
- **Curbs** are fun to jump, but, as with logs, be careful.
- **Curbside drains** are typically not a problem for bikes. Just be careful not to get a wheel caught in the grate.
- **Dogs** make great pets but seem to have it in for bicyclists. If you think you can't outrun a dog that's chasing you, stop and walk your bike out of its territory. A loud yell to "Get!" or "Go home!" often works—so does a sharp squirt from your water bottle right between the eyes.
- **Cars** are tremendously convenient when we're in them, but dodging irate motorists in big automobiles becomes a real hazard when you're riding a bike. As a cyclist, you must realize that most drivers aren't expecting you to be there—and often wish you weren't. Stay alert and ride carefully, clearly signaling all of your intentions.
- **Potholes,** like grates and back-road canyons, should be avoided. Just because you're on an all-terrain bicycle doesn't mean you're indestructible. Potholes regularly damage rims, pop tires, and sometimes lift unsuspecting cyclists into a spectacular swan dive over the handlebars.

Techniques to Sharpen Your Skills

Although power, strength, and endurance have their place in mountain biking, athletes with finesse, balance, agility, and grace develop their skills and techniques much faster. They find a way to make the bike an extension of their bodies. Slight shifts in the hips or knees can have remarkable results. Experienced bike handlers flash down technical descents, cruising over obstacles with the graceful controlled movements of a ballet dancer. Inexperienced riders and riders who try to power their way down trails often find themselves on the ground. No matter how strong a rider is, that tree or boulder is going to be stronger. It's better to work with the terrain than against it. The following riding tips won't make you a pro. Nor will this information be all you need to know about mountain biking. But it is more than enough to get you in the saddle and rolling down the trail. Like everything else, you get out of it what you put into it. The more time you spend spinning those pedals, the further your skills will develop and the more fun you'll have.

Braking

The more weight a tire is carrying, the more braking power it has. When you're going downhill, your front wheel carries more weight than the rear. Don't be afraid to use your front brake more often. About 70 percent of a bike's braking force originates at the front wheel, but the amount of stopping power changes with the conditions of the terrain. Moisture and mud inhibit rear stopping power more than it does in the front. Experienced mountain bikers know they can change the amount of braking power applied to either wheel by shifting their weight forward or backward. Braking with the front brake will help keep you in control without going into a skid. When applying considerable force to the front brake, be sure to shift your hips out over the back of the saddle. Otherwise, you'll be doing a nose dive over the front wheel. And don't neglect your rear brake! When descending, shift your weight back over the rear wheel, thus increasing your rear braking power as well. This will balance the power of both brakes and give you maximum control.

Good riders learn just how much of their weight to shift over each wheel and how to apply just enough braking power to each brake, so not to "endo" over the handlebars or skid down a trail.

Climbing Those Treacherous Hills

- **Shift into a low gear.** Before shifting, ease up on your pedaling so there is not too much pressure on the chain. With that in mind, it's important to shift *before* you find yourself on a steep slope, where it may too late. Find the best gear for you that matches the terrain and steepness of each climb.
- **Stay seated.** Standing out of the saddle is often helpful when climbing steep hills on a bike, but you may find that on dirt, standing may cause your rear tire to lose its grip and spin out. Climbing is not possible without traction. As your skills improve, you will likely learn the subtle tricks that make out-of-saddle climbing possible. Until then, have a seat.
- **Lean forward.** On very steep hills, the front end may feel unweighted and suddenly pop up. Slide forward on the saddle, and lean over the handlebars. Putting your chin down near your stem will add more weight to the front wheel and should keep you grounded. It's all about using the weight of your head to your advantage. Most people don't realize how heavy their noggin is.
- **Relax.** As with downhilling, relaxation is a big key to your success on steep, rocky climbs. Smooth pedaling translates into good traction. Tense bodies don't

balance well at low speeds. Instead of fixating grimly on the front wheel, look up at the terrain above, and pick a good line.

- **Keep pedaling.** On rocky climbs, be sure to keep the pressure on, and don't let up on those pedals! You'll be surprised at what your bike will just roll over as long as you keep the engine revved up.

Downhilling—The Real Reason We Get Up in the Morning

- **Relax.** Stay loose on the bike, and don't lock your elbows or clench your grip. Your elbows need to bend with the bumps and absorb the shock, while your hands should have a firm but controlled grip on the bars to keep things steady. Breathing slowly, deeply, and deliberately will help you relax while flying down bumpy singletrack. Maintaining a death-grip on the brakes will be unhelpful. Fear and tension will make you wreck every time.

- **Use your eyes.** Keep your head up, and scan the trail as far forward as possible. Choose a line well in advance. *You* decide what line to take—don't let the trail decide for you. Keep the surprises to a minimum. If you have to react quickly to an obstacle, then you've already made a mistake.

- **Rise above the saddle.** When racing down bumpy, technical descents, you should not be sitting on the saddle but hovering just over it, allowing your bent legs and arms to absorb the rocky trail instead of your rear. Think jockey.

- **Remember your pedals.** Be mindful of where your pedals are in relation to upcoming obstacles. Clipping a rock will lead directly to unpleasantness. Most of the time, you'll want to keep your pedals parallel with the ground.

- **Stay focused.** Many descents require your utmost concentration and focus just to reach the bottom. You must notice every groove, root, rock, hole, and bump. You, the bike, and the trail should all become one as you seek singletrack nirvana on your way down the mountain. But if your thoughts wander, so may your bike—and you may instead become one with the trees!

Repair and Maintenance

Fixing a Flat

TOOLS YOU WILL NEED

- Two tire irons
- Pump (either a floor pump or a frame pump)
- No screwdrivers!!! (This can puncture the tube.)

REMOVING THE WHEEL

The front wheel is easy. Simply disconnect the brake shoes, open the quick release mechanism or undo the bolts with the proper sized wrench, then remove the wheel from the bike.

The rear wheel is a little more tricky. Before you loosen the wheel from the frame, shift the chain into the smallest gear on the freewheel (the cluster of gears in the back). Once you've done this, removing and installing the wheel, like the front, is much easier.

REMOVING THE TIRE

Step one: Insert a tire iron under the bead of the tire and pry the tire over the lip of the rim. Be careful not to pinch the tube when you do this.

Step two: Hold the first tire iron in place. With the second tire iron, repeat step one, 3 or 4 inches down the rim. Alternate tire irons, pulling the bead of the tire over the rim, section by section, until one side of the tire bead is completely off the rim.

Step three: Remove the rest of the tire and tube from the rim. This can be done by hand. It's easiest to remove the valve stem last. Once the tire is off the rim, pull the tube out of the tire.

CLEAN AND SAFETY CHECK

Step four: Using a rag, wipe the inside of the tire to clean out any dirt, sand, glass, thorns, etc. These may cause the tube to puncture. The inside of a tire should feel smooth. Any pricks or bumps could mean that you have found the culprit responsible for your flat tire.

Step five: Wipe the rim clean, then check the rim strip, making sure it covers the spoke nipples properly on the inside of the rim. If a spoke is poking through the rim strip, it could cause a puncture.

Step six: At this point, you can do one of two things: replace the punctured tube with a new one, or patch the hole. It's easiest to just replace the tube with a new tube when you're out on the trails. Roll up the old tube and take it home to repair later that night in front of the TV. Directions on patching a tube are usually included with the patch kit itself.

INSTALLING THE TIRE AND TUBE
(This can be done entirely by hand.)

Step seven: Inflate the new or repaired tube with enough air to give it shape, then tuck it back into the tire.

Step eight: To put the tire and tube back on the rim, begin by putting the valve in the valve hole. The valve must be straight. Then use your hands to push the beaded edge of the tire onto the rim all the way around so that one side of your tire is on the rim.

Step nine: Let most of the air out of the tube to allow room for the rest of the tire.

Step ten: Beginning opposite the valve, use your thumbs to push the other side of the tire onto the rim. Be careful not to pinch the tube in between the tire and the rim. The last few inches may be difficult, and you may need the tire iron to pry the tire onto the rim. If so, just be careful not to puncture the tube.

BEFORE INFLATING COMPLETELY

Step eleven: Check to make sure the tire is seated properly and that the tube is not caught between the tire and the rim. Do this by adding about five to ten pounds of air, and watch closely that the tube does not bulge out of the tire.

Step twelve: Once you're sure the tire and tube are properly seated, put the wheel back on the bike, then fill the tire with air. It's easier squeezing the wheel through the brake shoes if the tire is still flat.

Step thirteen: Now fill the tire with the proper amount of air, and check constantly to make sure the tube doesn't bulge from the rim. If the tube does appear to bulge out, release all the air as quickly as possible, or you could be in for a big bang. Place the wheel back in the dropost and tighten the quick release lever Reconnect the brake shoes.

When installing the rear wheel, place the chain back onto the smallest cog (farthest gear on the right), and pull the derailleur out of the way. Your wheel should slide right on.

Lubrication Prevents Deterioration

Lubrication is crucial to maintaining your bike. Dry spots will be eliminated. Creaks, squeaks, grinding, and binding will be gone. The chain will run quietly, and the gears will shift smoothly. The brakes will grip quicker, and your bike may last longer with fewer repairs. Need I say more? Well, yes. Without knowing where to put the lubrication, what good is it?

THINGS YOU WILL NEED

- One can of bicycle lubricant, found at any bike store
- A clean rag (to wipe excess lubricant away)

WHAT GETS LUBRICATED

- Front derailleur
- Rear derailleur
- Shift levers
- Front brake
- Rear brake
- Both brake levers
- Chain

WHERE TO LUBRICATE

To make it easy, simply spray a little lubricant on all the pivot points of your bike. If you're using a squeeze bottle, use just a drop or two. Put a few drops on each point wherever metal moves against metal, for instance, at the center of the brake calipers. Then let the lube sink in.

Once you have applied the lubricant to the derailleurs, shift the gears a few times, working the derailleurs back and forth. This allows the lubricant to work itself into the tiny cracks and spaces it must occupy to do its job. Work the brakes a few times as well.

LUBING THE CHAIN

Lubricating the chain should be done after the chain has been wiped clean of most road grime. Do this by spinning the pedals counterclockwise while gripping the chain with a clean rag. As you add the lubricant, be sure to get some in between each link. With an aerosol spray, just spray the chain while pedaling backwards (counterclockwise) until the chain is fully lubricated. Let the lubricant soak in for a few seconds before wiping the excess away. Chains will collect dirt much faster if they're loaded with too much lubrication.

Last-Minute Check

Before a ride, it's a good idea to give your bike a once-over to make sure everything is in working order. Begin by checking the air pressure in your tires to make sure they are properly inflated. Mountain bikes require about 45 to 55 pounds per square inch of air pressure. If your tires are under inflated, there is greater likelihood that the tubes may get pinched on a bump or rock, causing the tire to flat.

Looking over your bike to make sure everything is secure and in its place is the next step. Go through the following checklist before each ride:

- **Pinch the tires to feel for proper inflation.** They should give just a little on the sides but feel very hard on the treads. Use a pressure gauge if you have one.
- **Check your brakes.** Squeeze the rear brake and roll your bike forward. The rear tire should skid. Next, squeeze the front brake and roll your bike forward. The rear wheel should lift into the air. If this doesn't happen, then your brakes are too loose. Make sure the brake levers don't touch the handlebars when squeezed with full force.
- **Check all quick releases on your bike.** Make sure they are all securely tightened.
- **Lube up.** If your chain squeaks, apply some lubricant.
- **Check your nuts and bolts.** Check the handlebars, saddle, cranks, and pedals to make sure that each is tight and securely fastened to your bike.
- **Check your wheels.** Spin each wheel to see that it spins through the frame and between brake pads freely.
- **Have you got everything?** Make sure you have your spare tube, tire irons, patch kit, frame pump, tools, food, water—and guidebook.

Need more info on mountain biking? Consider reading *Basic Essentials Mountain Biking* published by The Globe Pequot Press. You'll discover such things as choosing and maintaining a mountain bike; useful bike handling techniques; preparing for long rides; overcoming obstacles such as rocks, logs, and water; and even preparing for competition.

Ride Index

Smoothest Singletrack

Thigh-Burning Lung-Exploding Climbs

Toughest Technical Challenges

Fastest/Longest Descents

Dirtiest Mud Fest (During the rainy season)

11   Tiger Mountain—Preston Railroad Trail and Northwest Timber Trail
28   Capitol State Forest—Rock Candy, Lost Valley Loop, Larch Mountain Loop
29   Tahuya State Forest
19   Victor Falls
26   Lake Padden
16   South Sea Tac (Des Moines Creek Park)
25   Walker Valley ORV Park

APPENDIX A:

Clubs, Organizations, and Killer Web Sites

Backcountry Bicycle Trails Club
Their motto: Education, Recreation, and
Advocacy on behalf of mountain bikers.
Affiliated with the International Mountain Bicycling Association (IMBA), the
BBTC (founded in 1989) has more than
400 members and is run completely by
volunteers.
P.O. Box 21288
Seattle, WA 98111-3288
(206) 283–2995
bbtc@cycling.org
www.bbtc.org

**B.I.M.B.O. (Bainbridge Island
Mountain Bikers Organized)**
Established in 1996 in response to
possible trail closures on Bainbridge
Island. Primarily an advocacy group,
B.I.M.B.O. works with local government
and other groups to keep the trails open.
(360) 842–9779

Blackhills Mountain Bike Club
Established in 2000, the club focuses on
the Capitol Forest area and has made
progress in establishing a positive
relationship with the Department of
Natural Resources.
1169 Waddell Creek Road Southwest
Olympia, WA 98512
(360) 704–3315

Capital Bicycling Club
For mountain bikers and road bike riders into racing or group rides, this
group has been active since 1978.

P.O. Box 642
Olympia, WA 98507
(360) 956–3321
www.capitalbicycleclub.org

Cascade Bicycle Club
This is the largest cycling club in the
United States, with more than 5,000
members. They strongly promote safe
cycling, host many road bicycling
events, and are very active in cycling
advocacy and education.
P.O. Box 15165
Seattle, WA 98115-0165
(206) 522–3222
www.cascade.org/

Different Spokes
Seattle's gay and lesbian bicycling club,
they offer many organized rides for all
levels of interest and abilities.
P.O. Box 31542
Seattle, WA 98103
Rtyrell@evansgroup.com

Dirtworld.com
The largest grassroots mountain bike
racing team in the country and one of
the coolest Web sites on the World
Wide Web. More than 1,000 trails,
more than 1,000 races, product reviews,
and an online store.
support@dirtworld.com
(888) 832–2339
www.dirtworld.com

The Downhill Zone

The only bike shop in the area dedicated to downhill riding.
5236 University Way Northeast
Seattle, WA 98105
(206) 523–3337

Emerald Tea & Cycling Society

Formerly sponsored by the Rainier Brewery, this group was formed just for fun. ("Tea" refers to the prohibition word for alcoholic beverages. The club name used to be Team Green Death.) Meets monthly; rides for all abilities and interests.
6019 Fifty-first Avenue Northeast
Seattle, WA 98115-7077
(206) 522–3701 (residence)

Green River Bicycle Club

This group has been around since 1982. Rides are both on and off-road in the Green River Valley and beyond.
P.O. Box 1209
Auburn, WA 98071-1209
(360) 897–8026 (residence)
simploe@TC-NET.com

Northwest Bicycling

Home of the Memorial Weekend Bicycling tour of Orcas Island, Washington. Food and three-day cabin stay, round-trip ferry ticket, and the works included for under $100. Since 1974; open to mountain bikers and road bike riders.
6512 115th Place Southeast
Bellevue, WA 98006
(425) 235–7774

Northwest Mountain Bikers

Spur-of-the-moment fun. This loosely organized mountain biking group promotes races, rides, exploration, and some advocacy.
6304 Sixth Avenue
Tacoma, WA 98406
(253) 565–9050

Now Bike

A nonprofit advocacy group promoting "More People Bicycling More Often, Safely." They influence bicycle transportation, develop education programs for safe cycling, and encourage bicycle commuting.
Susie Stevens
P.O. Box 2904
Seattle, WA 98111
(206) 224–9252

PeteFagerlin.com

Awesome online mountain bike videos!
www.petefagerlin.com

Port Townsend Bicycle Association

Not a club, but an organization dedicated to promoting bicycling through educational, recreational, and sporting events. Host of The Roadie Tour in May to explore and discover the rural roads of Jefferson County.
P.O. Box 681
Port Townsend, WA 98368
(360) 385–3912
jdmcc@olympus.net

Redmond Cycling Club

Road bike riders who ride together for inspiration, camaraderie, and fun. The club offers rides that "cover the spectrum of cycling, from casual social jaunts to the most challenging ultramarathons to be found in the Northwest." Organizers of the Ride Around Mount Rainier in One Day (RAMROD), Don's End of the Year Century, many training rides, the fully supported two-day ride to Mazama through the North Cascades to the Methow Valley and back, and other rides.
P.O. Box 1841
Bothell, WA 98041-1841
(425) 739–8609
info@redmondcyclingclub.org
www.redmondcyclingclub.org/

Singletrack Mind

This club was originally formed with the thought that you never leave anyone behind. Primarily a recreational-paced group, the club also has specific organized group rides for racers. They average twenty-five rides per month and organize five or six huge mountain biking camping trips per year in Washington and Oregon. The club began in 1994 and has 200 members, promoting cycling through stewardship and education.
6824 Nineteenth Street West #147
Tacoma, WA 98466
(253) 565–5124
www.members.aol.com/STMClub/
stmclub/html

Skagit Bicycle Club

Organizers of weekly mountain biking and road biking rides for all ability levels.
1325 North Nineteenth
Mount Vernon, WA 98273
(360) 428–9487

Spokeswoman

Mountain Bike Camps for women designed by women.
Whistler Blackcomb
(800) 766–0449
www.spokeswomen.com

Tacoma Wheelmen's Bicycle Club

This club has been around since 1888 and welcomes road bicycle riders of all skill levels. They promote safe bicycling for recreation, health, and alternative transportation, sponsoring two organized rides each year: the Daffodil Classic and the Peninsula Metric.
P.O. Box 112078
Tacoma, WA 98411
(253) 759–2800
www.twbc.org/

West Sound Cycling Club

Founded in 1985, this club now has about one hundred members. Their main focus is promoting bicycling as a safe and healthful form of recreation and an environmental form of transportation. The club gets involved in some legislative issues and conducts several educational clinics. The two main sponsored rides each year are the Countryside Classic in July and the

Tour de Kitsap in September. Weekly
social rides on Saturday and Sunday for
all levels and bimonthly Welcome
Rides for new members. They meet
the first Wednesday of every month.
P.O. Box 1579
Silverdale, WA 98383
(360) 698–3876

**Whatcom Independent Mountain
Pedalers (WIMPs)**
A group of mountain bikers who wel-
come all skill levels to wander the
backroads and trails in northwestern
Washington.
Craig Stephens
1410 Girard Street, Suite 9
Bellingham, WA 98225
(360) 671–4107

APPENDIX B:

Cyclopedia of Terms

Air: Leaving the ground, the sensation of floating.

Allen key/wrench: A small L-shaped hexagonal wrench that fits inside the head of a bolt or screw.

Auger-in: To crash in such a manner that brings rider and bike to abrupt stop.

Bar ends: Miniature handlebar add-ons that fit on the ends of mountain bike bars to add another riding position, usually for increased climbing ability.

Biff: To crash.

Blowdowns: Obstacles created when trees, vines, drunks, or other big stuff falls across a trail.

Blow up: To be suddenly unable to continue at the required pace due to overexertion.

Bonk: See "blow up."

BMX: Bicycle Motocross—a type of racing done on a closed dirt track over obstacles usually on 20-inch-wheel bikes with one gear.

Bunnyhop: Flex your elbows and knees and spring/jump upward in a quick motion, lifting the bike off the ground.

Cadence: The rate of pedaling, measured in revolutions per minute (rpm) of one foot.

Cage: On a front derailleur, a pair of parallel plates that push the chain from side to side; on a rear derailleur, a set of plates on which pulleys are mounted to hold and guide the chain from cog to cog.

Calipers: Brake arms that reach around the sides of a wheel to press brake pads against the wheel rim.

Cantilever brakes: Rim brakes with pivoting arms mounted on fork blades or seatstays.

Cassette: The set of gear cogs on the rear hub; also called a freewheel, cluster, or block.

Cassette hub: A type of rear hub that has a built-in freewheel mechanism.

Catch or cop air: To fly through the air with the greatest of ease; to ride with both wheels off the ground when your bike hits a natural rise or dip in the trail.

Categories: The division of racers into groups based on ability and/or experience.

Century: A 100-mile ride

Chain: A series of links pinned together that connects the chainwheel to the cogs on the back wheel and allows one to pedal the bike (see "derailleur chains").

Chainring: A sprocket attached to the right crankarm to drive the chain.

Chainring nut spanner: A special tool used to loosen the slotted chainring bolts (the ones behind the inner ring) that fasten a chainring to a crankarm.

Chainstays: The two tubes of a bicycle frame that run from the bottom bracket back to the rear dropouts.

Chainsuck: When the chain doubles back on itself in the middle of a gear shift and gets jammed either between chainrings or between the inner chainring and the frame.

Chain whip or chain wrench: A tool consisting of a metal bar and two sections of chain, used in changing cogs on a cassette.

Chrome moly (chrome molybdenum): A type of high-quality steel tubing.

Circuit: A race course or area with several different trails that's ridden two or more times to comprise the race or ride.

Clinchers: Conventional tires with a separate inner tube.

Clincher tire: A tire whose edges hook under the curved-in edge of a rim.

Clipless pedals: Pedals that use a releasable mechanism like that of a ski binding rather than toe clips or straps to lock onto cleated shoes.

Cleat: A metal or plastic fitting on the sole of a cycling shoe that engages the pedal.

Cog: A sprocket attached directly to the rear hub on a single-speed bike and mounted on a cassette on a multispeed bike.

Corncob: A term used to describe a cluster of cogs on a racing cassette because of the small variation in number of teeth on adjacent cogs. "Straight block" is another term for a corncob.

Cottered crank: A crankset in which the crankarms are fastened to the axle by means of threaded cotters and nuts.

Cotterless crank: A crankset in which the crankarms are fastened to the axle by means of a taper and nuts or bolts (instead of cotters).

Crankarm: A part, one end of which is attached to the bottom bracket axle and the other holds a pedal, whose forward rotation provides the leverage needed to power the bicycle.

Crankarm bolt: The bolt that holds a crankarm on the end of the axle in a cotterless crankset.

Crankset: Includes the bottom bracket, two crankarms, and one or more chainrings.

Crash: Also known as a wipeout, biff, rag dolling, yardsale, to pack it in, pile up, and to stack.

Cross-country: The standard mountain bike race, in which cyclists ride over hills, through woods, across streams, to Grandmother's house we go.

Cross-country bike: A mountain bike suited to racing the cross-country event at NORBA events; features include wide-range gearing with super lows, at least front suspension, great brakes, and a light performance-oriented frame

Cyclocross: A fall or winter event contested mostly or entirely off pavement. Courses include obstacles, steps, and steep hills that force riders to dismount and run with their bikes across their shoulders.

Dab: To put a foot down to prevent toppling over.

Dabbing: Removing your foot from the pedal and touching the ground due to the inability to maintain momentum or balance.

Derailleur: A lever-activated mechanism that pushes the chain off one sprocket and onto another, changing the gear ratio.

Diamond frame: The traditional men's bicycle frame, the principal parts of which form a diamond shape.

Domestique: A racer who sacrifices individual results to work for the team leaders.

Double-crown fork: A type of suspension fork that resembles a motorcycle fork; it has crowns above and below the head tube, which increase stiffness.

Downhill bike: A bike designed for racing down mountains; features include long-travel dual-suspension frame, great brakes, single chainring, long saddle, and riser handlebars.

Down tube: The frame tube running from the headset to the bottom bracket, one part of the main triangle on a bicycle frame.

Drafting: Tucking in closely behind another rider so he or she breaks the wind, saving you energy.

Drivetrain: The derailleurs, chain, freewheel, and crankset of a bike.

Dropout: A slot in the frame into which the rear wheel axle fits.

Dropout hanger: A threaded metal piece that extends below the right rear dropout, used as a mount for the rear derailleur.

Drops: The lower, straight portion of a turned-down-type handlebar.

Doubletrack: A wide path that looks like parallel singletrack; also called a jeep trail.

Downhill: An off-road event usually contested at ski areas. The fastest rider to the bottom wins.

Dual slalom: Similar to skiing, in which riders maneuver around gates on a short downhill course.

Dual-suspension bike: A bike with front and rear suspension.

Dualie: See "dual suspension bike."

Dump: Crash.

Endo: To crash by going over the handlebar; short for end-over-end.

Equestrians: Horse lovers who think they deserve exclusive rights to the trails. Make nice—they are better organized and have more money than the mountain bike community does.

Face plant: Going over the bars and landing on your face. Plastic surgeon anyone?

Fire road: A road maintained chiefly for emergency vehicle access.

Flash: Climbing or ascending a hill in the first attempt, or any attempt, without dabbing or dismounting to walk.

Freeride bikes: Light, inexpensive dual-suspension bikes.

Granny gear: The smallest chainring combined with largest cog; used mainly for climbing.

Grill: Face, teeth, forehead.

Hammer: To ride as hard and as fast as you can for as long as you can.

Headset: The parts at the top and bottom of the frame's head tube, into which the handlebar stem and fork are fitted.

IMBA: International Mountain Bike Association.

Jam: See "hammer."

Lactic acid: A by-product of anaerobic exercise that accumulates in the muscles, causing pain and fatigue.

NORBA: National Off Road Bicycling Association, the governing body of off-road racing in America; a division of USA Cycling.

NORBA National: While NORBA sanctions hundreds of events, only a handful are part of its national championship series. In each of these races, points are awarded to top finishers. The final point total determines the NORBA national championship.

Off-camber turn: The surface slopes sway from the curve, making it difficult and dangerous to navigate with speed.

Oxygen debt: The amount of oxygen that needs to be consumed to pay back the deficit incurred by anaerobic work.

Saddle sores: Skin injuries in the crotch and thighs that develop from chafing caused by pedaling action. Sores can range from tender raw spots to boil-like lesions if infection occurs.

Saddle time: Time spent cycling.

Sag wagon: A motor vehicle that follows a group of riders, carrying equipment and lending assistance in the event of difficulty; also called the broom wagon.

Sandbagger: A racer who stays in an easier category instead of moving up. USA Cycling rules mandate an upgrade after a certain number of top finishes.

Snakebite: A two-holed flat you get when you slam hard on under inflated tires.

Spin: To pedal at a high cadence.

Squirrely: When a nervous or unstable rider can't be trusted to maintain a steady line, or a bike feels unstable.

Stack: Going over the bars and landing on your face or your head as though you are a pile being driven into the ground.

Switchback: A 90-degree or greater turn. Switchbacks are difficult to ride and are usually on the side of some mountain.

The East Side: Land of the yuppies, Beamer Country, Bill Gates's Kingdom—Bellevue, Redmond, Kirkland, Bothell.

The North End: Land of big hair, mullets, Cameros, Mustangs, and keggers in the fields.

The South End: More big hair, mullets, Cameros, Mustangs, and keggers in the fields—Renton, Federal Way, Kent, Auburn, Puyallup, Sumner.

About the Author

Santo Criscuolo, a 1990 University of Washington graduate, is one of the original founders of the online mountain bike guides *Dirt Northwest* and *Dirtworld.com*. Prior to launching the two Web sites, Criscuolo worked as a radio and TV sales executive and an online advertising sales manager, and he was the editor for *Northwest Skier* magazine in the early 1990s. Currently he is an advertising sales manager for MSN. His first book, *Ski America—The Pacific Northwest & British Columbia,* is one of Amazon.com's top-ten-selling books in the Seattle market every winter. His in-the-dirt and on-the-trail experience includes seven years of cross-country racing; starting Team Dirtworld.com, the largest amateur mountain bike racing team in the nation; and searching for singletrack all over Western Canada, the United States, and Central America. Rain or shine, you are sure to find him in the saddle somewhere in the Puget Sound region.

FALCON GUIDES®

From nature exploration to extreme adventure FalconGuides lead you there. With more than 400 titles available, there is a guide for every outdoor activity and topic including essential outdoor skills, field identification, trails, trips, and the best places to go in each state and region. Written by experts, each guidebook features detailed descriptions, maps, and expert advice that can enhance every outdoor experience.

You can count on FalconGuides to lead you to your favorite outdoor activities wherever you live or travel.

MOUNTAIN BIKING

These guides selectively cover the best rides in a state or region. Mountain bikers of all abilities will enjoy the assortment of rides that vary in length and difficulty and are appropriate for a variety of skills and fitness levels.

6 x 9" · paperback · maps · photos elevation graphs

A FALCON GUIDE
Rob Ginieczki

Mountain Biking
Pennsylvania

A FALCON GUIDE
Gregg Bromke
Second edition

Mountain Biking
Colorado

A FALCON GUIDE
Gregg Bromka

Mountain Biking
Utah